Future of Business and Finance

The Future of Business and Finance book series features professional works aimed at defining, describing and charting the future trends in these fields. The focus is mainly on strategic directions, technological advances, challenges and solutions which may affect the way we do business tomorrow, including the future of sustainability and governance practices. Mainly written by practitioners, consultants and academic thinkers, the books are intended to spark and inform further discussions and developments.

More information about this series at http://www.springer.com/series/16360

Annette Hofmann

The Ten Commandments of Risk Leadership

A Behavioral Guide on Strategic Risk Management

Springer

Annette Hofmann
Academic Director, Carl H. Lindner III Center for Insurance and Risk Management
Virgil M. Schwarm Associate Professor of Finance and Investments
Carl H. Lindner College of Business
University of Cincinnati
Cincinnati, OH, USA

ISSN 2662-2467 ISSN 2662-2475 (electronic)
Future of Business and Finance
ISBN 978-3-030-88796-4 ISBN 978-3-030-88797-1 (eBook)
https://doi.org/10.1007/978-3-030-88797-1

This Springer imprint is published by the registered company Springer Nature Switzerland AG
The registered company address is: Gewerbestrasse 11, 6330 Cham, Switzerland

Preface

> *"If only we could put aside the fear of losing, we might jump at the chance to win. But instead, the fear holds us back, chaining us to the status quo even when change is clearly in our best interest."*
>
> —Francesca Gino[1]

This quote says a lot about us humans. We evaluate risks in terms of upside and downside effects, pretty much like we evaluate losses more negatively than we enjoy gains of similar magnitude. Fear holds us back when we indeed have a chance to gain, but gain may imply change and not all of us like change. Our nature is driven not only by pure rationality but rather by emotional psychology in many cases where we should rather think clearly and focus on the numbers game at hand.

Managers are often seen as powerful decision-makers with sophisticated information-processing capability who make risk-related decisions based on economic incentives and the fullest available range of all risk-relevant variables and information. Well, as it turns out, managers are also humans and prone to a variety of wired-in cognitive mistakes in the way they interpret and react to risk-related information—as we all are! In their professional careers, this is highly consequential since the cognitive mistakes most managers are exposed to in their day-to-day business erode the objectivity of their risk-related decisions, which ultimately hurts the financial well-being of their firms. This book is the first behavioral strategic risk management guide for managers and other interested readers. The last decades have offered various insights into how human nature often gets in the way of rational decision-making. Using examples from economic theory, behavioral finance, and game theory, this book studies the hidden forces that drive our decision-making processes under risk and uncertainty. An important focus is on behavioral bias.[2] The book offers a deep discussion on how risk perception depends on an observer's cognitive biases and views of the world, which are responsible for their risk-related

[1] Francesca Gino is an award-winning Harvard Business School behavioral scientist, p.31 in: Rebel Talent—Why it pays to break the rules at work and in life, 2019, Pan Books.

[2] In statistics, a *bias* refers to the case when an estimate of a variable does not converge to the true value in the population, even when adding more observations to a sample. In a similar way, a behavioral bias refers to the cases when people systematically behave in a certain way that deviates from a rational way.

decisions. The insights from behavioral risk economics are then discussed in the face of managerial decision-making in the hope to teach today's decision-makers how to become better risk leaders.

Each chapter offers a summary of its main insights presented in the form of a commandment to become a better risk leader. After having read this book, you will be aware of the many psychological traps when making decisions under risk, and this will hopefully improve the way you think about and approach your everyday risk-related problems. This book should also be on every shelf in a firm since being a better risk leader will ultimately improve the well-being of the firm.

Cincinnati, OH, USA Annette Hofmann

Contents

1 **Introduction** 1
Risk Management Versus Risk Leadership 2
References 4

2 **Risk and Risk Perception: Why We Are Not Rational in the Face of Risk** 5
Risk and Uncertainty 5
Risk, Probabilities, and Rationality 9
Psychological Aspects on Risk Perception 12
Risk Metrics 14
Risk Aversion 16
Key Takeaways for Risk Leadership 20
References 21

3 **Expected Utility, Prospect Theory, and the Allais Paradox: Why Reference Points Are Important** 23
Bernoulli and Expected Utility Theory 23
Why Expected Utility Does Not Work 26
The Allais Paradox 27
Prospect Theory 28
Reference Points and Loss Aversion 30
The Isolation Effect 33
Framing 34
The Safety Effect 34
The Reflection Effect 35
The Insulation Effect 36
So How Do We Contextualize Risks in Practice? 36
Key Takeaways for Risk Leadership 37
References 37

4 **Confirmation Bias and Anchoring Effect: Why the First Piece of Information is Key in Negotiations** 39
Confirmation Bias 39
Anchoring Effect 44

Anchoring and Being a Good Negotiator . . . 47
Key Takeaways for Risk Leadership . . . 48
References . . . 49

5 **Framing and the Ostrich Effect: Why Our Decisions Depend On How Information Is Presented** . . . 51
Framing and the Ostrich Effect . . . 51
Framing and Loss Aversion . . . 53
Framing and Financial Literacy . . . 54
Distortions in Risk Perception . . . 55
Distortions in Risk Transfer . . . 57
Empirical Investigations into the Ostrich Effect . . . 58
Key Takeaways for Risk Leadership . . . 59
References . . . 59

6 **Emotions and Zero Risk Bias: Why We Make Bad Decisions and Overspend on Risk Avoidance** . . . 61
Zero-Risk Bias . . . 61
When We Hate to Lose: Aversion to a Sure Loss . . . 63
Key Takeaways for Risk Leadership . . . 64
References . . . 65

7 **Endowment Effect and Status-Quo Bias: Why We Stick with Bad Decisions** . . . 67
Risky Decisions and the Endowment Effect . . . 67
Endowment Effect and Loss Aversion . . . 68
Status Quo Bias . . . 71
Experimental Tests on Static Decisions . . . 72
Experiments on Sequential Decisions . . . 73
Explanation 1: Rational Decision-Making . . . 73
Explanation 2: Psychological Commitment . . . 74
Explanation 3: Cognitive Misperceptions . . . 77
Applications of the Endowment Effect to the Status Quo Bias . . . 77
Escalation of Commitment . . . 80
Key Takeaways for Risk Leadership . . . 80
References . . . 81

8 **Overconfidence and Self-Blindness: Why We Think We Are Better Than We Actually Are** . . . 83
Managerial Overconfidence . . . 83
Overestimation . . . 86
Forecasts and the Planning Fallacy . . . 86
Illusion of Control . . . 87
Overplacement . . . 88
Overprecision . . . 89

Overconfidence and Gender 90
The Confidence Gap 91
Imposter Syndrome: Underconfidence in Women 92
Men Promote Men: Narcissism or Old Boys'Club? 93
Managerial Overconfidence, Corporate Risk Management, and Selective Self-Attribution 94
Key Takeaways for Risk Leadership 94
References 95

9 The Low-Probability Puzzle: Why We Insure Our Cellphone But Not Our Home 99
Emotions Override Probability For LRHC Events 99
The Catastrophe Insurance Market Puzzle 100
Transaction Costs 101
Inefficient Financial Markets 103
Asymmetric Information 103
Limited Liability 105
Diversification in Time 105
Regret Aversion 106
Key Takeaways for Risk Leadership 108
References 108

10 Fairness, Diversity, Groupthink, and Peer Effects: Why Other People Matter for Our Risky Decisions 111
Fairness and Cooperation: Lessons from Game Theory 111
Prisoner's Dilemma 112
Dictator Game 113
Ultimatum Game 114
The Impact of Groupthink 116
When Does the Phenomenon Occur? 117
What Are the Symptoms of Groupthink? 118
What Are Symptoms of Defective Decision-making in Groups? 119
Debiasing Strategies to Limit Groupthink 120
Diversity and Independent Directors 122
Peer Effects, Stereotypes, and Company Culture 123
Peer Effects 123
Company Culture 124
Stereotypes 125
Key Takeaways for Risk Leadership 126
References 126

11 Hindsight Bias: Why We Think We Are Good Predictors Even Though We Are Not 129
Hindsight Bias 129
Why Do People Exhibit Hindsight Bias? 131

Consequences of Hindsight Bias in Practice 134
Myopia 134
Overconfidence 134
Effect Size 136
What Can We Do About Hindsight Bias? 136
Consider-the-opposite 136
Expertise 138
Visualisation Techniques 138
Key Takeaways for Risk Leadership 139
References 139

12 The 10 Commandments and How We Can Develop Strategic Risk Leadership Competencies 141
The 10 Commandments 141
Insights from Behavioral Sciences on Our Decision-Making Processes 142
Self-Leadership and Habits 143
Confidence 145
References 146

Appendix 1: Probability Fundamentals 147

Appendix 2: Decision Theory Fundamentals 153

Appendix 3: Risk Aversion and Expected Utility Fundamentals 159

Appendix 4: Game Theory Fundamentals 165

References 179

Index 181

Introduction 1

Why would you need a book on risk leadership and strategic thinking under risk and uncertainty? The short answer is: To develop *risk literacy* as a leadership skill. The longer answer is that competent decision making under risk and uncertainty needs training and practice given the many strategic mistakes people make every day.

Gerd Gigerenzer, a German psychologist and behavioral economist who has studied bounded rationality and heuristics in decision-making under risk, became well-known to the scientific community when he started highlighting, in several very impactful studies, that risk is something our human brains have difficulty grasping and dealing with in a rational way. He defines *risk literacy* as an essential tool needed for being a savvy citizen in today's world. While literacy in general is often referred to as the ability to read and write, which is of course indispensable for every citizen in today's world, risk literacy refers to acquiring knowledge about our modern technological society in order to efficiently deal with risk and uncertainty. He states that[1]

> The breakneck speed of technological innovation will make risk literacy as indispensable in the twenty-first century as reading and writing were in previous centuries. Without it, you jeopardize your health and money, or may be manipulated into unrealistic fears and hopes. One might think that the basics of risk literacy are already being taught. Yet you will look in vain for it in most high schools, law schools, medical schools, and beyond. As a result, most of us are risk illiterate.

According to his insights, since we cannot properly deal with risk and uncertainty, using *heuristics* is important. Complex problems do not require a complex but rational calculation or even a solution-generating algorithm but rather a good heuristic that helps solving the problem at hand quickly and without complexity. In many cases, more information is not always helpful in generating a "good" solution.

[1] Gigerenzer (2014), p. 2.

A. Hofmann, *The Ten Commandments of Risk Leadership*, Future of Business and Finance, https://doi.org/10.1007/978-3-030-88797-1_1

This insight follows Herbert Simon, Nobel Prize winner 1978 in economics, who argued that when decision-making involves cost—like time to gather important information on a problem at hand—then it is not rational to spend an extremely long amount of time simply to optimize all possible details and facets. Instead, it makes sense to follow rules of thumb that allow to get to acceptable or good outcomes. However, when these rules of thumb are used in situations that would be better optimized with investing significant time and effort, a suboptimal decision might be quite hurtful to an individual or a company.

Based on research by the Center for Creative Leadership, great leaders consistently possess the following ten core leadership skills: Integrity, Ability to delegate, Communication, Self-awareness, Gratitude, Learning agility, Influence, Empathy, Courage, and Respect. While self-awareness is paramount as a leadership skill, an important part of it is risk competence or risk literacy, an ingredient mainly neglected in leadership research!

Risk Management Versus Risk Leadership

Understanding individual risk perception, risk aversion, risk perception-related behavior and how emotions respond to risk and which cognitive biases are the result—these are all crucial elements in making better risk-related decisions and becoming better risk leaders. For managers, understanding cognitive biases is even more important than for the general population since managerial decisions have much greater consequences than individual decisions that only aim at improving an individual's situation. The long-term survival of the firm is at stake and a better decision-making process ensures overall better survival and profitability of the firm. It hence makes sense to differentiate between what I call "competence in risk management" and "competence in risk leadership". Broadly following Anderson and Young (2020, p.53), I will refer to risk management versus risk leadership as

- *Risk Leadership*: a situation where understanding of risk and uncertainty—along with other skills and knowledge—is put in the service of (risk) communicating, envisioning, initiating, persuading, decision-making, and leading a resilient company.
- *Risk Management*: a situation where understanding of risk and uncertainty—along with other skills and knowledge—is put in the service of (the more technical aspects of) anticipating possible losses by designing and implementing procedures that minimize the occurrence of such losses and their financial impact by planning, prevention, budgeting, coordinating, and monitoring.

As a subcategory of risk management, we may follow the Actuarial Standards Board and refer to *Enterprise Risk Management* (ERM) as "the discipline by which an organization in any industry assesses, controls, exploits, finances, and monitors risks from all sources for the purpose of increasing the organization's short- and long-term value to its stakeholders."[2] Traditionally, risk was managed in silos, which concentrated on how individual business units perform. For instance, insurance risk, technology risk, financial risk, all managed independently in separate compartments. Managing risk in silos created a limited view and unidentified risk relationships. Enterprise risk management solves these problems by breaking down the silos and combining them to the management of all risks together. Furthermore, in Enterprise Risk Management, the management of risks is integrated and coordinated across the entire organization, with the goal to create, protect, and enhance shareholder value. ERM is a discipline that has gained much attention in the last few years. The centralization of the risk management function is critical to its overall effectiveness, whereby the focus is on the highest priority risks. In order for Enterprise Risk Management to succeed, it must ultimately be a part of the firm's culture. RM goes beyond traditional risk management: while the traditional risk management approach deals mainly with so-called *pure* risks (i.e. there are only the possibilities of loss or no loss, like in the case of natural disasters or auto accidents), ERM also takes into account *speculative* risks (i.e. risks where both profits and losses are possible, like in the case of training with stocks or other financial instruments). ERM requires a company to take a portfolio view of risk by including managing speculative and pure risks simultaneously and exploiting chances where individual risks interrelate.

In this way, we make a distinction between risk leadership and risk management, and in particular ERM, to highlight the insight that these are in fact different approaches to dealing with risk. This view is developed from the striking discrepancy between the rationality-based approach outlined in the risk management literature and ERM frameworks on how companies should behave and what we observe companies really do in practice.

Risk leadership is an important discipline when we take into account that leaders in organizations are often expected to provide direction and guide the company through tough times by recognizing and coordinating efforts to deal with major risk exposures, anticipating opportunities to avoid risks, and implementing a risk-related strategy to ensure company survival and long-term success.

So, who are the risk leaders in a company? It seems that organizations have come to learn that a person who has knowledge in risk management has actual value for a firm and should be placed near the CEO in the hierarchy to best serve the firm's interests. Many new titles have emerged in the last decade, ranging from Chief Risk Officer (CRO), Director of (Enterprise) Risk Management, Chief Financial Officer, Risk Management Officer to Vice President Risk Services, Vice President Risk Services, or similar titles.

Leadership is about relationships. In his recent book, "The Leader's Brain", Wharton's Neuroscience Professor Michael Platt describes how key areas in our brain work and how insights from this can be used to teach us how to develop better leadership abilities. While some techniques may work well in improving team

[2] See Proposed Actuarial Standard of Practice; http://www.actuarialstandardsboard.org/asops/risk-treatment-enterprise-risk-management-2/

leading competence, a general leadership training seems challenging. For instance, when it comes to ethical behavior and moral reasoning abilities, a study used brain scans of MBA students and their moral development. It found that connections within the brain between the ventromedial prefrontal cortex and amygdala tended to be stronger in students with higher levels of moral reasoning. However, the question remains whether the stronger neural connections are responsible for students to develop higher levels of moral reasoning or, the other way around, whether higher moral reasoning levels strengthened these connections over time. It thus remains to be shown whether education and training exercises in moral reasoning can make us better leaders.

Indeed, while ethical decision-making and moral reasoning are more difficult to develop and train, improvements in risk literacy are relatively easy is accomplish as you will see when reading this textbook. The task consists mainly of acquiring knowledge about the risk-related biases our brains are commonly exposed to and gaining insights into how these biases can be avoided. Understanding the hidden forces that drive our decision-making processes under risk and uncertainty, we can be trained to make more "rational" decisions. Main insights will be summarized as commandments to become better risk leaders in our society today.

References

Anderson, T. J., & Young, P. C. (2020). *Strategic risk leadership - engaging a world of risk, uncertainty, and the unknown*. Routledge.

Gigerenzer, G. (2014). *Risk savvy: How to make good decisions*. Pengiun Books.

Risk and Risk Perception: Why We Are Not Rational in the Face of Risk

2

The most important single key takeaway from this chapter is

> **The 1st Commandment of Risk Leadership:** Measure risk even if you think you know about it—what is measured can be optimized!

Understanding individual risk psychology and perception, risk aversion, risk perception-related behavior and how our emotions respond to risk and uncertainty as well as which cognitive biases are the result—these are all crucial elements in making better risk-related decisions and becoming better risk leaders. For managers, understanding cognitive biases is even more important than for the general population given that managerial decisions have consequences for the long-term survival of the firm. By quantifying and measuring risk, we can manage the risk before it manages us. It is important to be aware of the fact that you and others may act in a way towards risk that is not rational. This is the first commandment of risk leadership, which basically leads to the others that follow in subsequent chapters. Making use of the ten commandments is important to manage your risk management style over time, given that we as humans often fall prey to many mistakes. Indeed, being actively aware of our weaknesses—and the weaknesses of our opponents—can make us stronger and better risk leaders.

Risk and Uncertainty

Risk is an inherent piece of any business in any industry. With that, risk management should be a major goal of firms looking to run a profitable enterprise. The point of risk management is not to eliminate risk, but to manage it. So what is risk? Defining "risk" is a puzzling subject, primarily because of its ambiguous roots. Risk—derived from early Italian origin—translates to *risicare*, which means "to

A. Hofmann, *The Ten Commandments of Risk Leadership*, Future of Business and Finance, https://doi.org/10.1007/978-3-030-88797-1_2

dare". When assessed within this context, risk is presumed to be a choice rather than an act of fate. And to make such a choice implies that there is a corresponding benefit or reward to making the "right" decision. The ability to define a person's capability to assess what may happen in the future and prescribe a treatment for such possible collection of future events lies at the heart of risk management. Risk touches every aspect of our lives: whether it's crossing the street; traveling in a car or aircraft; which job to choose; where to go on vacation; or safeguarding our wealth and financial investments. Our individual appetite to take risks, along with identifying and having the capacity to manage it, requires making forward-looking choices, all of which are key elements that drive the decision-making process. In the following chapters, we will find out about how and why we are often subject to errors when following our intuition when it comes to dealing with risks, and how we can become better risk managers in our private and professional lives. Another focus will be to understand how we can support and improve the practice of strategic risk management by helping ourselves and others build psychological skills to complement existing quantitative and communication skills.

Economists make a distinction between *risk* and *uncertainty*. This is important because risk and uncertainty should be treated differently in any risk management approach. While risk refers to a situation in which the probabilities assigned to outcomes or payoffs can be estimated with some reliability or even precisely stated, uncertainty refers to situations in which probabilities are either completely unknown or rather vague. More formally, we can define.

- *Risk*: a situation where probabilities of outcomes can be reliably estimated using distributions of previous outcomes
- *Uncertainty*: a situation where probabilities of outcomes cannot be reliably estimated—this may be due to an event being unique or unprecedented

We may add to this list a situation of *unknowability*, where things cannot be foreseen in any way (unknown unknowns) and may be due to complex dynamic systems leading to unexpected results—a situation that might be interpreted as a subcategory of uncertainty. As a consequence, when all alternatives, their consequences and probabilities are known, we make a *decision under risk*; this requires a *statistical mindset*. If, however, this is not the case and we do not know the probabilities, we make a decision *under uncertainty*; this requires an *intuitive mindset*, which does not necessarily mean that we act rational, but we can improve our intuitive actions by applying rules of thumb ("heuristics") to make smarter decisions. These two very different mindsets, the statistical one and the intuitive one, both of which I hope you will strengthen while reading this book, can be improved upon by continuing training and acquiring risk management knowledge. Distinguishing between risk and uncertainty leads to better practical decision-making, as we will see in this book. First, the analysis tools for risk are different from those for uncertainty. Second, our cognitive biases influence us to behave differently toward risk than toward uncertainty. There is some evidence that we are conditioned to think primarily in terms of risk rather than uncertainty—mainly because we can simply transform any situation of uncertainty into a situation of risk simply by attaching an equal probability to every possible state of nature. This principle is known as the *principle of insufficient reason*. Also, most of our social institutions, from government to nonprofit organizations to the insurance industry, encourage us to think in terms of risk. After all, the idea that these institutions can anticipate, measure, and thus manage all upheavals in our lives strengthens their legitimacy. We also naturally gravitate toward thinking in terms of risk—which we can control—rather than in terms of uncertainty—over which we have little control. Indeed, it appears that feeling in control reduces our anxiety and so we just think in terms of risk. Ultimately, we tend to stick to certain biases and simplified modes of thinking, even though these biases implicitly trade-off the effectiveness of many decisions.

The following example will introduce you to your own risk-versus-uncertainty brain. Imagine there are two urns filled with red and black balls. Urn A contains 50 red balls and 50 black balls, while urn B also contains 100 red and black balls but in an unknown ratio. You are asked to choose an urn, and then you can draw a ball at random from your chosen urn—of course without looking. If the ball is red, you win a prize of $100. Which urn would you choose?

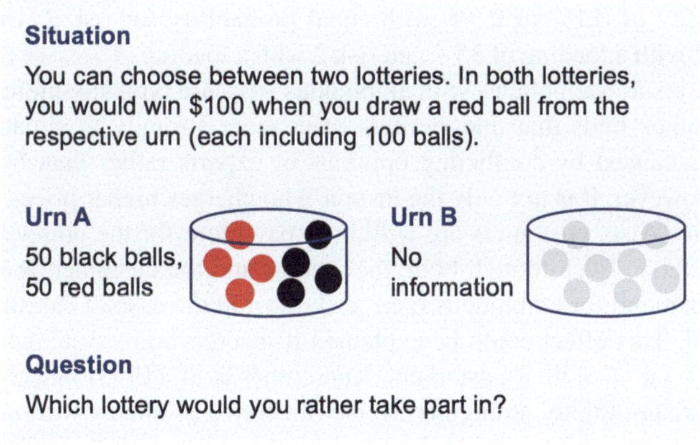

Well, if you are like most people, you will strongly prefer to draw a ball from urn A. This makes perfect sense, right? It seems that urn A is the better choice given the known probability of drawing a red ball—which is ½. However, being now perfectly rational in the face of these two lotteries, think about your preference again: If you really prefer to draw a red ball from urn A rather than urn B, then your (subjective) probability of drawing a red ball from urn B must be less than ½. Since probabilities always add up to one, this implies that your (subjective) probability of drawing a black ball from Urn B must be greater than ½, and you should therefore prefer it to drawing a red ball from urn A, which carries a probability of winning of ½. Put differently, we can also simplify the problem to evaluating urns containing only two balls. Urn A would then contain a red and a black ball, respectively, while urn B has also two balls in it, but we do not know of which color they are. Obviously, the probability of drawing a red ball from urn A is ½. For urn B, there is a 1/3 chance that there are two black balls in it, a 1/3 chance that there are two red balls in it, and a 1/3 chance that there is one red and one black ball in it. Adding these up, the overall chance of drawing a red ball from urn B is thus equal to $1/3 + 1/3 \times ½ = 3/6 = ½$. So you can see now that it makes no difference which urn you draw from!

The previous example is a very prominent one, that has been asked many different people with different cultural backgrounds and ethical standards—it is called *Ellsberg Paradox*.[1] According to Ellsberg, humans tend to maximize (subjective) expected utility in judgements involving risk (like in the case of urn A) and tend to maximize minimum utility in judgements involving uncertainty (like in the case of urn B). This tendency implies treating risk and uncertainty differently, and the strong preference for the known probabilities over the unknowns is called *ambiguity aversion*. Most people, when confronted with a situation like this one here with the two urns, overwhelmingly decide for the setting with known probabilities. It seems that we have this inherent preference for the knowns rather than the unknowns, and we tend to avoid situations where the probabilities of outcomes are not known to us.

Cabantous (2007) argues that ambiguity aversion is highly relevant for insurance markets. In her experiment, 78 underwriters priced two risks. In both cases, the loss is determined by a fixed amount L with probability of 0.2% for risk 1 and ambiguous probability of 0.1% or 0.3% with equal probability for risk 2. Underwriters priced risk 1 with a loading of 35% and risk 2 with a loading of 78% of the actuarial value. Thus, insurance policies with ambiguous risks are typically more expensive. Also, the author finds that underwriters react more strongly to situations where ambiguity is caused by conflicting opinions of experts rather than by imprecise forecasts. However, it is not only the insurer who charges higher prices in ambiguous situations. Also, customers are willing to pay more for the policy, as they are ambiguity averse. Even though both, the insurer and the customer, are ambiguity averse, the demand for ambiguous risks, as known in the case of catastrophe risks, is very small. This effect could be explained if insurers were systematically more ambiguity averse than their customers. Kunreuther et al. (1993) indeed found that many insurers are highly ambiguity averse. Incentive problems with underwriters who are usually more penalized when underestimating a risk than when overestimating it are a rationale for this effect.

Kunreuther et al. (1993) present two approaches to address the insurance market effects caused by ambiguity aversion. First, public, state-owned reinsurers could serve as a 'second line of defense' in case of high loss events such as earthquakes. Secondly, insurers could improve transparency of extra charging due to ambiguity by different actors, such as underwriters and actuaries within the organization. They thus would avoid to double charge extra loadings due to ambiguity.

Recent research by Jia et al. (2020) shows that learning about the Ellsberg Paradox reduces, but does not eliminate, ambiguity aversion in people. The authors test a setting where ambiguity aversion leads to lower earnings. In particular,

[1] Also referred to as the Ellsberg-Fellner Paradox, the paradox has been first introduced by political analyst Daniel Ellsberg and economist William Fellner. It was first published 1961 in the *Quarterly Journal of Economics*. See Ellsberg (1961).

participants needed to choose between a reference lottery with a 50% chance of winning $5, and another lottery with higher potential outcome but whose outcome probability was either below 50% or unknown. After learning about their ambiguity aversion, either by calculating the objective winning probabilities or by observing these calculations, participants became more tolerant of ambiguity.

In more complex situations, it becomes apparent that we are not only exhibiting ambiguity aversion regarding choices in the areas of risk and uncertainty, but we are also not deciding rationally when we are in a clear world of risk—without any uncertainty. The following example will introduce you to a setting of probabilities, where the task is to update your beliefs after gaining additional information about the situations.

Risk, Probabilities, and Rationality[2]

We are often first introduced to probabilities and probability theory in high school. Probabilities can often easily be determined by simply applying logical thinking. For example, when a coin is tossed, there are two possible outcomes: heads and tails, and thus we can conclude that the likelihood of each coming up is ½ or 50%. Another example is when a single die is thrown: then there are six possible outcomes: 1, 2, 3, 4, 5, 6. As a result, we can conclude that the probability of any one of them is 1/6. However, this reasoning and interpretation of probability is not very satisfying in practice, since for most problems such objective a priori probabilities simply do not exist (an exception possibly is gambling).

Do people respond rationally to risks and probabilities? You might have guessed it: The answer is no. In fact, it cannot be overstated that, unfortunately, people do *not* respond rationally to probabilities and risks. Here are some fun facts about probabilities I believe you wouldn't have guessed:

- In a random sample of only twenty-three people, there is a 50% chance that at least two people share a birthday. In a sample of 70 people, this probability jumps to over 99%.
- The likelihood of being crushed by a vending machine is higher than that of being attacked by a shark.
- There are 8.06e + 67 different ways to shuffle a deck of cards.
- You are 1860 times more likely to be hit by a world-ending asteroid than getting bombed by a terrorist.
- The odds of dying in an airplane crash are 1 in 205,552; this is not nearly as bad as compared to cars or motorcycles, on which you have a 1 in 846 chance of dying, according to the National Safety Council.[3]

While the above risks can be calculated by applying logical reasoning or using data, some probabilities cannot be calculated or are difficult to find out. This is why

[2] See Appendix 1 on probabilities for more information.

[3] https://injuryfacts.nsc.org/all-injuries/preventable-death-overview/odds-of-dying/

we tend to treat situations very differently, depending on how we personally evaluate the risk involved. For instance, in his prominent book on the history of risk, Peter Bernstein reports fascinating results from a study of 120 Stanford graduate students, who were asked to deliver probability estimates for dying from various causes (Bernstein, 1996).

Estimates of probabilities of death from various causes		
Cause	Subject estimates	Statistical estimates
Heart disease	0.22	0.34
Cancer	0.18	0.23
Other natural causes	0.33	0.35
All natural causes	**0.73**	**0.92**
Accident	0.32	0.05
Homicide	0.10	0.01
Other unnatural causes	0.11	0.02
All unnatural causes	**0.53**	**0.08**

The above table shows the probability estimates of one student group in the study, whereas another group was asked to estimate only the probability of death by natural versus unnatural causes. Interestingly, the students significantly *underestimated* the probabilities for natural causes, and vastly *overestimated* the probabilities for unnatural causes. It can be concluded from these findings that individuals tend to give more attention to worrying about the unnatural dangers and not enough to the natural dangers—a bias that is not easily explained.

So we have some problems estimating probabilities when it comes to real-life situations. Are we also as bad when it comes to making reasonable adjustments to probability estimates? Let's find out.

Do you think you can come up with a rationally adjusted probabilistic judgment of risk as new information about that risk arrives? The well-known rule to rationally update probabilities is the *Theorem of Bayes*. This theorem becomes useful in situations where we have limited risk information, as is the case for rare events or natural catastrophes. The principle is somewhat intuitive: start with your initial belief or what is called an *a-priori probability*. This is just your belief without having any additional information. Once the new information arrives, then scale your initial belief by what is called a likelihood ratio (measuring the strength of the new information). The likelihood ratio is used to adjust your initial belief to reflect the new information in your judgment of risk. The final adjusted probabilistic judgment of risk is called *a-posteriori probability*.

Unfortunately, humans are not very good at updating their probabilistic judgments of risks according to this principle. A possible reason is that the theorem seems complicated. However, it is possible for humans to become somewhat good Bayesian Updaters by practicising this task.

A very prominent example about our general inability to deal rationally with risk is the so-called *Monty Hall Problem*. This problem of probabilities impressively demonstrates how humans fail in the face of simple probability updating tasks. The *Monty Hall Problem* is famous since it heated the minds of a whole crowd of mathematicians and game theorists to the brink of despair in the 1980s. But first, let me introduce the game to you: In an American quiz show, a candidate stands in front of three locked doors, behind which in one case is a car and in two cases a goat. The contestant is now allowed to choose one of the doors; then the show-master opens one of the remaining two doors, always in such a way that one door with a goat is opened in any case, so that the car must be behind one of the still closed doors. He then offers the contestant to change the door now once again or to stay with the first selected door before it is opened. The candidate then gets to see what is behind the opened door she has finally chosen. Now, assuming that you prefer the car to the goat, what is the best way to play this game?

In a column by Marilyn vos Savant, someone asked whether it was better to switch in this situation or to stick with the original choice. Most people at that time thought that it didn't matter what you do. However, Marilyn vos Savant, who has the highest IQ ever measured and is therefore considered the most intelligent person in the world, answered succinctly with "switching is better", which triggered a whole discussion taking weeks for mankind to agree on the solution. Before that, however, she received nice letters saying: "You are the goat!", or: "You have made a mistake… If all these doctors were wrong, our country would be in serious trouble." The problem can be solved by applying the *Theorem of Bayes*. The problem can be illustrated as follows. Assume that your first choice is Door 1. The situation is as shown in the following table. Looking at the table, you can see that your chance of gain if you stick with Door 1—and so you do not switch doors after being shown what is behind the other closed door—is only 1/3. If, however, you decide to switch, your chance of gain is 2/3. As a result, by switching, you can double your chance of winning from 1/3 to 2/3.

Example: Assume your first choice is Door 1.

Door 1	**Door 2**	**Door 3**	***Result: not switch***	***Result: switch***
Car	Goat	Goat	Car	Goat
Goat	Car	Goat	Goat	Car
Goat	Goat	Car	Goat	Car

To illustrate this insight even more, assume that there are one million doors to choose from and assume you choose Door 1. Now you are asked whether you would like to stick to your original choice or whether you would like to switch doors. The moderator, who knows what's behind the doors and who always avoids the one door with the car, opens all doors except door number 222,222. Now you would immediately switch to this door, wouldn't you? This is because you have updated your guess about where the car might be after learning about the other doors with goats behind them. The *Monty Hall Problem* is not a multiplayer game but a game against nature (i.e. against the probability distribution of cars and goats behind doors). The quizmaster is not a decision maker who has to decide between two doors based on his own preferences, but he acts like an executing algorithm by always opening that door where there is certainly no car. Now—it seems easy to understand why this is about probability updating, and maybe you can see why people tend to have problems with it.

Psychological Aspects on Risk Perception

Given the fact that most people do *not* respond rationally to probabilities and risks, there is a need to become a better risk leader when we want to successfully deal with risks in our professional career. One of the reasons why it is so difficult for us to make "good" decision-makers under risk is that we are humans and, as humans, are driven by emotions that interact—and sometimes counteract—with our rationality. The psychological aspect is often neglected in economic theory of risk bearing and risk management. However, understanding psychology is fundamental in understanding the processes relating to risk management. It is important to know why humans behave the way that they do, react the way that they do in certain conditions, and why they make certain decisions in varying situations. Although it is important to understand the influences that psychology plays in risk and its management, it is difficult to overcome the conflicts that are natural to most humans. We may be well aware of our own biases or the influence that these conflicts can play in our decision-making processes; but even risk perceptions and judgements made by experts tend to be prone to a wide spectrum of psychological influences. Therefore, these influences can be learned, understood, and managed, but they cannot be ignored (Shefrin, 2017).

Research in psychology over the last 40 years has shown that processes where we are identifying and quantifying risk are extremely vulnerable to judgmental biases. People overestimate and underestimate some risks, while completely overlooking others. A Harvard Business Review article also thoroughly explains why assessing risk is such a challenge for managers. Managers often attach their estimates to the most readily available information, "despite the known danger of making linear extrapolations from recent history to a highly uncertain and variable future" (Kaplan, and Mikes 2012). Risk managers often entangle this issue with a confirmation bias, which also influences people to be receptive to data that supports their positions, while ignoring information that is contradicting to their positions (Kaplan and Mikes 2012).

Looking into the psychology literature related to decisions under risk and uncertainty, it is shown that we assess risks not only by using available cognitive skills (such as logic and reasoning) when we think about risk and uncertainty, but we also use individual emotional appraisals (fear and intuition), the outcome of which can be a decision that is far from rational. For instance, the *perception of risk* can be influenced by many factors, including.[4]

Control. Some real or at least perceived level of control over risky outcomes matters for us. This explains why some people are not afraid of driving a car, even though automobile accidents kill thousands of people every year but may be afraid of using a train or flying in an airplane. Indeed, dying due to our own error seems more acceptable than dying due to the error of a machine or algorithm. In March 2018, for instance, when a self-driving vehicle being tested by Uber killed a pedestrian in Tempe, Arizona, triggered a discussion on the safety of self-driving cars. A

[4] See Housel (2020) and Ropeik (2002).

poll in January 2018 had shown that 35% of survey participants considered self-driving cars to be less safe than regular human-driven cars. The same survey question was administered by the same pollster shortly after the Uber accident, and now the number of self-driving vehicle skeptics climbed to 50%.[5] Consider those ancient times when elevators were the new technology and operators were needed to open and close elevator doors. Since people started to fear driverless elevators when they were first introduced, a big red stop-button was added to improve the users' feeling of control; however, the button did not add any control over the elevator's operating system: it did only connect to a remote human operator when pushed. Today, Google's driverless car has a red e-stop button, as well, directing the system to stop the car safely. So the question that comes to mind is: How much control do we need to trust? Research suggests that a small amount of control is enough.

Origin. People are less concerned about risks they incur themselves than the ones that others impose on them. This helps explain why people often get upset when they see someone talking on the phone while driving—and yet think nothing of doing so themselves.

Scope. *Cataclysmic* events capable of killing many people at the same time are perceived to be scarier than *chronic* events killing only a few at one point in time but many over time. This explains why a hurricane or an earthquake feels scarier than heart disease or diabetes. The terrorist attacks of September 11, 2001, have been accompanied with high media attention over a longer period of time after they happened, and most people even remember what they did on this day. A large number of people lost their lives that day. However, a similar number of people also lost their lives in the same year due to car accidents, but nobody discusses these deaths. The effect here is that many people died due to one singular event on 1 day rather than due to many smaller events over time. Consequences can be irrational market reactions. For example, after 9/11 many people took the car to get to another city or location far away from their home rather than taking a plane, resulting in many more deaths due to car accidents after 9/11 than before. All these deaths from car accidents could have been avoided by good risk communication by the media—educating the public that the airplane is the safest vehicle to get from A to B. Indeed, the most dangerous part of the whole trip is the part of safely getting to the airport!

Awareness. Long-term media coverage of high-profile disasters raises awareness of particular risks at the time it is covered more than others. This is why we often see a peak in flood insurance demand right after an event happened! This is an irrational response since the likelihood of the disaster is not elevated right after one occurred! Likewise, an event that hits close to home, such as having a friend or family member being diagnosed with a deadly disease, heightens individual perception for that specific risk.

Individual History. Risk perception also depends on an individual's own personal history and time he or she was born. For instance, for a person born in 1960's USA, perception of inflation risk and its impact on the own economic conditions would be high; in contrast, for a person born in the 1990's USA, perception of

[5] Hosanagar (2019), p. 157.

inflation risk would be negligible. From a psychological perspective, every decision a person makes can be justified by taking into account their personal circumstances and history, the information available to them at the current moment and by plugging it into their mental model of how the system works.

Before we dig deeper into the psychological aspects of managing risks (better), let's find out more about how we deal with risk in a general fashion.

Risk Metrics

How a person decides in a risky situation also heavily depends on the *metric* he or she uses to quantify the risk. People use different risk metrics. As an example, assume you are a stockowner and consider your potential future investment returns. Which risk metric should you use? Well, it might make sense to limit your risk perception when it comes to stocks you own to "downward risk" only, that is, you would only worry about a stock going down but not going up—since this is when you make money on the stock. Below is a graph of the overall variation in the daily returns of the S&P 500. People can interpret risk now as the overall variation or simply the below-the mean semi deviation of returns over time. As a consequence, risk is measured differently depending on the risk metric that is used.

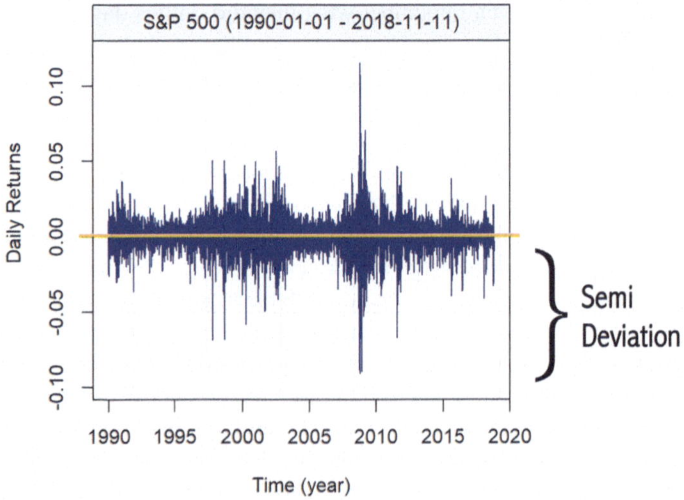

Assume now you are the risk manager of a firm which faces three different risky payoffs, say D, E, and F. You want to reduce or even eliminate risk so that the firm derives the highest mean payoff for each unit of total risk. How best to then combine these three risks depends on the actual metric you will use to quantify the risk. As an example, below you see the payoffs from each of three risks over a period of time as well as the mean aggregate payoff per unit of total risk given three different risk measures. The payoffs from the individual risks are below; the mean aggregate payoffs per unit of total risk are on the right.[6]

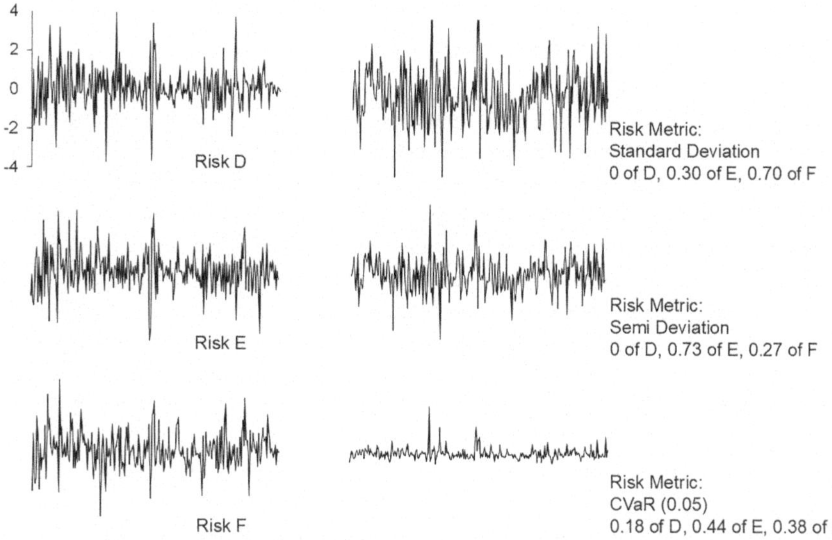

The top, right graph above depicts the results of the manager's decision if risk is measured as standard deviation. The manager should retain none of Risk D, retain 30% of Risk E and retain 70% of Risk F. The graph shows the aggregate payoff over time that results from the retained risk. The middle, right graph of the graph depicts the results of the manager's decision if risk is measured as below-the-mean semi-deviation. In this case, "upside risk" in terms of variability above the mean is ignored. The risk manager should continue retaining none of Risk D, but should now retain 73% of Risk E and only retain 27% of Risk F. The bottom, right graph depicts the results of the manager's decision if risk is measured as "tail risk" of the worst 5% of the payoff distribution. The risk metric is conditional value at risk or CVaR.[7] These examples of different risk metrics suggest that how risk is acted upon

[6] All graphs are on an identical scale. Risks D, E, and F are payoffs from randomly selected firms. Risks D, E, and F follow a logistic distribution with respective parameters (0.05, 0.55), (0.07, 0.55) and (0.03, 0.55). The association among risks is estimated using Pearson correlation. The correlation between Risks D and E is 0.58, between Risks D and F is 0.61 and between E and F is 0.53. The resulting distribution for the aggregate payoffs where standard deviation and semi-deviation are the measures of risk are logistic (0.12, 0.83) and (0.06, 0.50), respectively. The resulting distribution of the aggregate payoffs (where conditional value at risk is the measure of risk) is log-logistic (−0.62, 0.67, 5.19). The optimization analysis is performed using Monte Carlo simulation.

[7] The conditional value at risk (CVaR) specifies which variation in the occurrence of the tail risk is to be expected when exceeding a percentile threshold, often referenced as value at risk (VaR). The mathematical expression is thus a conditional expected value, $\mathrm{CVAR}(X) = E(X|X > \mathrm{VaR}(x))$. With CVaR as the risk metric, the manager should retain 18% of Risk D, 44% of Risk E, and 38% of Risk F.

clearly depends on how risk is measured. As a result, you should always ask which metric is being used to measure risk! Different metrics lead to different decisions.

Risk Aversion

Let me invite you to think about participating in an interesting game. Assume there are two players in this game and you are player 2. Player 1 begins and flips a fair coin. If the coin reveals heads, this player will pay the other player \$2, and the game is over. If the coin lands on tails, it is tossed again. If the second toss lands heads, the first player pays \$4 to the second, and the game is over. If the second toss lands tails, the coin is flipped again. Thus, the game continues until the first head appears, and then the first player pays the second $(\$2)^n$, where n signifies the number of tosses required to reveal the first head. Since a head will turn up eventually, the second player wants a long preceding run of tails. The problem is: how much will the second player, this means you, be willing to pay to participate in this game?

Obviously, the probability of heads for the first coin toss is equal to 1/2. Since coin tosses are independent events, the probability of having heads again in the second coin toss equals 1/2 × 1/2 = 1/4. The payout series is depicted below, where *T* represents tails and H represents heads. The payoff in dollars is written below each coin toss.

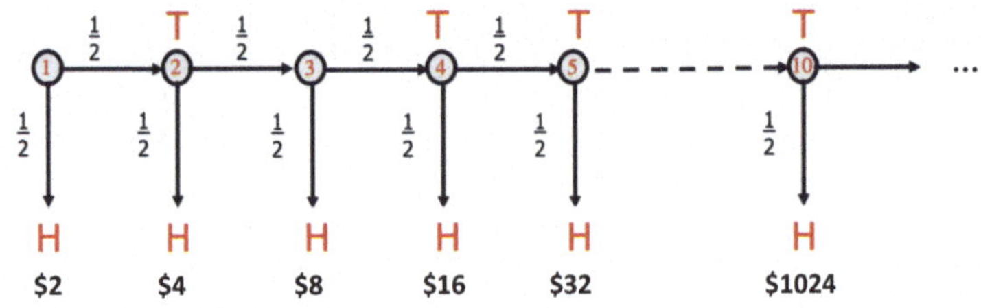

You can see from the picture that, witch each additional tails-event, the probability goes down while the payoff goes up in the same proportion. Indeed, when taking into account all probabilities and payoffs, the mean amount of money you will go home with from the payout series of this game is:

$$\text{Mean payoff} = \$2 \times ½ + \$4 \times ¼ + \$8 \times 1/8 + \ldots. = 1 + 1 + 1 + \ldots =$$
infinitely large amount of money!

So, would you invest all your money to participate in this game? I guess not. But why is it that people will typically only pay a few dollars to participate in a game that has an infinite mean payoff? People often calculate the mean or average payout when confronted with decisions involving risk. But clearly, the idea of following the average payout is broken here dramatically. What causes the mean principle to fail here?

The answer is that risk is ignored in the concept of average. We can illustrate this with another simple example: assume you need to compare two prospects A and B with each other. Gaining $10 with certainty (prospect A) is clearly very different from a 50–50 gamble for $20 or $0 (prospect B). The finding that people generally have a preference for A over B and the small entry price to participate in the game above indicate that the quality of variability in payouts is an adverse factor when we make decisions under risk, even given equality in averages. Most people prefer choices with less risk rather than more risk. This does not mean that people will never choose risk when it can be avoided. The average payout of one prospect may be so advantageous in comparison with a competing prospect that aversion to risk is overcome.

By the way, Daniel Bernoulli, an eighteenth century Swiss mathematician and physicist as well as professor of mathematics at the Russian Academy in Saint Petersburg, invented this classic game, which has come to be known in the literature as the *St. Petersburg Paradox.*

The next question, therefore, is: How can such preferences toward risk be defined? In risk economics, an individual is considered *risk-averse* if he or she prefers a certain payment over a lottery with the same average payment (or expected value). Risk aversion is considered to be common for most people. In one of my risk management lectures in 2020, for instance, a group of 20 students were asked to take part in a poll to assess their risk attitude using a basic example. This was done before defining risk aversion, in order to minimize interference with the results of the survey. Students were to choose between a certain payment of $100 (a), a gamble between gaining $200 or $0 with a probability of 50% each (b), or saying they were indifferent between (a) and (b) by choosing (c). In this setting, choosing (a) would mean that the student is risk-averse. If a student chooses (b), he or she would be considered risk-loving, and if (c) were chosen, the individual would be considered risk neutral.

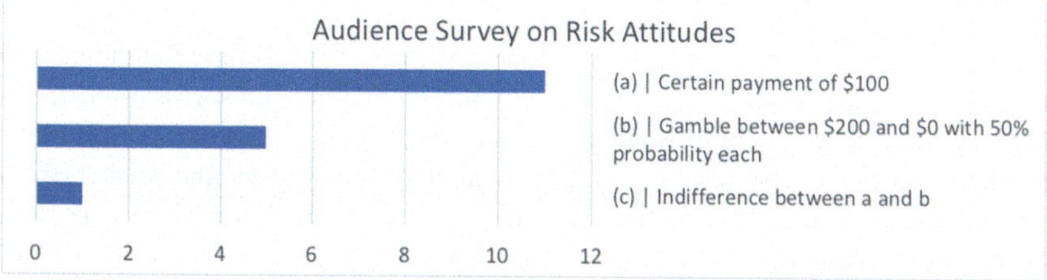

Of the 17 students taking part in the poll, 11 chose answer (a) and should therefore be considered as risk-averse individuals. Furthermore, five chose answer (b), making them risk-loving in this setting. Only one student opted for answer (c) and can therefore be considered risk-neutral. Hence, most students showed a risk-averse attitude, which is consistent with empirical findings in general.

Having established that people are generally risk-averse, the next question to address is whether this preference is a stable one and how it is possibly changing.

An individual's risk aversion can be influenced in a variety of ways. Some experiments with twins found that an individual's overall risk attitude can be divided into two general components: Approximately 20% of the expression of risk preferences can be due to genetic disposition; accordingly, the remaining 80% is determined by environmental influences.[8] Looking closer at these two main components, we can say that an individual's level of risk aversion is usually influenced by the following factors:

Wealth. The level of wealth and permanent income are very important risk aversion determinants. A richer person is less risk-averse than a poor person. Why? Well, if you give $1 to a poor individual, he or she will simply value it more than Bill Gates. As we become richer, our risk aversion generally goes down and we become more "playful" with money. This is confirmed in a study by Riley and Chow (1992), who evaluated individual asset allocation decisions and found that risk aversion tends to decline with wealth. Noteworthy is that cross-sections with the least wealth and the most wealth tend to exhibit less risk aversion than those with intermediate levels of wealth, as shown by Barsky et al. (1997).

Gender. Halek and Eisenhauer (2001) examine aversion against both pure and speculative risks. The authors find, confirming previous research, that women are significantly more risk averse than men. Why? Well, taking an evolutionary perspective on risk aversion suggests that males tend to be better equipped to handle physical threats simply by virtue of strength, speed, and endurance, and this is why they may have acquired a more risk-prone attitude than others in society by way of natural selection. In contrast, social identity theory suggests that our personal identity is derived from social group memberships, such as nationality, religion, ethnicity, professional environment, and gender identity. A study by Powell and Ansic (1997) evaluated samples of college students' responses to experimental questions regarding insurance and foreign currency exchange. This study also found, in line with multiple earlier studies, that women tend to be more risk averse than men. Interestingly, the gender differences do not depend on age or level of education but were affected by race and having children. Dohmen et al. (2011) and Gupta et al. (2011) find that women's choices are more driven by risk attitudes compared to men's choice. Other researchers find that women in the financial sector often act in a more conservative way. For instance, Niessen and Ruenzi (2007) find female managers invest in a more risk-averse way than male managers. Powell and Ansic (1997) find men are more likely to choose investment strategies which increase the portfolios' risk variations. Their findings confirm that women are less risk-seeking than their men counterparts.

Experience. Another factor that has an impact on an individual's risk preference is the experience a person has with a certain risk. A chain of prior successes or prior failures can lead to changes in the risk attitude over time. In a study by Brocas et al. (2019), an influence of prior gains or losses was observed in the behavior of almost half of subjects. The majority of these individuals took more risk after a gain. This phenomenon, that people will be willing to take greater risk after a prior gain, is

[8] See Cesarini et al. (2009), p. 834 as well as Ahern et al. (2014), p. 3213.

often called the *House Money Effect*. It has also been shown in several experiments that people are less likely to take risks after prior losses.[9] Sometimes, a minority of subjects takes more risks after a loss. This can partially be explained by what Thaler and Johnson describe as the *Break-Even Effect*. It describes that options with outcomes that would offer the possibility to break even with a prior level of wealth are perceived as being especially attractive.

Age. Riley and Chow (1992) find that risk aversion tends to decline with wealth, level of education, and age, until the age of 65, at which risk aversion goes up again. Maybe, as we get older, we get more aware of the fact that our remaining life expectancy is approaching its limits.

Level of Education. As found in Halek and Eisenhauer (2001), at the margin, education increases individual risk aversion to pure risk but also increases the willingness to accept a speculative risk. This may relate to a desire to control one's environment: an individual must actively seek out speculative risks, whereas he or she reacts to the pure risks that are thrust upon him or her. Dohmen et al. (2011) also point out the impact of family background in terms of parental education. The level of education of one's parents seems to play a major role in determining individual risk attitudes, demonstrated by a positive correlation between parental education and a child's willingness to take risks.

Genetics. You night ask yourself the question about genetics. What is the role of genetics in risk aversion? Barnea et al. (2010) analyze data on the asset allocation of over 37,000 twins from the Swedish Twin Registry. While they study the effects of different factors on investment behavior, namely stock market participation and asset allocation decisions, and not specifically on risk aversion, risk aversion in itself is a very important determinant for investment behavior. Their research showed clearly that a third of the variation in individual investment behavior can be explained by a genetic factor. This finding even holds for identical twins that are rarely or never in contact with each other. It is interesting that the effect does not disappear with age. When controlling for a genetic factor, the influence of other factors decreases. Hence, whether you as a person are risk-averse or risk-loving is indeed, at least partially, influenced by your genetics and this behavior might have developed over thousands of years. However, Barnea et al. (2010) also find a significant effect of the family environment as well as the non-shared environment. While the effect of the family environment is important for younger ages, it disappears quickly as soon as individuals gain their own experiences relevant for investment decisions.[10]

In general, it seems that wealth, experience, gender, and age are the most important drivers of risk aversion. This is confirmed by Dohmen et al. (2011) pointing out the important drivers of peoples' willingness to take risks "in general" to be gender, age, height, and parental background; these drivers all have an economically significant impact on peoples' general willingness to take risks. Interestingly, in this study,

---

[9] See Thaler and Johnson (1990), p. 644.

[10] See Barnea et al. (2010), pp. 584–588.

height appears to be also a determinant of an individual's risk attitude, with taller individuals of both genders being found to be more willing to take risks.

Finally, another factor that has an impact on individual risk preferences is experience with a certain risk. A chain of prior successes or prior failures can lead to changes in a person's risk attitude over time. In a study by Brocas et al. (2019), the impact of prior gains or losses was observed in the behavior of almost half of subjects. The majority took more risk after a gain. This phenomenon, that people will be willing to take greater risk after a prior gain, is often referred to as the *House Money Effect*. In the same way, it has also been shown in several experiments that people are less likely to take risks after prior losses. It is, however, not rational to change your risk-related behavior depending on the consequences of a prior decision, if the prior outcome did not have any influence on the expected outcome of the next decision.

Are risk preferences generally stable over time? A fascinating article by Schildberg-Hörisch (2018) summarizes a variety of studies and offers a projection on how risk preferences are not stable but somewhat predictable for all of us. Findings confirm previous empirical evidence that individuals become more risk-averse over their life cycle. There may be downward shifts of abrupt mean-level changes in individual risk preferences, for instance following exogenous shocks like economic crises. In addition, the general trend is accompanied by temporary variation in risk preferences, for instance temporary variations in emotions, self-control, or stress levels causing preferences to vary slightly around an average level.

Key Takeaways for Risk Leadership

Understanding individual risk psychology and perception, risk aversion, risk perception-related behavior and how our emotions respond to risk and uncertainty as well as which cognitive biases are the result—these are all crucial elements in making better risk-related decisions and becoming better risk leaders. For managers, understanding cognitive biases is even more important than for the general population given that managerial decisions have consequences for the long-term survival of the firm.

Given that many of the common biases are predictable once you are aware of them, you will be less vulnerable to manipulation. These biases also provide the necessary ingredients to improve our decision-making processes as managers, which is the aim of this book. As we go forward, we will gain deeper insights into the different biases that distort our decision-making. Understanding important aspects of risk psychology is fundamental in understanding the processes relating to risk management. We may be well aware of our own biases or the influence that these conflicts can play in our decision-making processes; but even risk perceptions and judgements made by experts tend to be prone to a wide spectrum of psychological influences. But the good news is: while they cannot be ignored, these influences can be learned, understood, and managed.

How a person decides in a risky situation heavily depends on the metric he or she uses to quantify risk. Awareness about different types of measurement of risk and consequences of using either one or another metric should be trained.

Risk aversion is the common risk preference that most humans exhibit when confronted with risky situations, and this is not necessarily a disadvantageous human trait. In many situations, it is likely even better to be risk-averse when making important decisions. Risk aversion is influenced by several factors and varies with a person's age. It is noteworthy that there are quite a few effects regarding risk preferences that may influence the decision-making process of an individual in a non-rational way. For example, it may not be rational to change your risk-related behavior depending on the consequences of a prior decision, if the prior outcome did not have any influence on the expected outcome of the next decision. Unfortunately, being inconsistent over time is quite common in human risk-related decision making.

The most important single key takeaway from this chapter is to measure risk even if you think you know about it—this is because what is measured can be optimized! By quantifying and measuring risk, you can manage the risk before it manages you. By actively managing your own risks, even if you need to make simplifying assumptions about probabilities, you can improve your perception of risk, evaluate your risk aversion, avoid zero-risk bias, and be aware of the biases discussed later in this book. You should also be actively aware of and manage your risk management style over time. In particular, be aware of the fact that you and others may act in a way towards risk that is not rational. This is the first commandment which basically leads to the others that follow in subsequent chapters. It is important to manage your risk management style over time, given that we as humans often fall prey to these many mistakes. Being actively aware of our weaknesses (and the weaknesses of our opponents) makes us stronger and better risk leaders.

References

Ahern, K. R., Duchin, R., & Shumway, T. (2014). Peer effects in risk aversion and trust. *Review of Financial Studies, 27*(11), 3213–3240.

Barnea, A., Cronqvist, H., & Siegel, S. (2010). Nature or nurture: What determines investor behavior? *Journal of Financial Economics, 98*, 583–604.

Barsky, R. B., Thomas, F. J., Kimball, M. S., & Shapiro, M. D. (1997). Preference parameters and behavioral heterogeneity: An experimental approach in the health and retirement study. *Quarterly Journal of Economics, 112*(2), 537–579.

Bernstein, P. (1996). *Against the gods: The remarkable story of risk*. John Wiley & Sons.

Brocas, I., Carrillo, J. D., Giga, A., & Zapatero, F. (2019). Risk aversion in a dynamic asset allocation experiment. *Journal of Financial and Quantitative Analysis, 54*(5), 2209–2232.

Cabantous, L. (2007). Ambiguity aversion in the field of insurance: Insurers' attitude to imprecise and conflicting probability estimates. *Theory and Decision, 62*(3), 219–240.

Cesarini, D., Dawes, C. T., Johannesson, M., Lichtenstein, P., & Wallace, B. (2009). Genetic variation in preferences for giving and risk taking. *Quarterly Journal of Economics, 124*(2), 809–842.

Dohmen, T., Falk, A., Huffman, D., Sunde, U., Schupp, J., & Wagner, G. (2011). Individual risk attitudes: Measurement, determinants, and behavioral consequences. *Journal of the European Economic Association, 9*(3), 522–550.

Ellsberg, D. (1961). Risk, ambiguity, and the savage axioms. *Quarterly Journal of Economics, 75*(4), 643–669.

Gupta, D., Poulsen, A., & Villeval, M. (2011). Gender matching and competitiveness: Experimental evidence. *Economic Inquiry, 51*, 816–835.

Halek, M., & Eisenhauer, J. G. (2001). Demography of risk aversion. *Journal of Risk and Insurance, 68*(1), 1–24.

Hosanagar, K. (2019). *How algorithms are shaping our lives and how we can stay in control – a human's guide to machine learning*. Viking.

Housel, M. (2020). *The psychology of money – timeless lessons on wealth, greed, and happiness*. Harriman House Ltd..

Jia, R., Furlong, E., Gao, S., Santos, L.R., & Levy, I. (2020). Learning about the Ellsberg Paradox reduces, but does not abolish, ambiguity aversion, In: PloslOne Open Access, published March 4, 2020.

Kaplan, R. & Mikes, A. (2012). Managing risks: A new framework, Harvard Business Review. https://hbr.org/2012/06/managing-risks-a-new-framework. Last accessed January 10, 2022.

Kunreuther, H., Hogarth, R., & Meszaros, L. (1993). Insurer ambiguity and market failure. *Journal of Risk and Uncertainty, 7*(1), 71–87.

Niessen, A. & Ruenzi, S. (2007). Sex matters: Gender differences in a professional setting, Center for Financial Research (CFR), Univeristy of Cologne (Germany), Working Paper No. 06-01.

Powell, M., & Ansic, D. (1997). Gender differences in risk behaviour in financial decision-making: An experimental analysis. *Journal of Economic Psychology, 18*(6), 605–628.

Riley, W., & Chow, K. V. (1992). Asset allocation and individual risk aversion. *Financial Analysts Journal, 48*(November/December Issue), 32–37.

Ropeik, D. (2002). Understanding Factors of Risk Perception, Nieman Reports, 2002.

Schildberg-Hörisch, H. (2018). Are risk preferences stable? *Journal of Economic Perspectives, 32*(2), 135–154.

Shefrin, H. (2017). *Behavioral risk management: Managing the psychology that drives decisions and influences operational risk*. Palgrave Macmillan.

Thaler, R. H., & Johnson, E. J. (1990). Gambling with the house money and trying to break even: The effect of prior outcomes on risky choice. *Management Science, 36*(6), 643–660.

3 Expected Utility, Prospect Theory, and the Allais Paradox: Why Reference Points Are Important

The most important single key takeaway from this chapter is

> **The 2nd Commandment of Risk Leadership:** Reference points have significant implications for the way we evaluate risky opportunities.

Humans do *not* follow logical axioms used in common economic theory when making decisions under risk and uncertainty. In contrast, reference points and loss aversion are rather important when we make our risk-related decisions. Here, we tend to rely on a number of simple heuristics—thereby reducing the complex task of assessing and evaluating probabilities and predicting gains and losses to much simpler judgmental operations. While these heuristics can be quite useful and save time and energy for the brain, they can also imply severe and systematic errors.

Bernoulli and Expected Utility Theory[1]

How do humans make decisions under risk? The Swiss mathematician and physicist Daniel Bernoulli, a member of the famous Bernoulli family of distinguished mathematicians from Basel, gave this question deeper thought in the early 1700s.[2] He was the first to suggest that individuals facing the same lottery tend to value it differently. He found that this is due to their different risk preferences or, in other words, their different (psychological) attitudes towards the same risk. He argued that the actual 'value' of a lottery to an individual is generally not equal to its (mathematical) expected value but differs between individuals. According to Daniel

[1] See Appendix 2 for more details.

[2] The original article 'Specimen theoriae novae de mensura sortis' appeared in 1738 and has been translated into English in Bernoulli (1954).

A. Hofmann, *The Ten Commandments of Risk Leadership*, Future of Business and Finance, https://doi.org/10.1007/978-3-030-88797-1_3

Bernoulli's idea, instead of using mathematical expected value, a lottery should be valued according to expected utility that it provides, i.e., the expected value of the utility of wealth. His basic idea was to suggest that there usually is a non-linear relationship between monetary wealth and utility - or satisfaction - of consuming this monetary wealth. In other words, utility is a scale of measurement of the person's satisfaction derived from money. Given that an individual has 'rational' preferences, we may - under reasonable assumptions - represent this relationship by some utility function that attributes every outcome a level of utility. Expected Utility theory is used throughout economics as the main standard tool of analysis for studying human behavior under risk and uncertainty from a theoretical standpoint.

To represent utility, we can reasonably order levels of satisfaction according to the rule "more wealth is always preferred to less wealth." Second, we can assume that incremental utility, or satisfaction, from unit increases in wealth decreases as wealth increases. Why? Well, if somebody is very poor, an additional $1,000 to his wealth will make a considerable impact on his level of satisfaction. However, if somebody is extremely rich, these same extra $1,000 will still increase his satisfaction, but only at the margin. Indeed, the rich guy would barely feel the increase in his wealth. In economics, we refer to these concepts as the law of diminishing marginal utility. Since different individuals will scale different levels of wealth in different ways, utility functions look different for these individuals.

While it is not possible to make a direct comparison of different individuals' tastes for wealth, comparing utility functions gives insight into individual risk attitude. For one individual, the shape of her utility function may change slope more rapidly than for another person. In the graph below, there are two different individuals with different levels of attitudes toward risk. Individual B is more risk-averse than individual A, which is indicated by B's more intense curvature of her utility function.

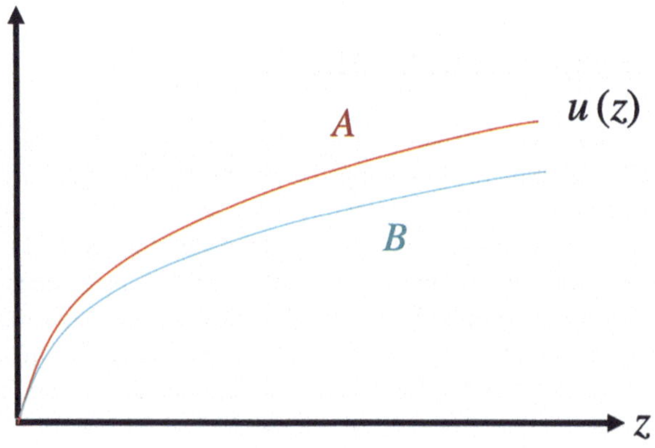

The following principle, often referred to as the *Bernoulli Principle*, has proven to be a powerful technique for analyzing choices under risk. The Bernoulli principle is an axiomatically based decision criterion. It is based on a set of formal axioms, and we will see that it can be used to provide some very important preliminary insights into risk-management problems. The following decision principle for risky outcomes is called.[3]

Bernoulli Principle. *An individual should choose the alternative that maximizes the expected value of utility over all states of the world.*

Under this principle, the possible outcomes are weighted according to their respective probabilities and according to the utility scale of the individual. The substitution of outcomes measured in utility terms for money outcomes ensures that individual risk preferences can be impressed on the decision process. It is noteworthy that the principle is based on four fundamental assumptions (or *axioms*) about individual preferences:

1. *Completeness* (the individual can tell a preference over lotteries).
2. *Transitivity* (the individual's preference order is consistent).
3. *Independence over lotteries* (the individual's preference stays the same when adding an identical risk).
4. *Continuity* (the individual's preferences are continuous).

The axiom of *completeness* states that for each pair of choices or lotteries A and B, the individual can make a comparison and determine his or her preference ordering such that $A > B$, $A < B$ or $A \sim B$, or in other words: "A is better than B", "A is worse than B" or "I am indifferent between A and B".

The axiom of *transitivity* states that the individual's preferences are transitive such that if he or she prefers option A over option B ($A > B$) and option B over option C ($B > C$), then it must follow that option A is preferred over option C ($A > C$). Stated more briefly, transitivity means that $A > B > C \Rightarrow A > C$. Transitivity is an intuitive rationality assumption, which is unfortunately often violated in practice. It requires a preference order of an individual to be consistent in the following way: Assume the individual thinks A is better than B, and B is better than C, then the individual logically must also think that A is better than C, right? Well, assume you ask people about their preferences regarding beer, whiskey and wine consumption. A person might say he prefers wine over beer, and beer over whiskey, but then he might express that, if given the choice between whiskey and wine only, he likes the whiskey better. This would represent inconsistent preferences in the sense of transitivity.

The axiom of *independence* states that if the individual prefers A over B, this preference is independent of any transformations that are the same for both outcomes. In other words, if $A > B$, then this preference will not change for all outcomes C and all probabilities $p \in [0,1]$, such that $pA + (1 - p)C > pB + (1 - p)C$. As a consequence, the individual is indifferent between a lottery and its certainty equivalent.

The axiom of *continuity* states that for uncertain events A, B and C, if he or she thinks that $A > B > C$, then a probability p exists such that he or she is indifferent

[3] The principle is shown formally in Appendix 3.

between B with certainty and playing a lottery where (s)he receives A with probability p and C with probability (1 − p). In other words, it is always possible to construct a combination of choices A and C that are equally valuable to the individual as the certainty equivalent B.

It should be noted that Bernoulli was thinking of rational individuals without any flaws. But looking into field and laboratory experiments reveals that humans share many common flaws and do (unfortunately) not behave in the predicted way. In particular, the above preference assumptions are not always fulfilled when we look at real-life decision-making outcomes of many individuals—maybe except in certain easy-to-understand basic probability choices. Indeed, individual decision-making could only be deemed to be really rational if choices were made in adherence with these axioms.

Why Expected Utility Does Not Work

The Expected Utility (EU) model is useful for streamlining our thinking about decisions under risk and uncertainty and the generated results can be used as first approximations for meaningful and reasonable solutions to risk management problems. The application of this model in practice is, however, very limited. While the EU model can be seen as a handy tool to analyze decision-making under risk in theory, it is often not a good predictor of actual decision-making under risk in many practical situations. First, this is because we need to know exactly the shape of an individual's utility function in order to calculate results. While finding such a function is possible using a survey method, the data is mostly not available in practice and so an exact function is unknown. The best available data is often some broad measure of individual risk aversion, which can be used to find some general range of potential solutions. Second, the assumption that a firm can somehow be treated like an individual with a utility function is rather unrealistic given the many different stakeholders and shareholders forming the entity as a whole.

It is well documented in the literature that the overly rational decisions assumed under the EU model are most often inconsistent with findings from laboratory and field experiments. Many experimental economists have increasingly begun to question the descriptive validity of the model due to its limitations. For instance, the EU model cannot explain why some individuals purchase insurance contracts to reduce or avoid certain risks, while also at the same time playing the lottery or going to a casino and thereby actively seeking situations involving risk. Furthermore, the EU model predicts a rational individual to purchase insurance for a high-consequence risk, but empirical evidence shows that only a small proportion of the insured population demands insurance to protect them from natural disasters—and this is even the case when catastrophe insurance is highly subsidized (see Chap. 10). Similar effects can be observed in the long-term care insurance and agricultural insurance markets.[4] Another issue when thinking about rationality is that people sometimes over-insure certain risks, a phenomenon observed in the markets for homeowners and auto insurance. This behavior can only be explained using the EU model by assuming unrealistically high degrees of individuals' risk aversion.[5]

The following is a famous simple example to illustrate why the EU model generally will not work in practice. It may help to think about what your own choices would have been in this situation.

The Allais Paradox

The Allais paradox is a choice problem designed by Allais (1953), a French physicist and economist, to show an inconsistency of actual observed choices with the predictions of expected utility theory. Allais was the first to suggest that expected utility theory cannot correctly depict human behavior. Please think about which of the following gambles you would prefer, 1A or 1B. The situation is as follows: In gamble 1A, you gain $1 million with certainty (cool, right?). In gamble 1B, however, you have a 89% chance of winning $1 million, a 1% chance of winning nothing at all, and a 10% chance of winning $5 million. Do you prefer 1A or 1B?

Experiment 1

Gamble 1A		Gamble 1B	
Winnings	Chance (%)	Winnings	Chance (%)
$1 million	100	$1 million	89
		Nothing	1
		$5 million	10

Well, most people prefer 1A in this experiment, simply because there is no risk involved and the $1 million represent a certain win. We can rewrite this decision more formally in EU terms as follows, where U(.) depicts the individual's utility function and ">" simply means "is perferred over":

$$U(1\,\text{mill.}) > 0.89\,U(1\,\text{mill.}) + 0.01\,U(0) + 0.1\,U(5\,\text{mill.}) \Rightarrow$$
$$0.11\,U(1\,\text{mill.}) > 0.01\,U(0) + 0.1\,U(5\,\text{mill.})$$

In a second experiment, there is always some risk involved. Here, in gamble 2A, you have a 89% chance of winning nothing at all (too bad, right?), and an 11% chance of winning $1 million. In gamble 2B, you have a 90% chance of winning nothing at all (even worse, right?), but a 10% chance of winning $5 million.

Now please think again about which of the following gambles you would prefer, 2A or 2B?

[4] See Gollier (2005), Brown and Finkelstein (2009), Mahul and Stutley (2010) as well as Volkman-Wise (2015).

[5] As shown by Sydnor (2010) and Barseghyan et al. (2013).

Experiment 2

Gamble 2A		Gamble 2B	
Winnings	Chance (%)	Winnings	Chance (%)
Nothing	89	Nothing	90
\$1 million	11	\$5 million	10

Most people now prefer 2B because there is a much higher amount of money that can be won with an only slightly lower chance. Again, we can rewrite this decision more formally in EU terms as follows:

$$0.9\,U(0)+0.1\,U(5\,\text{mill.})>0.89\,U(0)+0.11\,U(1\,\text{mill.})=>$$
$$0.01\,U(0)+0.1\,U(5\,\text{mill.})>0.11\,U(1\,\text{mill.})$$

So far, this all makes perfect sense. However, when looking into the formally expressed preferences, we see from experiment 1 that the individual has preference.

$$0.11\,U(1\,\text{mill.})>0.01\,U(0)+0.1\,U(5\,\text{mill.})$$

while from experiment 2, the same individual has preference.

$$0.1\,U(0)+0.1\,U(5\,\text{mill.})>0.11\,U(1\,\text{mill.}).$$

Whoops!—This cannot be right! And so, as a result, the Allais paradox predicts a *systematic violation* of the Bernoulli Principle, in particular the *independence axiom*!

Prospect Theory

Americans spend more on lottery tickets than movies, games, and music together. Isn't that amazing?! And why are the lottery tickets mostly purchased by poor people with less "extra" funds available for play? Indeed, the lowest-income households in the U.S. spend \$412 a year on average on lottery tickets, which is four-times as much as the highest-income households. By and large, this lowest-income-but-highest-lottery-spending group also indicates that it cannot come up with \$400 in case of an emergency.[6] Why would these people risk their annual financial safety net for a winning chance of 1-in-14-million? It may seem irrational from your point of view but it does not from theirs.

Psychologists Daniel Kahneman and Amos Tversky formulated what they called *Prospect Theory* in 1979 and published their theory in *Econometrica*, one of the most prestigious academic economics journals.[7] Prospect theory wants to describe

[6] See Housel (2020), p. 18.

[7] Daniel Khaneman was born in Tel Aviv, Israel, and earned his bachelor's degree in psychology, with a minor in mathematics, from Hebrew University in Jerusalem, Israel in 1954, and also obtained his Ph.D. in psychology from the University of California, Berkeley in 1961. Amos

how individuals behave under risk "in the real world" rather than how they should behave in a theoretical world assuming perfect rationality. For instance, it is assumed that individuals evaluate risky outcomes as deviations from a *reference point* rather than looking at absolute net asset levels that can be achieved and selecting the alternative that provides the maximum payoff. Put simply, a reference point means that an individual's decisions are highly influenced by where he or she starts. It is also assumed that individuals attribute higher weight to losses than to comparable gains, and that individuals tend to be generally risk-averse regarding possible gains and risk-loving regarding possible losses. Through a series of experimental empirical demonstrations of human choices under risk and uncertainty, Kahneman and Tversky identified specific "idiosyncratic properties of value functions and decision weights that people employ to make decisions under risk: showing that people make systematic mistakes" (Szpiro, 2020). Their publication "Prospect Theory: An Analysis of Decision Under Risk"explored a new and differing theory to the more traditional expected utility framework. Their research and work paved the way for how we view behavioral economics today. What is most amazing about their collaboration is that it was one-of-a-kind in the sense that they really did everything together.

Preceding prospect theory, normative theories of rational choice dominated higher cognitive process analysis. Note that a major limitation of the EU model was that is does not allow for personal influences on choice selection due to the decision maker's cognitive limitations, history or personal values. Prospect Theory highlights that

> the way decisions are presented and processed can produce systematic violations of expected utility theory's basic assumptions. (…) When making strategic decisions, decision-makers' choices reflect the risk, simplifications, and preference reversal characteristics of prospect theory. (Sebora & Cornwall, 1995).

Prospect theory describes the decision-making process in two distinct phases: an editing phase and an evaluation phase. The editing phase, also referred to as the *framing effect*, explains how individuals characterize their choice options. The framing effect reflects on how an individual's choice is influenced by the order, method, or wording in which the setting is presented. In the evaluation phase, individuals tend to behave as if they would decide based on all potential outcomes and choose the option with the highest utility. This phase consists of two components, the value function, and the weighting function; it uses statistical analysis to measure and compare each prospect's outcomes.

Prospect theory can explain the most important and empirically proven violations of expected utility theory, called *psychological biases*, that individuals suffer from when making decisions under risk and uncertainty: reference points, the anchoring effect, and loss aversion.

Tversky was also born in Israel and obtained his bachelor's degree at Hebrew University in 1961. Amos went on to receive his doctorate from the University of Michigan in 1965. Daniel and Amos went on to teach at their alma mater.

Reference Points and Loss Aversion

As experimental evidence associated with prospect theory has pointed out, when analyzing risks, people only consider the potential gains or losses they can achieve - but they do not analyze these potential gains and losses with concurrence to their overall wealth. Therefore, whenever a person is presented with a risk, they will analyze potential losses before potential gains when making their decision according to the loss aversion principle. The principle can be traced back to our ancestors, who lived in forests and were often considered potential prey. Our ancestors focused on survival and avoiding predators more than harvesting a few extra berries or nuts. They were focused more on avoiding losses rather than acquiring a potential of more gains, which illustrates the loss aversion's motivational forces very well. In a similar way, aversion to a certain loss occurs when a person is willing to take an unfavorable bet with the hopes that they will beat the odds and wind up breaking even. The motivation behind these decision-makers is their strong abhorrence of losses, which motivates them to the point of taking on risks just in the attempt to avert a certain loss.

As a result, an important finding in experimental studies is that people tend to make decisions based on individual *reference points*. These reference points are different for different individuals with different wealth levels, risk aversion, income, etc. The position of the reference point usually resembles the current wealth or asset position of the individual or simply the starting position in a game of chance.

For instance, a typical scenario where reference points come into play is in a casino. Imagine you are sitting at a blackjack table together with a very wealthy man and a man living on a low income. They are both likely to experience the same levels of joy or suffer the same levels of pain based on their gains and losses when, in reality, they probably should not. The very wealthy man hypothetically should not be as upset when he loses a hand, simply because he has plenty of other money readily available to play, nor should he be as happy when he wins a hand, for the same reason. This view takes into account the decreasing value of additional income on wealth. Yet, the rich guy will likely experience the same amount of joy or sorrow as the man on the lower income scale. Why? Well, this can be explained by the phenomenon that people only focus on gains and losses relative to a reference point - and this reference point is where they started their casino day. Maybe they both put in $2000 as play money for the day. These individuals do not translate those gains and losses to their overall wealth situation. If reference points were *not* a factor in this scenario, the low-income man would be tremendously more affected by the outcome of the game because he does not have as much money to spare as the wealthy man. A huge gain would indeed make him very happy. But, unfortunately, he is not taking into account his overall wealth while he is experiencing these gains and losses but rather evaluates outcomes relative to what he initially invested: the $2000 play money for the day.

However, a deviation of the reference point from the current asset position is often possible due to several other influencing factors. Expectations and goals of the decision-maker are another possible cause. In the expectation of a supposedly secure profit, a decision-maker can form a reference point which already includes it and is therefore above his current asset position. If this gain is then unexpectedly not realized, the decision-maker perceives this as a loss although in fact no loss has occurred. In addition, individuals can be influenced externally in determining their reference point by a number of psychological effects.

For instance, the *anchoring effect* can play a major role here. Here, the decision maker is influenced in the determination of his reference point by providing selected quantitative information. For instance, it can be shown that participants can be significantly influenced in the determination of a "fair price" for a property by given price demands. In a similar way, expectations of wealth levels can also be influenced, which affect the formation of the reference point.

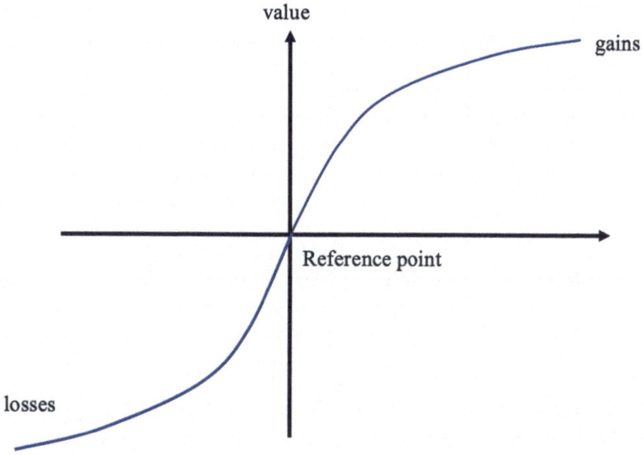

As can be seen from the graph, people behave in a risk averse manner for possible gains relative to the reference point and in a risk seeking manner for possible losses relative to the reference point. So even while we know that most individuals are risk averse, they often don't respond rationally to risks when they evaluate them relative to their current situation or status quo.

The phenomenon called *loss aversion* refers to an individual's preference to prefer avoiding losses to acquiring gains of the same magnitude. Loss aversion was first explained in 1975 by Kahneman and Tversky, who described an individual's utility of losses being different than their utility of gains. In essence, it is when an individual's utility function is convex over losses and concave for gains. This phenomenon has been observed in numerous studies since prospect theory's invention. Loss aversion, given its characteristic of describing an individual's higher sensitivity to losses than to gains of the same magnitude, has important implications on the way people evaluate risk and risky opportunities in practice. Would you participate in this lottery?

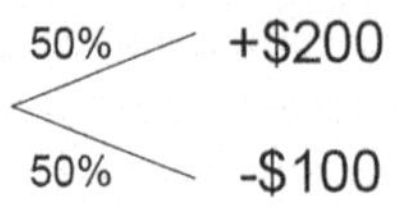

Following Kahneman and Tversky (1992), 50%+ of respondents do not want to participate in this lottery due to loss aversion although the lottery clearly has a positive expected value! Indeed, any project will be assessed according to its reference point and relative gains and losses. As demonstrated by Kahneman and Tversky (1992, p.313),

> "a sure gain of $100 is equally as attractive as a 71% chance to win $200 or nothing, and a sure loss of $100 is equally as aversive as a 64% chance to lose $200 or nothing."

The irrational behavior becomes even more apparent when people need to make decisions regarding low-probability-high-impact events, such as catastrophes or stock market crashes. Since these events are usually associated with huge emotional reactions on the human side, the probability of the event happening plays a minor role in the choices people make. The reason behind this affect bias is that losses cause more emotional misery than gains of the same magnitude cause emotional happiness, and here comes the name of the phenomenon called *loss aversion*.

A recent example of this happened on March 16th, 2020, at the beginning of the Corona pandemic in the United States, where stock markets perceived a massive hit. For example, the S&P 500 dropped significantly around 12% that day, wiping off over 2 trillion in equity value in 24 h. This should go on to illustrate that the market is not acting rationally, but rather with emotions and cognitive biases, such as loss aversion, resulting in mass selloffs of equities and creating the domino effect of decreasing equity prices.

Loss aversion was first explained in 1975 by prospect theory where Kahneman and Tversky described an individual's characteristic in which the utility of losses is higher than the utility of gains. In essence, it is when an individual's utility function is convex over losses and concave for gains. This phenomenon has been observed in numerous studies since prospect theory, and describes a characteristic where an individual is more sensitive to losses than to gains of the same value. For example, an individual who exhibits loss aversion will lose more happiness by losing 100 dollars than he would gain happiness for an equivalent gain of 100 dollars. Interestingly, studies have also shown that an individual will weigh a loss almost twice as heavy as a comparable gain.

Does level of loss aversion change for different magnitudes of loss? For example, how much would a gain of $1000 have on your level of happiness compared to a loss of $1000? Now, what about a gain of $1 compared to a loss of $1? A study in 2017 attempted to ask the question if loss aversion was magnitude dependent and measured the prospective affective judgments in regard to gains and losses. By conducting gambling scenario experiments with experiments in the context of fluctuating prices, they concluded that loss aversion doesn't exist in lower magnitudes. However, for the same participant, they were able to find loss aversion for higher magnitudes. Interestingly, they also found that loss aversion was non-existent for higher magnitudes when contextually a larger anchor was provided, thus providing more evidence for the anchoring bias. Their results implied that the value function in prospect theory is magnitude dependent; therefore, changing the way future research is analyzed with respect to prospect theory.

Option	Consequences
A	300% increase in knife attacks
B	Increase in knife attacks from 100 to 400 in 100,000 people

Similar to what studies have shown when asking a question like this, our respondent also answered A rather quickly. However, A is not rational without knowing the exact number of knife attacks, to begin with. What if it was one? A 300% increase would, therefore, be 4 knife attacks for a total increase of 3 extra knife attacks. Now, looking at it this way, we would agree that this is not as bad as answer B that had an extra 300 knife attacks. This goes to show that we are more affected by ratios, rather than absolute risk. Interestingly, in our question, both answers are a 300% increase.

> "The Literature on risk effects of pollutants and pharmaceuticals commonly reports relative risk, [...] rather than the difference. Yet, this difference [...] is most relevant for decision-making [...]." - Jonathan Baron

Like our question above, this difference as mentioned in the quote by Baron is largely ignored. This happens because people have difficulties differentiating between relative risk and absolute risk, unless either more information is added or if the situation is reframed. In essence, people worry more about the proportion of risk reduced than the actual or absolute amount of risk reduced. According to Baron, the extreme form of this cognitive bias is what has become known in psychology as the zero-risk bias (see Chap. 4).

The Isolation Effect

The *isolation effect* occurs when individuals are presented with two options with the same outcome but different routes. In this case, individuals tend to cancel out similar or overlapping information to simplify a problem at hand, and conclusions tend to vary depending on how the options are framed. The *isolation effect* also occurs when people are given two solutions with the same result but different paths to the outcome. Khaneman and Tversky created a scenario to explain the isolation effect:

Scenario 1: Participants start with $1000. They then can choose between:

A. Winning $1000 with a 50% probability (and winning $0 with a 50% probability), or
B. Getting another $500 for sure.

Scenario 2: Participants start with $2000. They then can choose between:

A. Losing $1000 with a 50% probability (and losing $0 with a 50% probability), or
B. Losing $500 for sure.

This effect explains how, even though these two different scenarios appear different, they are the same. If individuals decide to choose option B or D, the results are the same, even though they are from two different scenarios. Options A and C are equivalent. Even though in the isolation effect decision-makers choose the risk-averse option (Option B) from scenario 1 and loss adverse option (Option C) from scenario 2. People will respond to negatively framed messages very differently than they would respond to a positively framed one. Prospect theory outlines several psychological influences that motivate people when making decisions regarding risk. There are several main applications discussed in the book which help in illustrating this motivation. Some of these applications are loss aversion, aversion to a sure loss, and framing effects. Each application gives insight into the psychological processes that occur in people when making decisions regarding risks.

Framing

Another application featured in prospect theory is framing. Framing is the way how elements of a risky situation are described. Prospect theory tells us that framing will have a significant impact on the decision an individual will make. Prospect theory states that how the risk alternative is explained, or framed, will influence what people place on their mental scales. This will undoubtedly have an impact on the motivation behind a person's decision. Several other psychological principles are emphasized within prospect theory. One of these principles is found in the limitations of human cognitive abilities. Human brains process registering changes rather than final positions, which is why the prospect theory is focused on gains and losses. This psychological principle also has a significant impact on a person's decision-making. Framing is discussed in more detail in Chap. 5.

The Safety Effect

Kahneman and Tversky (1979) observed that individuals do not value gains and losses in decision problems under uncertainty in a linear fashion. Individuals tend to attribute a particularly high weight to the certainty of a result in a game of chance. Accordingly, the perceived increase in benefit is greater when the probability of a desired outcome of the gambling game increases from 99% to 100% than when it increases from 50% to 51%. Kahneman and Tversky (1979) call this cognitive distortion the safety effect.

The inconsistency with expected utility theory resulting from the certainty effect was already noticed by Maurice Allais in 1953. This can be illustrated in the following experiment. In a first decision problem, test participants could choose between two options. Option A led to a certain profit of one million dollars. Option B led to one of three possible results. The participants could either win a million dollars with a probability of 89%, 5 million dollars with a probability of 10% or nothing with a probability of 1%. The majority of the respondents preferred option A. Subsequently, in a second decision problem, the test participants were asked again about their preference. This problem differed from the first in that the probability of winning one million dollars for the options was reduced by 89% points. As a result, the participants in the experiment were only 11% likely to win 1 million dollars for option A and 89% likely to win nothing. Option B, on the other hand, led to a profit of 5 million dollars with a probability of 10% and no profit with a probability of 90%. According to the independence axiom of the expected utility theory, this modification of the problem should not influence the order of preference of the respondents, since in both options the probability of winning $1 million was reduced equally. Nevertheless, the modification of the problem led to the majority of respondents now preferring option B, which is in direct contradiction to the independence axiom (Allais, 1953). In parallel to the security effect, a so-called possibility effect can also be identified, which refers to very small probabilities of occurrence. This states that a higher benefit is obtained if the probability of occurrence of an evil, e.g. a reactor accident, is reduced from low to zero than if it is reduced by the same number of percentage points but the possibility still exists (e.g. from 10% to 5%). Kahneman and Tversky (1979) conclude that individuals weight objective probabilities. According to them, moderate to high probabilities are underweighted and low probabilities are overweighted.

The Reflection Effect

In addition to the safety effect, Kahneman and Tversky (1979) observed that individuals have opposite risk preferences for gains and losses in decisions under uncertainty. When it comes to the possibility of winning, individuals generally behave in a risk-averse manner and therefore prefer a secure, albeit smaller, gain over a higher, but riskier gain. With regard to losses, individuals are generally risk-averse and therefore prefer to take a risk for a higher loss if there is a chance of losing nothing. The order of preference is therefore reflected at a reference point. Kahneman and Tversky (1979) call this effect the *reflection effect*. Risk aversion with regard to profit opportunities, as well as risk affinity with regard to loss opportunities, can be attributed to the overweighting of security and thus to the security effect. In the case of potential gains, security is perceived as positive, in the case of potential losses as negative. From the reflection effect it can be deduced that in decision problems not always safe options are preferred to risky options. However, since the expected utility theory does not consider profits and losses separately, it is not able to describe this behavior.

The Insulation Effect

Another observation of Kahneman and Tversky (1979) is that individuals in decision-making situations under uncertainty try to simplify the problem. An essential step is to neglect the components of a decision problem that share options. Instead, decision-makers concentrate exclusively on the differences between the options. This effect is called the *insulation effect* by Kahneman and Tversky (1979). Because the subdivision into common and different components can be done in several ways, it is possible that inconsistencies in the order of preference will arise.

Kahneman and Tversky (1979) illustrate this inconsistency by means of two different views of a two-stage game of chance. In the first stage of the game there is a 75% probability that the game will end without a win. If the second stage is reached, the decision maker can choose between two options. Option A has an 80% probability of winning $4000, option B has a sure win of $3000. Individuals tend to ignore the first stage and focus on the second stage. They therefore ignore the part of the decision problem that is the same for all options. In line with the certainty effect, the majority of the participants in one experiment chose the $3000 sure win, but when the decision problem is considered as a whole, including the first stage of the game of chance, there is a 20% probability of winning $4000 and a 25% probability of winning $3000. Under this approach, the majority of the participants preferred the $4000 chance of winning with a 20% probability. The isolation effect can also be seen in other examples. When individuals are confronted with a decision problem after their wealth level has been increased shortly before, they usually do not include this change in their initial situation in their decision. The decision is made independently of the change in wealth, since this change is the basis for all options and therefore does not play a role in the differentiation of options.

The assessment of a decision-making problem therefore depends not only on the decision-making problem as such, but also on the way in which the decision-maker views the problem and the way in which he simplifies it. This again represents a violation of the expected utility theory according to which a different view of a decision problem should not influence the preference order.

So How Do We Contextualize Risks in Practice?

Individuals perceive threats more strongly when they emerge at the same time rather than each at a different time, even if these threats are all independent. Such a perception is consistent with the observation that people evaluate their well-being relative to a recent change in its quality than by its overall quality. Hence managers will employ resources to counter loss events that occur close to each other - even if the managers would have ignored those same events in isolation.

Events like the terrorist attacks in September 11, 2001, where many people die at the same time are generally perceived as a bigger catastrophe than if the same amount of people die due to cancer over a given period. The reason is the same: an event occurring at a point in time with many deaths is subjectively perceived as worse than an event occurring over a period of time with the same number of deaths.

Knowing that individuals also tend to contextualize gains and losses according to a personal reference point, they will adjust their reference point more quickly for gains than for losses. Thus, managers will perceive losses, even if they are aligned with the long-term trends of the firm, subjectively more strongly if such losses succeed a loss-free period. As a result, managers may plan to employ resources to counter those losses even though the loss is part of the firm's normal cycle of business.

Key Takeaways for Risk Leadership

Humans do *not* follow the logical axioms of expected utility theory when making decisions under risk and uncertainty. In contrast, reference points and loss aversion are rather important when we make such decisions. Indeed, we tend to rely on a number of simple heuristics—thereby reducing the complex task of assessing and evaluating probabilities and predicting gains and losses to much simpler judgmental operations. While these heuristics can be quite useful and save time and energy for the brain, they can also imply severe and systematic errors—some of which will be addressed in the next chapters.

References

Allais, M. (1953). Fondements d'une Théorie Positive des Choix Comportant un Risque et Critique des Postulats et Axiomes de l'Ecole Américaine, in: Colloques Internationaux du Centre National de la Recherche Scientifique, 40 (1953). Translated into English, with additions, as "The Foundations of a Positive Theory of Choice Involving Risk and a Criticism of the Postulates and Axioms of the American School," in: Allais, M. and Hagen, O. (eds.) (1979). *Expected utility hypotheses and the allais paradox* (pp. 27–145). Dordrecht: Reidel.

Barseghyan, L., Molinari, F., O'Donoghue, T., & Teitelbaum, J. C. (2013). The nature of risk preferences: evidence from insurance choices. *American Economic Review, 103*(6), 2499–2529.

Bernoulli, D. (1738). Specimen theoriae novae de mensura sortis. *Commentarii Academiae Scientiarum Imperialis Petropolitanae, 5*, 175–192.

Bernoulli, D. (1954). Exposition of a new theory on the measurement of risk. *Econometrica, 22*(1), 23–36.

Brown, J. R., & Finkelstein, A. (2009). The private market for long-term care insurance in the United States: A review of the evidence. *Journal of Risk and Insurance, 76*, 5–29.

Gollier, C. (2005). Some Aspects of the Economics of Catastrophe Risk Insurance, CES Ifo Working Paper No. 1409.

Housel, M. (2020). *The psychology of money – timeless lessons on wealth, greed, and happiness*. Harriman House Ltd..

Kahneman, D., & Tversky, A. (1979). Prospect theory: An analysis of decision under risk. *Econometrica, 47*, 263–291.

Kahneman, D., & Tversky, A. (1992). Advances in prospect theory: Cumulative representation of uncertainty. *Journal of Risk and Uncertainty, 5*, 297–323.

Mahul, O., & Stutley, C. J. (2010). *Government support to agricultural insurance: challenges and options for developing countries*. The World Bank Publications.

Sebora, T., & Cornwall, J. (1995). Expected utility theory vs. prospect theory: Implications for strategic decision makers. *Journal of Managerial Issues, 7*(1), 41–61.
Sydnor, J. (2010). (O)verinsuring modest risks. *American Economic Journal: Applied Economics, 2*(4), 177–199.
Szpiro, G. (2020). Sunk costs, the gambler's fallacy, and other errors. In *Risk, choice, and uncertainty: three centuries of economic decision-making* (pp. 188–205). Columbia University Press.
Volkman-Wise, J. (2015). Representativeness and managing catastrophe risk. *Journal of Risk and Uncertainty, 51*(3), 267–290.

4 Confirmation Bias and Anchoring Effect: Why the First Piece of Information is Key in Negotiations

The most important single key takeaway from this chapter is

> **The 3rd Commandment of Risk Leadership:** Negotiating effectively means being a leader in providing information. Be the first to set an anchor by fixing an acceptable range of possible or outcomes for your negotiation!

Being aware of the impact of the confirmation bias, disciplining ourselves to actively seek opposing data and using techniques to change our perspectives before deciding, we might be able to mitigate the effects of the confirmation bias. The same holds true for the anchoring effect. Almost inevitably, anchor values will establish an "invisible range of reasonable terms" and influence decisions, valuations and negotiations. Both effects—the confirmation bias and the anchoring effect—show why the first piece of information is key. They provide a powerful tool to govern the outcome of real-life situations without requiring authority over our counterparts.

Confirmation Bias

Both the confirmation bias and anchoring effect relate to the topic of cognitive psychology, which includes the biases deeply rooted into the structure of our thinking. The field of biases clouding the objectivity of our thinking is to a large extent pioneered by the work of Kahneman and Tversky, who analyzed many of the well over 100 biases uncovered by academic research so far. While in court settings, public prosecutors and defense attorney deliberately argue very biased storylines, Nickerson (1998) argues that the cognitive biases often work in a more sublime and not intentional way. This chapter sheds light on two central thinking patterns: the confirmation bias and the anchoring effect.

A. Hofmann, *The Ten Commandments of Risk Leadership*, Future of Business and Finance, https://doi.org/10.1007/978-3-030-88797-1_4

In the 1960s, a prominent psychologist named Peter Wason developed an experimental setting to evaluate the thought process humans use to find out whether or not a particular statement is true or not (Wason, 1960, 1968). The following experiment was performed where people were asked about a simple setting. In this setting, four cards are placed on a table. The only known information provided is that *there is always a letter on one side of a card and a number on the other side of the card.* The following four cards are laid out on the table: a b. 2. 3

The challenge now is to test the following hypothesis as efficiently as possible, that is, by only selecting a minimum number of cards that will determine whether the hypothesis is true or false. Here is the hypothesis: "*Any card having a vowel on one side has an even number on the other side.*" Of the four cards, which ones would you turn over to reveal information about the hypothesis?

In order to find the minimum, it makes sense to evaluate which card has the potential to reveal information on whether the hypothesis is true or false. These cards are "a" and "3"—why? Well, we need to test whether a vowel card has an even number on the other side, and if the other side of the "a" card reveals an odd number, the hypothesis can be rejected as proven false. The "b" card cannot deliver such revealing information. Additionally, in the same way, if the other side of the "3" card reveals a vowel the hypothesis can be rejected as proven false. The "2" card cannot deliver such revealing information.

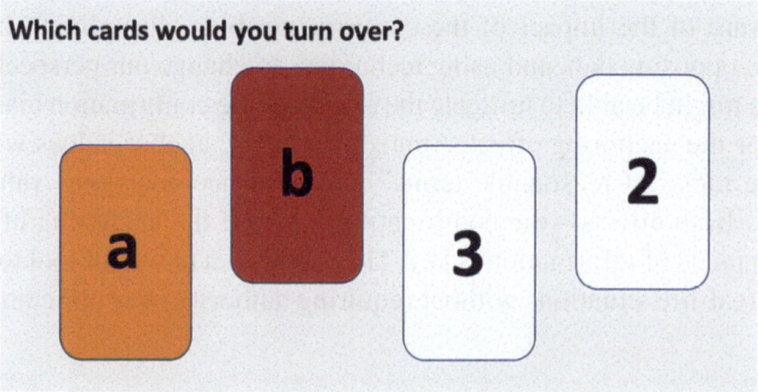

Many people tend to turn over the "2" card in order to confirm that an even-number-card has a vowel on the other side; however, finding a consonant does not help. Peter Wason suggested that people have a strong tendency to overweigh "confirming evidence" and underweigh contradictory evidence, a phenomenon he referred to as *confirmatory bias.*

Today, we define *Confirmation bias* as the tendency to look for data that confirm our beliefs, as opposed to looking for data that challenge our beliefs. The confirmation bias is well described by Nickerson (1998), who summarizes that the term "connotes the seeking and interpreting of evidence in ways that are partial to existing beliefs, expectations or a hypothesis at hand.". Therefore, in very brief terms, the confirmation bias describes a process, which is not governed by objectivity, but rather a tendency to seek information in line with our views and beliefs, instead of pursuing evidence, which could challenge our view in an effort to secure the validity of a hypothesis. Darley and Gross (1983) add that this tendency also involves interpreting ambiguous or mixed information to confirm our existing theories.

Another one of these experiments comes to be known as Wason's triplet of numbers, which shows a sequence of three numbers (2, 4 and 6). Participants in the experiment were informed that the number triplet adheres to a certain rule and are asked to find out that rule by testing other triplets. When testing sequences, the vast majority tested sequences of increasing even numbers and certain rules of adding a number, for example, adding two for each subsequent number of the sequence.

The testing approach observed by Wason (1966) is diagnostic for the confirmation bias: Suspecting the rule of increasing even numbers, the experiment participants focus to find confirming evidence that would align with their initial hypothesis. Very few of the participants test number sequences challenging the initial intuition, e.g. testing increasing odd numbers or even decreasing numbers. By seeking affirmative testing results only, the participants precluded themselves from finding the actual rule behind the triplet 2, 4 and 6, which is "any three numbers in an increasing order". Interestingly, we could confirm the same result in a much smaller setting in the context of our class presentation on "cognitive biases". Out of the 10 obtained number triplets, which were submitted to find out about the sequence rule, the vast majority of nine responses are sets of increasing even numbers and only one sequence to test the sequence 5, 10, and 15. This distribution of answers adheres to Wason's findings and highlights—even though in a much smaller setting—that the confirmation bias holds true even if we have a basic suspicion about a task with a hidden twist.

The confirmation bias occurs in academic experimental settings across a wide domain of tasks. Interestingly, the confirmation bias remains relevant irrespective of the degree of our personal involvement. As pointed out by Nickerson (1998) we proceed in judging a question in a biased fashion even it involves the testing of thesis that we do not have any material stake in. Cherry (2020) provides the example of people often holding the belief that "left-handed people are more creative than right-handed people". Following this belief with a personal nexus will certainly provide more personal involvement than pursuing random numbers. However, the literature shows the confirmation bias is independent of personal involvement contouring two forms of the confirmation bias: The motivated cases of confirmation bias with personal involvement and the unmotivated forms of the confirmation bias.

Fischhoff and Beyth-Marom (1983) find that we can partially attribute the confirmation bias to a systematic failure to appropriately consider likelihoods and likelihood ratios. Thereby, we preclude the possibility of interpreting the same data as supportive of any alternative explanation. Even under circumstances where we recognize the possibility of other beliefs, we allocate biased probabilities. If we suppose the same data might occur under two competing hypotheses, we overestimate the probability of our "preferred hypothesis" relative to the complement probability to make the same observations under the other hypothesis.

When evaluating a hypothesis using data, the human mind not only encounters problems to objectively consider probabilities under the confirmation bias. Also, our mind puts more weight on positive confirmatory instances. Pyszczynski and Greenberg (1987) show that we require less pieces of confirming evidence to be convinced to accept a developed hypothesis, than we need inconsistent evidence to reject a hypothesis. This implies that we overweight positive evidence and thereby play down the weight of negative and opposing evidence. With a concurring opinion Wason (1977) notes "there would appear to be compelling evidence to indicate that even intelligent individuals adhere to their own hypothesis with remarkable tenacity when they can produce confirming evidence for them". As an intuitive example for our tendency to overweight confirmatory instances, Nickerson (1998) considers the case of the fortune teller or mind reader: "When the mind reader, for example, describes one's character in more-or-less universal terms, individuals who want to believe their minds are being read will have little difficulty finding substantiating evidence in what the mind readers says if they focus on what fits and discount what does not and if they fail to consider the possibility that equally accurate descriptions can be produced if their minds are not being read.".

This very much ties into the findings of Snyder (1981), who finds that experiment participants very much "see what they are looking for". In an experiment, Snyder asks the subjects to judge a person they were about to meet. Before meeting one another, the judging participants were given a brief description about the other person—either that the person is an extrovert or an introvert type. The results support the thought behind the fortune teller example: If you give people a pattern to look for, they will find evidence irrespective of the pattern's actual existence. Along with this finding, Snyder (1981) also observed the participants to ask strongly confirmatory questions aimed to support the preconceived opinion. Also, participants asked very undiagnostic questions, i.e. questions which were likely to receive very similar answers irrespective of the true personality of the meeting person. Interestingly, participants indicated after the meeting that they found it easy to connect the description pattern to the actual person. Considering Snyder's observations, the confirmation bias possibly forms a basis for the common saying "the first impression counts".

Another element of the confirmation bias builds on the *illusion of correlations*. This illusion describes our tendency to perceive correlations where none exist. Research by Chapman (1967) illustrates this in an experiment where drawings of human figures were each combined with two random statements about the personality of the artist. Even though it was secured that no actual nexus between the statements and the picture exist, participants in the experiment see a direct relationship between the statements and drawings they are shown. In conjunction with other elements of the confirmation bias this means that the illusion of correlations tricks us into detecting a relationship, which does not exist, which we then one-sidedly support with evidence to arrive at a conclusion, which exceeds well "beyond what the evidence justifies" (Nickerson, 1998).

Further effects contribute to the confirmation bias: The primacy effect describes our tendency to better recall information, which we hear first compared to information we receive later. Bacon (1620) already proclaimed 400 years ago "the first conclusion colors and brings into conformity with itself all that come after", which also holds true for information. When a person must draw a conclusion by acquiring subsequently presented information, the earlier pieces of information carry more weight than the information following thereafter. A contribution by Bruner and Potter (1964) illustrates this in a visual experiment. They prepare a sequence of slides each showing the same picture, which becomes clearer and less blurry with each slide. After each slide the participants are asked to identify the object. The results strongly indicate the stickiness of the first impression. Even with the picture becoming clearer participants would not switch to the (almost obvious) correct identification of the object but stick to the early information of the blurry picture.

Once attached to a belief, we are persistent in retaining it. This belief persistence is also mirrored in experiments where two people with initially conflicting views can examine the same evidence and both will find reason to uphold their view using the same information. A great illustration of this observation is a study conducted by Wheeler and Arunachalam (2008) with 142 tax advisors in relation to a tax issue on the tax deductibility of a bonus payment. They were given identical sets of information (e.g. court decisions and tax commentaries) and asked to form an opinion if the bonus payment should be tax deductible or not. All participants were also given a client preference, some for one and the remainder for the other alternative. As a result of the investigation, each group confirmed the respective client preference, seeing strong evidence in the very same set of information. Our mind uses ambiguous information in a very one-sided way, even in situations where we consider ourselves to be experts. In adhering to our desired opinion, we apply a selective testing pattern whereby we look only or primarily for positive cases that affirm our individual hypothesis, which might collide with finding the "objective truth" and preclude us from accepting the correct hypothesis as also observed by Wason (1966) in the triplet of numbers experiment.

Nickerson (1998) also points out with further references that people have a tendency to better recall those facts and data points, which are in support of their belief, a phenomenon which came to be known as the preferential memory for evidence supporting existing beliefs. However, this research could be interpreted in two ways: Either people remember well only facts that support their position—or—they have the position on a certain subject because they can rather recall the facts that support this position. Related studies point more towards a biased memory based on existing beliefs: In these experiments, participants were more likely to recall evidence as being consistent with their theories than it was. Baron (1995) also finds that participants were more likely to recall one-sided arguments than two-sided arguments. Interestingly, people also rated the one-sided arguments higher (i.e. as more meaningful) than the two-sided arguments.

The cognitive confirmation bias also rests on the overconfidence we have in our own judgement. In general, we tend to overestimate the quality of our thinking when working towards a result as Kahneman and Tversky (1973) find. In an effort to find a strategy to mitigate the overconfidence effects, the authors find that by asking people to evaluate one's view and the strength of the provided reasons, we can substantially reduce our overconfidence even though it cannot be completely eliminated. Consistent with this insight into evaluating our own judgement, Murphy and Winkler

(1974) find that weather forecasters are potentially better calibrated with respect to their own judgement in comparison to other professional groups, which could be due to the fact that they also receive constant and timely feedback on their predictions.

Anchoring Effect

Along the confirmation bias there is another cognitive heuristic—the *Anchoring* effect. The anchoring effect might be best explained by considering a popular experiment conducted by Kahneman and Tversky (1974), who were among the first to research this cognitive bias. The experiment asks people to estimate various quantities, stated in percentages (for example, the percentage of African countries in the United Nations). For each question, a number between 0 and 100 was determined by spinning a wheel of fortune. The participants were subsequently asked to indicate first whether the random number displayed by the wheel of fortunes was higher or lower than the answer to the question they were asked and then to estimate the value of the quantity by moving upward or downward from the given number. To test for the anchoring effect, different groups were given different (random) numbers for each quantity. The results of the experiment by Kahneman and Tversky shows that the arbitrary numbers determined by the wheel of fortune had a significant effect on the estimates. For example, the results for the question on the share of African countries in the United Nations were very different depending on the starting point determined by the random number: The median estimates for the percentage of African nations in the United Nations was 25% for groups which received the random number 45 from the fortune wheel and the estimate was 45% for groups that received the random number 65 from the wheel of fortune as a starting point. This manipulation of the answers by the random number is what came to be known as the anchoring effect.

The anchoring effect is an active influence on our decision process and—as the experiment by Kahneman and Tversky (1974) shows—even unrelated reference points can guide our judgement. Our mind appears to automatically consider the anchor value as a plausible answer and then determines our answer in the "numerical neighborhood" of the anchor as explained by Strack and Mussweiler (1997). Anchoring effects apply throughout a wide domain of decision tasks—from general knowledge (freezing temperature of vodka or the mean temperature in Germany) to even more serious domains like legal judgements over prison sentences. A further example by Kahneman (2013) illustrates that anchoring effects can also occur indirectly through asking questions, which provoke certain ideas or images and then support the anchor. In his example, Daniel Kahneman contrasts the question on the average price of a German car sold in the United States. Under the first alternative, he asks the question if the average price is more or less than USD 100,000, in another version of the question he uses the reference amount of USD 20,000. He points out that the USD 100,000 presumed average price will evoke the association of luxury German cars like Mercedes Benz, while the lower price will center the respondents thinking around more affordable car brands like Volkswagen. The two ways to ask the very same question will therefore strongly influence the estimate given by the respondent.

We can also find the anchoring effect in business contexts. Looking at consumer behavior Wansink et al. (1998) finds that anchor-based promotions significantly increase sales. In a set of variations in a supermarket, the visiting customers were provided with different anchors. These anchors were set by (1) displaying multiple-unit prices instead of single unit prices (6 cans for USD 3 instead of 1 can for 50 cents), (2) introducing purchase quantity limits (up to 4 or 12 cans per person) and (3) using suggestive selling slogans like "buy snickers bars for your freezer" in an anchored version "buy 18 snickers bars for your freezer". All these strategies with anchoring effects significantly increased purchase quantities. The same logic applies to showing reduced prices to provide another real-world example of the anchoring effect. The undiscounted original price provides an anchor for the value estimate of the product in the consumer's mind, the discounted price is then perceived as a good price for the received value. Apple actually used this "trick" when first introducing the iPad. Back then Steve Jobs revealed the price using an anchor technique. First in his speech, he said there were great speculations about the price with experts estimating USD 999, but then told the audience that it will "only be 499 USD" and therefore "very affordable for many households".

Anchoring can also be observed for valuation settings. Mussweiler et al. (2000) conducts an experiment around valuing a car. What is remarkable about the car experiment is the realistic setting: Specifically, 60 male car experts were approached and asked to estimate the value of a 10-year old car (Opel Kadett). They not only received the typically relevant information on the car (e.g. model, make, year, mileage etc.) but had the actual car right in front of them and opportunity to inspect it for the experiment. The true value of the car was previously estimated to be around USD 1800 (buying price) and USD 2500 (selling price)[1]. When being presented with the car during the experiment, the participants were provided with different price estimates as anchors (the lower anchor around USD 1500 and the higher USD 2800). After inspection, they were asked whether they think the price estimate is too high or too low and to estimate an approximate selling price, which follows the question structure used by Kahneman and Tversky (1974). The experiment result confirmed heavy anchoring on the given price estimate—even among experts: The high anchor group indicated a value of USD 2000 for the car, while the low anchor group estimated USD 1250.

Another experiment by Galinsky and Mussweiler (2001) transfers the anchoring effect in valuations into the world of negotiations. The setting involved MBA students on their first day of class to negotiate the price of a pharmaceutical plant with identical information packages. In some negotiations the seller was given the opportunity to make a first offer, in other cases the buyer could make the first offer. In line

[1] All numbers presented here and in the following are rounded amounts and approximates to improve the readability. Some of the referenced numbers are also converted from another currency, which however does not change the relative amount distributions and resulting findings. For exact amounts, please refer to the respective source.

with common expectations, sellers made higher first offers (on average around USD 27 m) than buyers (on average roughly around USD 17 m). All negotiations reach a consensus and consistent with the anchoring effect, the negotiations with higher first offers made by the sellers led to higher final settlement amounts: In the negotiations that started with a seller offer, the agreed price averaged around USD 25 m, while the buyer-led negotiations resulted in a final price of roughly USD 20 m. As another interesting finding, Galinsky and Mussweiler (2001) show that the anchoring effect can be substantially reduced when people are additionally asked to focus on information that is inconsistent with the anchor offer and also take the perspective of the other party by estimating a "walk-away price".

We can also observe the anchoring effect in the marketing of car insurance policies. Shapira and Venezia (2008) ask amateurs and professionals to price insurance policies with varying deductibles and MBA students were asked to choose among a set of insurance options. The full coverage insurance premium for a car insurance was estimated around USD 180. Participants were then asked to also quote prices for the same insurance policy with varying levels of deductibles. When pricing the policy with deductibles, participants heavily anchored on the amount of the deductible and almost subtracted the amount of the deductible from the insurance premium. For example, the average price of an insurance policy with a USD 60 deductible comes down from USD 180 (price of the zero-deductible policy) to USD 125. If this "computation logic for pricing policies with deductibles" is representative for consumers, it could offer a reasonable explanation why consumers prefer low or no deductible insurances, apart from the frequent finding of strong risk aversion. In such case, consumers simply perceive a better price for the value of no deductible policies based on their "subjective pricing model". Interestingly, the observation of inefficient policy choices remains stable among a test group of MBA students that even attended a class on risk management. These MBA Students were offered insurance policies for a Toyota Corolla with several deductible levels. The majority still chose the lower deductible alternatives even though these were calculated to be inferior.

Despite the apparent drawbacks of anchoring effects in certain situations, the anchoring effect can also be a quite helpful tool in other situations. Again, considering the insurance industry, we actually use the anchoring logic to offer new products: One example can be seen in the evolution of the Directors & Officers (D&O) liability insurance industry in Germany in the 1990s. Considering this as a new product for the German market, insurers and reinsurers developed risk models based on US data, as no data was available for the new market in Germany. Therefore, the US data provided an anchor—even though our legal systems are very different—which led to roughly estimated premia in the beginning, which were subsequently corrected on the accumulating German data. Very similar to this, new environmental liability policies were calculated based on scoring models as data on big energy facilities was rather scarce. The scoring prices provided anchors for afterwards adjusted estimates. These two insurance examples show that anchoring can also be a useful tool, at least, as long as a certain degree of objectivity can be introduced by involving many different views opposed to just one person providing or using the anchor.

Having visited the many aspects of the two cognitive biases in question—the confirmation bias and the anchoring effect—we find a source for potentially misguided opinions and claims. If we trust the research, the benefits of the confirmation bias—if any—will most frequently be limited to self-esteem by protecting our beliefs and time savings (Nickerson, 1998). Certainly, we also must be careful when assessing the presence of the confirmation bias in the "real world". First, the experiments are not free of potential distortions. As pointed out by Nickerson (1998), a critical strand of literature claims that the judging experiments involving communication might suffer from a self-fulfilling prophecy problem. The opposition reasons that the pattern-hunting questions provoke confirmatory question for which respondents have a natural desire to answer in an affirmative way. The effect of altered communication is also shown by Snyder et al. (1977) in a previous experiment in which male participants were informed about the attractivity of a female counterpart, they would subsequently have a call with. Following the critics' argument, respondents actually adhere to the personality type the judging person is looking for and the experiment would not be suitable to substantiate the confirmation bias. Second, the experiments settings are often simplified scenarios, e.g. the number triplet, which might only represent our complex environment to a certain extent. After all, the confirmation bias might also suffer from a confirmation bias itself in the pursuit to prove an early developed claim about the way our thinking works. However, it should be hard to deny the existence of a tendency of what research describes under the concept of the confirmation bias.

But how important is this bias for decision-makers and their businesses exactly? Well, it turns out that the bias is there but that other biases (like overconfidence bias, for instance) are much more important. When Griggs and Cox (1982) applied a more real-world context to the problem with the four cards, the confirmation bias was greatly diminished. The authors offered their subjects a situation in a tavern with a barkeeper who followed the law about underage drinking. The challenge now reads: "Which two of these cards should you turn over to test the claim that in this bar, 'If you are drinking alcohol then you must be over 19'?" They found that almost three quarters of the respondents came up with the right choices.

Anchoring and Being a Good Negotiator

When making a decision, it is well established that humans tend to rely too heavily on the very first piece of information they encounter, and this tendency can have serious consequences for the final decision they end up making. In other words, we are influenced by the initial figure we learn when estimating the value of an item. This initial piece of information is interpreted as a "reference point" or benchmark (called anchor) that is being updated as more information comes in—the updating mechanism then builds on this initial point and adjustments are made but may not be enough to arrive at a "superior outcome". In other words, individuals using different starting points will end up with different end points or final estimates.

As all other people, managers are humans and are subject to common biases in decision-making. Most importantly, like all of us, managers are *over-reliant on the first piece of information* presented to them in a negotiation. When negotiating a take-over, for instance, whoever makes the first numerical offer range establishes an anchor of what others see as a range of reasonable possibilities regarding where to go in terms of final negotiated price. Managers also tend to listen more often to information that confirms their own preconception. This prevents them from being open-minded.

This type of cognitive bias is known as *anchoring effect*. It is a very interesting and important bias since it shows that, from a psychological perspective, humans can easily be manipulated! You can and should use this insight to your advantage in negotiations. It has been shown in a number of negotiation studies that this phenomenon has significant impact on negotiation outcomes. Indeed, it is fascinating how the anchor can even be established using arbitrary numbers when two consecutive events has nothing to do with each other! This has been shown by Tversky and Kahneman, where in one demonstration of the effect, participants were asked to spin a wheel showing random numbers from 0 to 100. The participants were then asked to adjust that number up or down to indicate the percentage of African countries in the United Nations. Those who spun a high number gave higher estimates while those who spun a low number gave lower estimates. The spin of the wheel influenced the participants' estimates in a powerful way. In each case, the participants were using that initial number as their anchor point to base their decision—although this initial number was the result of a random event and was of course independent of what should be their reasonable estimate. They relied on an irrelevant and totally uninformative anchor!

Key Takeaways for Risk Leadership

Understanding this chapter's biases is important because they can determine your financial well-being and thus be of long-term value to you. Being aware of the impact of the confirmation bias, disciplining ourselves to actively seek opposing data and using techniques to change our perspectives before deciding, we might be able to mitigate the effects of the confirmation bias. The same holds true for the anchoring effect. Almost inevitably, anchor values will establish an "invisible range of reasonable terms" and influence decisions, valuations and negotiations. Both effects—the confirmation bias and the anchoring effect—show why the first piece of information is key. They provide a powerful tool to govern the outcome of real-life situations without requiring authority over our counterparts. Moreover, anchoring and the confirmation bias can help us to navigate through uncertainty and seek new opportunities.

The anchoring effect implicitly serves as a psychological boundary for negotiations. So, in the future when you think about negotiating a salary increase with your boss, it might make sense to first think about what your request will be and then not hesitate to make an initial offer to your boss. Making the first offer may be the best you can do given that the anchoring effect will render that initial offer the starting point of your negotiation. In addition, setting the anchor will help bias negotiations in your favor by establishing the range of acceptable counteroffers your boss may make. When I had my first job interview after graduation from University, I was sitting in an office with the CEO of the company as well as his partner. The CEO had an empty piece of paper in front of him, and when it came to discussing my starting salary, he wrote down on the paper a relatively moderate starting salary—relatively spoken given my qualifications. From there, it was difficult for me to fight my way up, and I had not much negotiation power due to the fact that this was indeed my first real job and I could not offer much experience in the field. It took me many years to realize that the interview's resulting job offer and salary would have been much better had I told them my monetary expectations right from the beginning—thereby setting an anchor for further discussions.

References

Bacon, F. (1620). Novum Organum. In E. A. Burtt (Ed.), *The English Philosophers from Bacon to Mill* (pp. 24–123). Random House.

Baron, J. (1995). Myside bias in thinking about abortion. *Thinking and Reasoning, 1*, 221235.

Bruner, J. S., & Potter, M. C. (1964). Interference in the visual recognition. *Science, 144*, 424–425.

Chapman, L. J. (1967). Illusory correlation in observational report. *Journal of Verbal Learning and Verbal Behavior, 6*(1), 151–155.

Cherry, K. (2020). How Confirmation Bias Works. Last Accessed June 19, 2020. www.verywellmind.com/what-is-a-confirmation-bias-2795024#:~:text=Understanding%20Confirmation%20Bias&text=For%20example%2C %20imagine%20that%20a,supports%20what%20they%20already%20believe

Darley, J. M., & Gross, P. H. (1983). A hypothesis-confirming bias in labelling effects. *Journal of Personality and Social Psychology, 44*(1), 20–33.

Fischhoff, B., & Beyth-Marom, R. (1983). Hypothesis evaluation from a Bayesian perspective. *Psychological Review, 90*(3), 239–260.

Galinsky, A. D., & Mussweiler, T. (2001). First offers as anchors: The role of perspective-taking and negotiator focus. *Journal of Personality and Social Psychology, 81*(4), 657–669.

Griggs, R. A., & Cox, J. R. (1982). The elusive thematic-materials effect in Wason's selection task. *British Journal of Psychology, 73*, 407–420.

Kahneman, D. (2013). Anchoring, with Daniel Kahneman (author of Thinking, Fast and Slow). Uploaded February 1, 2013. https://www.youtube.com/watch?v=HefjkqKCVpo.

Kahneman, D., & Tversky, A. (1973). On the psychology of prediction. *Psychological Review, 80*(4), 237–251.

Kahneman, D., & Tversky, A. (1974). Judgment under uncertainty: Heuristics and biases. *Science, 185*, 1124–1131.

Murphy, A. H., & Winkler, R. L. (1974). Subjective probability forecasting experiments in meteorology: Some preliminary results. *Bulletin of the American Meteorological Society, 55*, 1206–1216.

Mussweiler, T., Strack, F., & Pfeiffer, T. (2000). Overcoming the inevitable anchoring effect: Considering the opposite compensates for selective accessibility. *Personality and Social Psychology Bulletin, 26*(9), 1142–1150.

Nickerson, R. (1998). Confirmation bias: A ubiquitous phenomenon in many guises. *Review of General Psychology, 2*, 175–220.

Pyszczynski, T., & Greenberg, J. (1987). Toward an integration of cognitive and motivational perspectives on social inference: A biased hypothesis-testing model. *Advances in Experimental Social Psychology, 44*, 297–340.

Shapira, Z., & Venezia, I. (2008). On the preference for full-coverage policies: Why do people buy too much insurance? *Journal of Economic Psychology, 29*(5), 747–761.

Snyder, M. (1981). Seek, and ye shall find: Testing hypotheses about other people. In P. Herman, M. Z. Edward, & T. Higgins (Eds.), *The Ontario symposium on personality and social psychology* (pp. 277–303). Lawrence Erlbaum Associates.

Snyder, M., Tanke, E. D., & Berscheid, E. (1977). Social perception and interpersonal behaviour: On the self-fulfilling nature of social stereotypes. *Journal of Personality and Social Psychology, 14*, 148–162.

Strack, F., & Mussweiler, T. (1997). Explaining the enigmatic anchoring effect: Mechanism of selective accessibility. *Journal of Personality and Social Psychology, 73*(3), 437–446.

Wansink, B., Kent, R. J., & Hoch, S. J. (1998). An anchoring and adjustment model of purchase quantity decisions. *Journal of Marketing Research, 35*(1), 71–81.

Wason, P. (1960). On the failure to eliminate hypotheses in a conceptual task. *Quarterly Journal of Experimental Psychology, 12*, 129–140.

Wason, P. (1966). Reasoning. In B. M. Foss (Ed.), *New horizons in psychology* (pp. 135–151). Penguin.

Wason, P. (1968). Reasoning about a rule. *The Quarterly Journal of Experimental Psychology, 20*, 273–281.

Wason, P. (1977): "On the failure to eliminate hypotheses in a conceptual task. ... – a second look." In Thinking: Readings in cognitive science, edited Philip N. Johnson-Laird and Peter C. Wason, 307–314, Cambridge University Press.

Wheeler, P., & Arunachalam, V. (2008). The effects of decision aid design on the information search strategies and confirmation bias of tax professionals. *Behavioral Research in Accounting, 20*(1), 131–145.

5 Framing and the Ostrich Effect: Why Our Decisions Depend On How Information Is Presented

The most important single key takeaway from this chapter is

> **The 4th Commandment of Risk Leadership:** Losses loom psychologically twice as much as gains. Being a risk leader means embracing gains as much as losses.

Being a successful leader requires a large set of different communication skills. A part of this set of communication skills is the skill to frame a problem at hand appropriately and effectively for others to understand and react in a certain way. As such, embracing gains as much as losses is part of successful risk leadership.

Framing and the Ostrich Effect

One aspect of us being human and obviously not rational is that we are easily influenced by our environment and the choices that are presented to us. Framing refers to the fact that the way how information is presented to us will have an impact on the choices that we will make. In other words, while rational decision-making stresses the reason and logic of a process and the use of information is supposed to reduce the level of uncertainty, the framing effect pertains to the way risk-related information is portrayed and how this distorts (optimal) decision-making. The main insight is that different representations of identical alternatives tend to cause considerable valuation differences depending on how the information is presented to indivdiuals.

The pioneering research study with respect to the framing effect was conducted by Kahneman and Tversky (1981). Their experimental approach was centered around hypothetical decision problems that were either framed as "gains" or "losses". They discovered that subjects are inclined to behave more risk-aversely

A. Hofmann, *The Ten Commandments of Risk Leadership*, Future of Business and Finance, https://doi.org/10.1007/978-3-030-88797-1_5

when alternatives are positively framed and that they tend to react in a more risk-seeking manner when alternatives are presented in negative domain. Framing effects are not solely restricted on loss and gain frames. In the "Asian disease task", Kahneman and Tversky (1981) asked a number of people about which scenario of alternative treatments for a disease they would prefer. The hypothetical scenario is as follows. Assume a dangerous epidemic breaks out and without any countermeasures undertaken, 600 people will die. There are two alternative medical programs available. Subjects had to choose one of them. The effects were described in the following two ways. First, call this formulation 1:

1. With medical program A, 200 lives can be saved.
2. With medical program B, with probability 1/3, 600 lives can be saved and with probability 2/3, nobody can be saved.

In this case, the result was that 72% voted for medical program A. Second, call the next formulation 2:

1. With medical program A, 400 people will die.
2. With medical program B, with probability 1/3, nobody will die and with probability 2/3, 600 people will die.

In this case, the result was that 78% voted for medical program B. Indeed, subjects are more likely to choose an alternative that lets one-third live over one that lets two-thirds die, even though this is just the same thing!

Individuals are very susceptible to the framing effect as we all have an aversion towards loss and will always look for gain. In prospect theory, a loss is perceived as more significant, and therefore more worthy of avoiding, than an equivalent gain. A sure gain is preferred to a probable one, and a probable loss is preferred to a sure loss. Since people want to avoid sure losses, they look for options and information with certain gain. The way something is framed can influence our certainty that it will bring either gain or loss. Therefore, people find it appealing when the positive features of an option are highlighted instead of the negatives. Framing occurs out of a consequence that mental processing and evaluating information from our environment takes time and energy. To speed up the process our mind often uses small shortcuts or "heuristics.". This is important in an evolutionary sense because encountering a large animal in the wild with sharp teeth will quickly frame up the situation as dangerous and cause you to act.

Availability heuristic, or information availability, contributes to the framing effect. The availability heuristic is our tendency to use information that comes to mind quickly and easily when making decisions. Studies showed that the framing effect is more common in older adults who have more limited cognitive resources, and who therefore favor information that is presented in a way that is easily accessible to them (Kahneman and Tversky, 1981). Because we favor information is easily understood and recalled, options that are framed in this way are favored over those that aren't. Framing is a cognitive shortcut for which we use our emotional state during decision-making, instead of taking the time to consider the long-term consequences of a decision. The existence of cognitive frameworks is the reason why we favor information and options that are framed to elicit an immediate emotional response.

Framing is applied in many areas where risk-related information is presented to individuals. Interestingly, it is found that dangerous or negative risk-related information is often ignored - just like an ostrich who buries his head in the sand in order to avoid being noticed - and this is why it is called the *Ostrich Effect*. In a similar way, research on investment behavior suggests that investors check the value of their portfolios less often in bear markets—and indeed, why should I spoil my day by looking at my declining stock portfolio value again?! Empirical research indicates that individuals operating in investment contexts generally benefit from the provision of information. In view of this, investors should always emphasize the broad acquisition of information. But what if investors do not want to acquire relevant financial information under certain circumstances irrespective of how the information is presented? The Ostrich effect refers to investors choosing to only be selectively exposed to financial facts. The aim of this chapter is to convey psychological insight with respect to the possible impact of our environment on financial and risk-related decision-making.

Framing and Loss Aversion

The term *framing* in psychology refers to the way logically equivalent choice situations differently described leading to different results or preferences. When people are confronted with a risky choice, they will evaluate their prospects in the matter of two frameworks: the "gain frame" and the "loss frame". In the gains frame, people prefer the sure choice over a risky venture, while in the loss frame, individuals prefer choices with higher risk. Research has illustrated that framing effects can have an impact on an individual's level of risk taking and loss aversion. By restating the question or by changing the description of the situation one's rationality when making decisions can be affected. For example, a study was conducted trying to promote breast self-examination (BSE) in women in order to find possible breast cancer sooner. Two different pamphlets were distributed. In the first, pamphlet A, it was stated that "Research shows that women who do BSE have an increased chance of finding a tumor in the early, more treatable sate of the disease." In the second, pamphlet B, it was stated that "Research shows that women who do not do BSE have a decreased chance of finding a tumor in the early, more treatable sate of the disease." The result was that pamphlet B gained more awareness because it was written in a so-called "loss frame" when compared to pamphlet A, which was written in a "gain frame".

The insights to gain from such experiments is that we can use framing effects combined with individual loss aversion tendencies to promote products or services. For instance, psychologist Ariely conducted an experiment to show how loss aversion and framing could be used to help promote employees to invest in employer match retirement accounts. The subjects of the experiment were given an annual salary of $60,000, which they were told to split up for different everyday expenses as well as their retirement, where the employer would match up to 10% of that salary put into the retirement account. Most of the subjects did not put any money on the retirement account, basically giving up free money, and only a few maximized their retirement contributions. In a slightly different version of the experiment, participants were told that the employer would put $500 in their retirement account at the beginning of the month. However, that money would only stay in the retirement account to the degree that it was matched by the own contributions of the participants. At the end of the month, every subject who did not entirely match the $500, received a reminder on the amount of money they lost. By making the loss explicitly clear, Ariely took full advantage of the loss aversion effect and the result was that participants began to maximize their monthly contributions (Ariely & Kreisler, 2017).

Framing and Financial Literacy

Financial literacy refers to finance knowledge and skills that allow for a good understanding of how to manage financial resources efficiently and taking into account the time value of money. A lack of these skills may make it difficult for an individual to decide on financial investments such that they are in his or her own best interest. This includes, for instance, private banking and retirement decisions as well as how to manage credit debt. Interestingly, early financial education does not seem to impact financial behavior later in life. The reason is that financial literacy is only improved when the knowledge can actually be applied in practice—which is many years after school. As a consequence, financial literacy is best taught in college or at a higher level to stick with a person.

It is important to understand that many financial institutions frame their products in such a way that is in their own best financial interest and not in the best interest of their customers. Multiple examples how financial institutions take advantage of lacking financial knowledge in the general population come to mind. Most of these examples involve the time value of money or hidden fees that are not directly observable by the client. A typical example are credit cards that involve extremely high interest rates for purchases or late payment fees. Another example is an institution that collects retirement contributions from employees and offers a "default plan" where the contributions will be put into when the employee does not explicitly indicate where the funds should be invested. This makes it easy for them and the default plan is often on the more expensive side when it comes to administrative fees associated with the plan. It makes sense to look at these fees and compare plans. Indeed, calculating accumulated fees over 30 years of retirement savings can easily add up $100 k which can be saved by switching from one plan to another. Sometimes, the next thing they make difficult for you is the act of switching itself. Some providers make switching a "two-step process", requiring the enrollee to indicate that not only past but also future contributions should be put into the new plan instead of the default plan. When you are not aware of this, the switch would only be for past contributions. You see, it is not easy to fight for your own financial interest, especially given the fact that many financial institutions act in theirs and don't have an interest in making it easy for you.

This is both a framing and a financial literacy problem. First, it takes framing knowledge and insight to see that the plans are framed in such a way that the institution maximizes overall fee income, and second, it takes financial literacy skills to evaluate which plan is right for you. Maybe you do not want to invest in risky equity but prefer less risky bonds. A default retirement fund is often structured in such a way that there is more equity investment at the beginning of the plan and that fades into more bonds at the end or later stages of the individual's working life. But this pre-determined structure might not be right for you given your individual risk appetite.

Distortions in Risk Perception

Johnson et al. (1993) offer exciting research on how to strengthen the theoretical evidence with respect to the presence of framing effects in insurance and risk contexts. One central assertion is that consumer errors may be ascribed to biases in any segment of the insurance decision. Accordingly, individuals may often have distorted perceptions of the probability of the risks they are confronted with. They may also have biased views regarding the benefits or costs of insurance policies.

In illustrating possible distortions in risk perception, especially anecdotal accounts serve as an important evidential means. In 1990, Iben Browning, an independent business consultant with a Ph.D. in zoology, made the claim that there was a fifty percent chance of a serious earthquake striking New Madrid, Missouri on December 1–5, 1990. Browning's prediction found broad public acceptance. One of the considerable causes for this was that the New Madrid seismic zone had seen great earthquakes in the past. However, it was a statement of David Stewart, then Director of the Center for Earthquake Studies at Southeast Missouri State University, which indirectly catapulted Browning's estimation into the limelight. Stewart initially expressed that the prediction was worthy of further attention. Key media outlets considered the statement to be an authoritative approval. Consequently, they covered Browning's claim extensively. A significant number of proven seismologists, however, did not agree with Browning's forecast. Their estimated probability of an earthquake occurring was about one in sixty thousand. An Ad Hoc Working Group even went as far as to show that Browning's assessment was neglectable. The predicted earthquake did not eventuate. It is important to also point out that sales for earthquake insurance in the affected area increased dramatically compared to the preceding year. What is to be extracted from this story is that there can be significant external influencing of prevalent risk perceptions. Johnson et al. (1993) indicate that biases with regard to the perceived probability of vivid causes of death are highly correlated with the volume of media coverage. Yet, the researchers also note that the surge in earthquake insurance purchases partly may have been caused due to an increased awareness of the true level of seismic risk.

Examining distortions in the perception of risk, Johnson et al. (1993) conduct several experimental surveys based on different hypotheses. They primarily focus on the ascertainment of the average willingness to pay for diverse hypothetical insurance contracts. The experimental approach is the same across the testing of the various hypotheses. Subjects are asked to value two separate insurance policies which cover mutually exclusive risks. The average willingness to pay for a third policy which provides insurance against a risk encompassing the prior mentioned two hazards is also obtained. It is noteworthy to mention that divergent experimental methods are presented in eliciting the average price of the all-encompassing policy.

Their first set of questions examines the pricing of hypothetical flight accident insurance policies based on different subject matters. The research objective was to deduce if circumstances related to the key terms "terrorism" and "mechanical failure" were more affecting than events characterized by the rather broad description "any reason". The first insurance contract was designed to cover death caused by any act of terrorism. The second policy insured a death occurrence due to any non-terrorism related mechanical failure. A third policy covered the individual's death due to "any reason". The insured sum in all these cases was \$100,000. All respondents had to assign values to all three alternatives among answering other unrelated insurance questions. The determined average willingness to pay of the first policy was around \$14, while the second contract had an average price of \$10.31. Surprisingly, the all-encompassing policy only had an average willingness to pay of around \$12, thereby being valued lower on average than a restricted insurance option. The results clearly show that the principle of inclusion is violated. The implication is that two disjoint subsets of an inclusive risk are deemed more probable than the overall risk itself.

Another survey conducted was centred around the pricing of disease-specific insurance options. A group of thirty individuals was questioned about their willingness to pay with respect to a specific insurance policy covering hospitalisation for any disease. Then they were asked to value an additional policy insuring hospitalisation for any accident, based on the hypothetical assumption that they had already purchased the first policy at their proposed price. Another group of respondents had to answer these two questions in the reverse order. In contrast to the Flight insurance survey, none of the first two groups were asked to price an all-encompassing policy. In this particular case, that question was put to two other groups. One of them priced a policy insuring hospitalisation for any reason, whilst the other revealed their willingness to pay for a policy covering any disease or accident. Essentially similar results to the first survey were obtained. The average willingness to pay for the insurance option covering any disease was higher than the average prices of all the remaining policies. In fact, the average willingness to pay for the first policy was more than twice as high as the average insurance fee assigned to the policy insuring hospitalization due to any cause. Obviously, the principle of inclusion is also violated in this particular context. Further, the results suggest that the isolation of vivid causes has a strong influence on the perceived value of insurance (Johnson et al., 1993).

Johnson et al. (1993) conclude, based on the results of the conducted surveys, that decision-making processes in insurance contexts could be affected by biased perceptions concerning the probability and size of certain risks. However, externally focusing on the slightly differing approaches with regard to both experimental surveys, some aspects should be looked at more critically. Especially the first survey bears the potential of respondents misunderstanding the hypothetical scenario. Since it is not clearly stated that the third insurance policy covers the subject matters of the first two policies, there may be a certain level of unclarity in assigning a price to this insurance contract. A common misunderstanding with respect to the term "any reason" lets the obtained results appear more reasonable. Furthermore, it must be noted again that in the second experimental survey the all-inclusive policy was priced by another group of respondents. It can be assumed that the observed discrepancies between the average willingness to pay for the first two policies and for the insurance option covering any reason for hospitalisation would have been considerably smaller if the first two groups had been asked to value this third policy directly. On the other hand, it is unclear whether the result pertaining to the violation of the inclusion principle would have been different.

Distortions in Risk Transfer

A typical risk transfer is insurance. As the insurance company is not able to observe the behaviour of the policyholder after buying this particular insurance contract and given the fact that policyholders tend to be more careless after buying an insurance contract, the insurance company has to account for the problem of moral hazard on the part of the policyholder. A possible solution lies in the implementation of a deductible. Implementing a deductible will not only give the policyholder an incentive to be more careful even after having bought an insurance contract. The policyholder is obliged to come up for the amount agreed on as part of the deductible in case of an insurance incident but there is also a decrease in the amount of the premium which has to be paid. Rationally seen, it is a "win-win" situation for both sides—insurance company and policyholder—but the policyholder usually does not feel that way as he frames the accumulated premiums paid and the obligation to come up for the amount agreed on in case of an insurance incident as segregated losses. Alternatively, the insurance company could design a more attractive insurance contract by implementing a rebate which will be financed with some additional premium charge giving the policyholder the opportunity to receive the whole rebate as a reward in case of claim free year(s) instead of a deductible. Will the insurance contract with the rebate policy be more attractive than the insurance contract with the deductible? The hypothesis reflected by the key message presented was tested within a survey. The respondents were asked if they would prefer choosing the insurance contract with the rebate policy or the insurance contract with the deductible. They were more likely to take the insurance contract with the rebate policy than the insurance contract with the deductible although the policy with the rebate policy was worse than the policy with the deductible, since the rebate in its dilution is basically an interest-free loan to the insurance company. Assuming any positive discount rate for money, the consumer would be worse off choosing the insurance contract with the rebate policy.

Another example with explicit numbers e.g. a standard disability insurance contract on the one side and a $20 per month more expensive disability insurance contract on the other side will emphasize the just discussed phenomenon even more. The $20 per month additionally charged are used to finance a rebate amounting to $1200 in case of five claim-free years. Again, considering the time value of money and the restriction of being claim-free in the 5 years, the insurance contract with the deductible should be preferred over the insurance contract with the rebate but again the majority of the respondents chose the insurance contract with the rebate policy (Johnson et al., 1993).

To sum up, the evidence provided by these examples suggests that people usually do not act in a rational way when in front of a risk-related financial contract. The way in which insurance premiums (and prices of other financial products) are framed can determine the attractiveness of coverage and other related characteristics. These findings are consistent with the research on framing effects in other domains.

Empirical Investigations into the Ostrich Effect

Given the theoretic background for the ostrich effect and its main manifestations, Karlsson and Loewenstein (2009) provide empirical evidence that if the ostrich effect is indeed exhibited by investors, they will look up their portfolios more often when the market goes up as compared to when it goes down. By the way, even the author of this book has seen this behavior manifest itself over time.

Using data from the Swedish Premium Pension Authority, the study evaluates how Swedish citizens who were allowed to choose how to invest 2.5% of their pre-tax income in equity and debt markets made their decisions. The time period of the chosen sample ranges from January 7, 2002 to October 13, 2004. According to the researchers, by 2004, about 5.3 million out of 9 million Swedish population used this new pension system. Additionally, the data contains the number of investors' reallocations, which are essentially the transactions. Also, the data includes the average daily number of logins, which is equal to 10,903, and of these, 1142 resulted in transactions. It is assumed that there are no other purposes of logging in other than to (1) check the value of the portfolio and (2) make an investment allocation, i.e. transaction. This allows us to calculate the number of *look-ups*, which is measured as the number of logins minus the number of transactions. A second dataset is provided by Vanguard Group. In this case, the time period is from January 2, 2006 to June 30, 2008. However, there is no data on the amount of investment allocations made, which can be replaced by the aggregate trading volume in the S&P500 to control for transactional logins in the regression analysis. The analysis clearly indicates that the previous S&P500 return positively influences the current number of investors' logins. In particular, a 1% increase in the prior average return will lead to an increase in the number of logins in the range from roughly 18′000 to 23′000 additional logins (which is 5–6% of the daily mean number of logins).

The researchers draw several interesting conclusions. First, the Ostrich effect implies that the loss aversion reference point should increase faster when the markets go up than when they go down. Since the Ostrich effect causes investors to ignore the negative information, the reference point updating will take place more slowly, while in the up markets—vice versa. Second, the ostrich effect might contribute to a well-documented relation of trading volumes and market returns. Third, the Ostrich effect might explain why investors have a preference for assets that are more liquid over less liquid ones. Fourth, the effect might add an explanation to the liquidity drying up during crises: investors do not want to come to terms with painful losses, which leads to less transactions and liquidity provided. Finally, the Ostrich effect has social consequences for the transmission of information. When markets are going up, people actively check their portfolios and exchange information, creating a "buzz", while in down markets, social transmission is suppressed, exacerbating the downturns.

Key Takeaways for Risk Leadership

Being a successful leader requires a large set of different communication skills, ranging from delivering a capturing speech to employees, motivating team members to push an important project forward for the company, or negotiating the best way to take over or beat a competitor in the market. A part of this set of communication skills is the skill to frame a problem at hand appropriately and effectively for others to understand and follow a leader and his or her decisions. Financial literacy contributes to a better understanding of given risky choices. In this way, psychologically embracing risk is part of successful risk leadership.

References

Ariely, D., & Kreisler, J. (2017). *Dollars and sense: How we misthink money and how to spend smarter*. HarperCollins.

Johnson, E. J., Hershey, J., Meszaros, J., & Kunreuther, H. (1993). Framing, probability distortions, and insurance decisions. *Journal of Risk and Uncertainty, 7*(1), 35–51.

Karlsson, N., & Loewenstein, G. (2009). The ostrich effect: Selective attention to information. *Journal of Risk and Uncertainty, 38*, 95–115.

Kahneman, D. & Tversky, A. (1981). The framing of decisions and the psychology of choice. *Science, 211*(4481), 453–458.

6 Emotions and Zero Risk Bias: Why We Make Bad Decisions and Overspend on Risk Avoidance

The most important single key takeaway from this chapter is

> **The 5th Commandment of Risk Leadership:** Don't let your emotions overrun your rationality! Avoidance of a risk may be a suboptimal choice!

Zero-risk bias manifests itself in many ways, some of which we can use to our advantage as decision-makers and others that we must be aware of more actively in our daily lives. For example, as managers, we must be aware not to allocate resources to a project that completely eliminates a risk if there are other projects that allow for a more efficient use of the firm's capital. As consumers, we must be aware to avoid purchasing full coverage insurance when it is obviously overpriced.

Zero-Risk Bias

Assume you are sitting at a negotiation table with your supplier company that produces parts for your final product (a nice car or a stylish coffee maker, for instance). The supplier discusses six possible software problems that can potentially occur in the final product, each with equal probability. Such a software problem, once it occurs, would make the product useless for the client since the product would simply stop working. The supplier company happily reports that they were able to eliminate two of these problems in the last month, leaving the company with only four remaining potential problems. Now, they might be able to eliminate the final two problems, which requires some significant effort on their side, and so they ask how much you would be willing to pay to have them eliminate these two remaining potential issues. Even if they could eliminate one more at a reasonable cost, assuming there was only one problem left, how much would you be willing to pay them in order to get rid of this one remaining problem? Most people would be willing to pay

A. Hofmann, *The Ten Commandments of Risk Leadership*, Future of Business and Finance, https://doi.org/10.1007/978-3-030-88797-1_6

more in the latter case, which is because in that case the chance of a problem occurring with the final product at all finally is reduced to zero. But this does not make sense from a pure statistical viewpoint: in the first case, you are reducing your risk of a problem by 50% or two out of four, while in the second case, you are reducing the risk by only 25% or 1 out of 4. How valuable is the final reduction to zero risk?

Another example is the following setting. Assume you are a health care manager with many responsibilities. The information presented to you by a team of experts is that X and Y are two equally dangerous types of cancer. You need to choose between treatment A and B, and due to financial restrictions of your company, only one treatment can be executed. With treatment A, a drug given to 100 people with cancer X will cure 60 of them. With treatment B, a drug can be given to only 50 people with cancer Y, but it will cure all 50 of them! Which treatment would you choose? Most people would choose treatment B. The reason is a preference for zero-risk. In other words, they exhibit the *zero-risk bias* as they prefer to eliminate one risk entirely even if treatment A would have saved an additional 10 lives for a cancer that is equally serious.

Zero-risk bias is a type of cognitive bias that causes individuals to make decisions that are statistically irrational due to a strong preference for zero-risk. Zero-risk bias is defined as the preference of an individual to prefer the complete elimination of a risk and thereby striving for safety while undervaluing very small risks. Complete elimination of a risk may be suboptimal though. Zero-risk bias has been shown to exist in many fields including the energy industry, the health care industry, and even the environment. One study, for example, surveyed a group of individuals with different backgrounds about which option they would prefer when it comes to clean up two hazardous waste sites in two different cities. The options of the study are shown in the table below. There were two versions of this questionnaire with the first version having equal amounts of lives saved in each option; however, one of the options, option B, completely eliminated the hazardous waste in one site. Those who ranked this option the best were considered to exhibit zero-risk bias. Version 2 went on to explore this bias to see if individuals would rank this option B higher, even if the total amount of lives saved was less than in the other options.

Option	Consequences on number of cancer cases	
	Big city	Small city
A: partial clean up in both cities	Prior: 8 Later: 4	Prior: 4 Later: 2
B: total clean up in smaller city; partial clean up in larger city	Prior: 8 Later: 6 (7 in V2)	Prior: 4 Later: 0
C: partial clean up in both cities, but concentrate on larger city	Prior: 8 Later: 3	Prior: 4 Later: 3

Setup of survey on attitudes toward hazardous waste by Baron et al. (1993)

In version 1, where every option would lead to the same reduction in cases of cancer, only 18% of the subjects exhibited zero-risk bias by choosing option B as the best option. However, in version 2, 42% exhibited zero-risk bias by ranking it higher than another option, which would save more lives. Also, in version 2, 11% preferred the complete elimination of risk and ranked option B as the best, even if it saved the least amount of lives. Surprisingly, judges, legislators, and environmentalists showed the greatest amount of zero-risk bias, while economists and experts showed it the least (Baron et al., 1993).

A slightly more extreme form of zero-risk bias in public policy was the Delaney clause in the Food Additives Amendment of 1958. The Delaney clause prohibited any amount of a chemical additive to food if that chemical was found to induce cancer in humans or animals. It sounds great when you first hear it, but when you dive a bit deeper you can see that it was irrational to induce such a *zero-tolerance policy*. For example, if a chemical were found to cause cancer in mice at 250 times the normal concentration, that chemical would be prohibited by the Delaney clause even if it were safe for humans to consume at lower doses. For these reasons, the clause was eventually repealed as it prevented too many additives that were actually safe for human consumption.[1]

Many implications result from zero-risk bias. Being aware of the zero-risk bias raises the question in regard to public policies if the money may be better spent on other projects that would in turn save more lives. So how can individuals be risk-averse and at the same time exhibiting zero-risk bias? According to some studies, it could be the result of a confusion about quantities. An interesting study in small children illustrated that children will confuse length and number. Although this study was conducted in small children, there may be a connection in how we think as adults in regard to our irrational decisions involving differences between relative and absolute risks.[2]

When We Hate to Lose: Aversion to a Sure Loss

In some situations, a person may choose the option to make an "actuarially unfavorable bet" because they are optimistic that their outcome will allow them to break even and avoid losing. Kahneman and Tversky coined this type of behavior with the term "aversion to a sure loss," which is different from loss aversion. Aversion to a sure loss is a different kind of animal due to the fact that with loss aversion, investors are afraid of suffering a loss and spend more time trying to avoid it as opposed to earning a gain of similar magnitude. On the other hand, aversion to a sure loss also occurs when a person is afraid of the loss but they try to avoid the loss by making risk-seeking choices.

We can easily identify someone acting with loss aversion versus someone acting with aversion to a sure loss. Assume participants are presented with two options:

[1] See Baron (2003), p. 1152.

[2] See Baron (2003) as well as Baron et al. (1975).

The first option is surely losing $500. The second option is a 2:1 risk where there is a 33.33% chance of losing $1000 and a 66.67% chance of losing $250. Although the expected payoffs for both options are the same (that is, losing $500), the choice the participants make indicates their type of aversion. In this experiment, those individuals who choose the sure loss of $500 are demonstrating loss aversion because they do not want to take the 33.33% chance of losing $1000. Those who choose the 2:1 risk are demonstrating aversion to a sure loss because they are optimistic that the odds will work out in their favor and they will only lose $250. In this experimental study, about 65% of the participants averted the sure loss (Shefrin, 2017).

In another experiment that relates to the subject of aversion to a sure loss, researchers had finance graduate students participate as investors. The beginning of the experiment required them to choose three unrelated stocks worth the same amount. The stocks varied based on their potential volatility which revealed the participant's risk behavior. They presented respondents the opportunity to utilize averaging down as part of their strategy which helped separated aversion to sure loss and ambiguity aversion. Aversion to a sure loss comes into play because when using this strategy, it makes the investors give a large amount of money to a stock that doesn't always increase back to its original value. They make this trade-off because this strategy helps to recover lost assets at a faster rate (Ferenčak et al., 2018).

The study results revealed that as stock prices diminished, the majority of students (87.64%), opted for averaging down once it was presented as an option despite knowing they could actually lose even more. For example, participants were given the chance to use averaging down starting at 9,00$ and the next one was at 8,35$ (the study specified that the median value set = 9 and standard deviation = 1.45). There was also an option to "do nothing" and as the stock price kept decreasing more people chose to sell and implement averaging down. All of this evidence points to aversion to a sure loss being the main factor as a way of explaining the investors' behavior once they witness the stock decreasing in value (Ferenčak et al., 2018).

Key Takeaways for Risk Leadership

Zero-risk bias manifests itself in many ways, some of which we can use to our advantage as decision-makers and others that we must be aware of more actively in our daily lives. For example, as managers, we must be aware not to allocate resources to a project that completely eliminates a risk if there are other projects that allow for a more efficient use of our firm's capital. As investors, we must be aware not to quickly offload equities into traditional zero-risk securities, such as treasury bonds, during market volatility or market downturns. As managers and marketing experts, we should charge more for a service or product while at the same time offering a free trial or thirty-day risk-free trial period of our product, by taking advantage of our customers' tendency for zero risks. As consumers, we must be aware to avoid purchasing full coverage insurance when it is obviously overpriced.

References

Baron, J. (2003). Value analysis of political behavior – self-interested, moralistic, altruistic, moral. *University of Pennsylvania Law Review, 151*, 1134–1167.

Baron, J., Gowda, R., & Kunreuther, H. (1993). Attitudes toward managing hazardous waste: What should be cleaned up and who should pay for it? *Risk Analysis, 13*(2), 183–192.

Baron, J., Lawson, G., & Siegel, L. S. (1975). Effects of training and set size on children's judgments of number and length. *Developmental Psychology, 11*(5), 83–588.

Ferenčak, M., Dobromirov, D., Radišić, M., & Takači, A. (2018). Aversion to a sure loss: Turning investors into gamblers. *Zbornik Radova Ekonomski Fakultet u Rijeka, 36*(2), 537–557.

Shefrin, H. (2017). *Behavioral Risk Management: Managing the psychology that drives decisions and influences operational risk*. Palgrave Macmillan.

7 Endowment Effect and Status-Quo Bias: Why We Stick with Bad Decisions

The most important single key takeaway from this chapter is

> **The 6th Commandment of Risk Leadership**: Although we prefer to keep things the way they are, change can be in our best interest. Don't let the status quo fool you!

It seems that the more emotional a decision is or the more different options there are, the more we prefer the status quo. Status quo bias influences decisions of private individuals as well as numerous strategical decisions in companies made by managers. Doing nothing is also making a decision! The more extensive the consequences of a decision, the more thoroughly we should examine whether we are influenced by this cognitive bias.

Risky Decisions and the Endowment Effect

How do you value your car? Any sentimental value you attach to it? The longer you have it, the more you become attached to it. Several experiments show the high influence of ownership on the perceived value of objects. The *endowment effect* is commonly known as the tendency for an individual to value something they own more than if someone else owned it. Many people believe that the endowment effect may be a result of loss aversion because losing something will cost you more happiness than to gain something of a similar value. And it does not need to be an object of particular beauty! For example, in the stock market, if someone owns a stock of a company, studies have shown that investors will hold the stock for way too long, even if the fundamentals of the company show a bleak future (Kahneman et al., 1991). Indeed, it can be shown that investors—who should be rational at least when it comes to their financial investments, right?—value a stock more because they feel

A. Hofmann, *The Ten Commandments of Risk Leadership*, Future of Business and Finance, https://doi.org/10.1007/978-3-030-88797-1_7

an attachment to it and they do not want to sell easily; maybe because they do not want to realize a permanent loss even though in the long run it would save them money. Additionally, the endowment effect has been observed in the real estate industry, where it is commonly seen that a seller wants to list his or her house at a much higher price than what their real estate agent recommends or what the market will be willing to pay. As a result, the listing might stay on the market for a very long time period if your real estate agent is not able to convince you to lower your valuation. This is very much the case, in a down market when sellers do not want to sell their home for less than what they paid for it, even if it is what the market is willing to pay.

Endowment Effect and Loss Aversion

When introducing Prospect theory, Daniel Kahneman and Amos Tversky proposed some characteristics of an individual's value function: First, the value function is defined on deviations from the reference point of the individual. Second, the value function usually is concave for gains and convex for losses, and third, it is steeper for losses than for gains (Kahneman and Tversky, 1979). There is high experimental evidence for these relations to be true. From the described characteristics of the value functions it follows that people typically weight losses stronger than gains. One is risk-averse with respect to gains and risk-seeking with respect to losses. This irrationality is called loss aversion. With loss aversion, preferences are in dependence on how potential outcomes are framed, i.e. whether they are presented as a loss or a gain compared to the current status quo as reference point. Status quo bias results from loss aversion if the consequences of an alternative of current status quo are framed as losses. Assumptions of standard utility theory are violated by this.

In 1980, Richard Thaler was the first to introduce the endowment effect as it is commonly known today. According to him, individuals value goods higher if they are their property than in case the same good would not be the individual's property. The reason for this is strongly connected with loss aversion. Not possessing an owned good anymore gives the individual the feeling of a loss, whereas adding a non-possessed good is recognized as a gain. As explained above, in general, losses are weighted stronger than gains. Thaler also expresses this as an underweighting of opportunity costs.

Kahneman et al. (1991) provided a set of examples and experiments that verifies the existence of the endowment effect. They introduce the endowment effect with a short example, which puts the effect in a nutshell: A colleague of them once bought a bottle of wine for $10, but did not drink it for some years. During these years, the bottle highly increased in value. After that time period, he would need to pay $200 to buy another bottle of that type. In his current situation, he neither would be willing to pay 200$ for another bottle, nor would he be willing to sell it for the new, higher price. Due to the fact that he owns the wine, he does not want to give it away now. Status quo remains because of the endowment effect.

In a laboratory experiment, Knetsch and Sinden (1987) wanted to prove the assumed existence of the endowment effect. The experimental setting is the following: Every participant gets one of two kinds of lottery tickets, randomly distributed. If one wins the lottery, one gets a price worth at least $50. Participants with the first kind of ticket are asked to pay $2 to keep their ticket and take part in the lottery. 50% of the people chose that option to participate. The other half preferred not to pay $2 of their money. In the group with the second kind of lottery tickets, people can participate in the lottery without paying an amount of money. Instead, they get an offer of $2 to resign from their lottery possibility. Rationally, one should expect that the distribution of decisions is the same as in the first group. But this did not materialize. 76% of the people in group two decided not to sell their ticket (Knetsch and Sinden, 1987). This seems to be a hint on an existing endowment effect, participants value their ticket higher if it belongs to them. However, concerning the experimental design, some economists criticized that the identified effect would not have been occurred if there were included a market environment and possibilities to learn from behavior of oneself and others.

To be able to prove the existence of an endowment effect, Kahneman et al. (1991) undertook some more experiments, which explicitly consider learning possibilities and a market environment. In their first experiment, participants are parted into two groups, one seller and one buyer group. Every person in the seller group gets a coffee mug which could be bought for $6 in a store nearby. For guaranteeing a setting comparable to real markets with learning opportunities, there are the following specifications introduced:

The coffee mugs are traded in four successive market trials, which enables the participants to learn about the market situation. Buyer and seller roles stay constant over the trials. In each trial, all participants are asked to determine the amount of money that they would buy or sell the mug for, depending on the role as buyer or seller in each trial. By this, supply and demand curves are created. After every market trial, the market clearing price, and the number of trades, resulting from the clearing price and the prices determined by the participants, were announced. A trade occurs if a buyer offers the clearing price or more to get a mug and a seller demands the clearing price or less for their mug. One of the four trials is randomly chosen. Only in this chosen trial, trades actually are executed.

Furthermore, they introduce four more successive markets, this time trading with ballpoint pens, whose store price was known as $3.98. Now, buyers from the mug markets get the pens, so that they will be in the seller role. Showing that a possible effect occurs not only in case of using mugs in the experiment, but also using other products like pens, would bring stronger evidence for the existence of the cognitive bias.

Economically, one has to expect that the mugs or the pens will be hold by the people who value them the most, because transaction costs and income effects play a negligible role in the experimental setting. One can think of the half of participants who like mugs the most as mug lovers and the half of participants who like mugs least as mug haters. With this implication and due to random distribution of mugs, half of the mug haters should have a mug, and because of this, half of the mugs should be traded by the mug haters to the mug lovers in theory.

This is not what resulted in the experiment: There were 22 mugs (and also pens) in the markets, so 11 trades would be expected. In fact, there were substantially fewer trades, with five as the highest number of trades in the four market trials. The reason for this was the reservation price for the mugs of buyers and sellers. Market prices laid between $4.25 and $4.75. Median sellers did not want to sell for less than $5.25 (willingness to accept), whereas median buyers were unwilling to pay more than $2.75 (willingness to pay), which is approximately half of the selling prices. In the pen trials, relation was almost the same. Replicating the experiment always led to the same result: Median seller price was twice as high as median buyer price, with the consequence that substantially fewer trades took place as expected. It seems that participants owning the mugs or pens value it higher than people not owning it. Even when explicitly considering a market environment and learning opportunities, an endowment effect is measurable and strengthens the preference for the status quo alternative—in case of the sellers: keep the mug (Kahneman et al., 1991).

A second experiment investigates whether a surprisingly low trading volume in an experiment as described above could be explained by a reluctance to buy or to sell. Kahneman, Knetsch and Thaler define a price range from $0.25 to $9.75 for coffee mugs. 77 students of an US American university are parted into three different groups. People from the first group are the sellers and have to tell at which prices in the given price range they would be willing to sell the mug they get. The buyers do not get a mug and have to tell at which prices they would buy one. As a third group, the choosers have the choice to either buy the mug at the prices in the price interval or get the equivalent amount of money. Objectively, choosers and sellers are in the same situation. For every price, they decide between getting money and having the mug. The buyer decides between losing money for a mug and retaining the amount of cash. Surprisingly, the behavior of the choosers was more similar to the buyer's decisions than to the seller's decisions. Concretely, the median reservation price of the sellers was $7.12, the price of the choosers was $3.12 and the one of the buyers was $2.87. From this, one could conclude that endowment played a substantial role in decisions: The low number of trades was predominantly triggered by the aversion against giving up a coffee mug, and less produced by the reluctance of giving up an amount of money. The endowment effect seems to be mainly relevant for real objects according to this experiment. Kahneman, Knetsch and Thaler additionally mention that in the experimental setting, the trivial income effect is excluded, because there is no difference in the economic situation of sellers and choosers.

Referring to two more experiments from other papers, the authors are presenting some further aspects connected to the endowment effect. They describe an experiment of Loewenstein and Kahneman, in which a group of students either gets pens or tokens exchangeable to an unspecified gift. Amongst others, one of the gifts are two chocolate bars. Shortly explained, all participants have to rank the attractiveness of the gifts and the pen. Half of the students get a pen, the other half gets a token. In a last step, the participants are given the choice between the pen and the chocolate bars as one of the gifts. 56% of the pen owners decided for the pen, whereas only 24% of the students who got assigned a token chose that option. As in the mug experiments, an endowment effect seems to influence the decision and strengthens status quo. Another interesting result is that in the attractiveness rating conducted before, the pen owners stated they did not consider the pens to be more attractive than the chocolate. From this, the authors conclude that the endowment effect mainly can be reasoned by the pain of giving up an endowment, less by an increasing appeal of the possessed good.

Besides, Knetsch (1992) analyzed the effect of loss aversion and the endowment effect on indifference curves. In microeconomic theory, indifference curves cannot cross, they represent different levels of utility. This is only given if the assumption of reversible indifference curves is fulfilled. With the following experiment, Knetsch shows that with loss aversion and endowment effect existent, this assumption is violated. Participants of the experiment get either 5 pens or $4.50. Afterwards, the individuals who got a pen have to decide whether they would accept to give away a specified number of pens for a specified amount of cash. In the same procedure, people initially provided with cash have to decide whether they would accept to get a certain number of pens in exchange for a specified amount of their money. With these data, individual indifference curves can be derived. In a next step, average indifference curves of the pen-group and the cash-group are calculated from the individual indifference curves (Knetsch, 1992).

When evaluating the results of the described laboratory experiments, it is important to keep in mind that it is extremely difficult to create an experimental setting that controls only for one type of cognitive bias. There will always be other effects influencing the outcomes, e.g. the *anchoring effect*, when trying to proof the endowment effect in an experiment. Additionally, a laboratory setting will differ in some ways from real-life situations. Nevertheless, due to consistent, significant results from the different experiments, there is high evidence for the existence of a substantial endowment effect.

Status Quo Bias

Another important human bias in decision-making under catastrophe risk is the *Status Quo Bias*: In many decision problems, one alternative inevitably carries the label status quo—that is, doing nothing or maintaining a current or previous decision is almost always a possibility. Faced with new options, decision-makers often stick with the status quo alternative, which means 'no insurance' here (Kahneman et al., 1991). Other non-insurance examples for this bias include doing nothing in order to (1) follow customary company policy, (2) elect an incumbent to stay another term in office, or (3) to purchase the same product brands over and over again, or finally (4) to stay in the same job. A tendency to prefer status quo norms and regular, habitual behavior compared to innovative acting is arising. Especially, behavior in the way of conventional social norms is supported by this. People often follow the conventional norms, just because it is the way of least resistance, not because it is the optimal decision in the specific situation. These aspects again lead to the result that the status quo alternative is chosen more often than it would be rationally correct (Samuelson & Zeckhauser, 1988).

The occurrence of the *Status Quo Bias* is explained in two main categories: First, if present, transition costs and/or uncertainty can influence the decision such that the status quo is rationally the best alternative. Second, psychological commitment makes people behave irrationally such that they try to avoid regretting past decisions or want to maintain staying in control regardless of efficiency.

Decision-making under uncertainty usually involves some status quo in which humans are currently set. This might be the case when there is an election or a renewal of a continuous contract in the insurance market. Although, there are no switching costs and decisions like the ones stated are completely independent from past decisions, one is prone to choose the alternative that is currently the selected one. Samuelson and Zeckhauser (1988) design various laboratory experiments which validate the existence of the status quo bias.

Experimental Tests on Static Decisions

Samuelson and Zeckhauser performed experiments with 486 students taken from economic classes at Boston University School of Management and the Kennedy School of Government at Harvard University. The participants were asked to decide between either four, three or two alternatives, varying across the participants. In the case that the participant receives four alternatives to choose from, one either may receive a neutral setting, i.e. where one does not have any currently selected alternative. Otherwise, one may receive one out of four possible status quo settings, where one alternative is already selected and may be continued or switched to another alternative at no costs. When the participant receives only three alternatives to choose from, one out of the four alternatives is left out. Then, one receives either a neutral setting or one out of three possible status quo settings. Lastly, the participant can also receive only two alternatives, i.e., choosing between the first two or the last, both settings again constructed as either a neutral or one of possible two status quo settings. Thus, the participants randomly receive one out of fifteen possible settings. Furthermore, the order in which the alternatives are presented will be permutated, excluding any order effect, e.g., choosing the first alternative more often out of convenience. The researchers constructed six different questions, all following the upper described scheme when presented to the participants.

As an example, one of the settings is to make a financial decision. In the neutral setting, you are supposed to consider an investment, choosing out of four different alternatives which you have selected previously due to reading financially related newspapers. However, your funds to invest are rather small. The four alternatives, in summary, contain a high risk and low risk investment, an investment in a treasury bill and an investment in a municipal bond, all having a 1-year time horizon. The corresponding status quo setting then states, that you have inherited a portfolio consisting of cash and securities from your great uncle. The great uncle has already invested a portion of this particular portfolio in one of the four alternatives which is hereby considered as the status quo alternative. However, there are no costs when you want to allocate the portfolio's resources to another alternative, i.e. there are no trading costs or commissions. In the case that the participants make rational choices, the given answer should not differ significantly across the different settings, since, in the previous example, both statistical first and second moments, i.e. the expectation and the variance do not differ in the alternatives. Furthermore, the subject's risk aversion should not change by framing the environment differently. Since there are no switching costs, an influence of the setting on the subject's answer can only be caused by the status quo bias.

If an alternative is framed as the *status quo alternative*, most likely, this alternative will then be chosen. The opposite effect occurs as expected: If the same alternative is framed as a change to the status quo, i.e. an alternative to the status quo, it is less likely to be picked compared to the neutral setting. When comparing the difference in the status quo bias between the different number of alternatives, the responses indicate that the status quo bias becomes relatively more severe if the number of alternatives is high. It should be noted that a lower number of alternatives induces a higher response rate naturally. Thus, the absolute status quo bias remains the same among the alternatives which induces that the relative status quo bias increases with the number of alternatives. The authors use an approximate chi-square test in order to test for a significant difference in the response rates. Hence, the authors could show a statistically significant difference in 57.4% of the settings. The rather weak statistical evidence is most likely caused by the high variance across the questions as well as the low sample size which is however a result of the high amount of different settings for each question. Nevertheless, it should be considered that the different settings are obligatory due to the possible influence of other psychological biases.

Experiments on Sequential Decisions

Samuelson and Zeckhauser extend their experimental design to a sequential decision-making test with a two-period setting. The subjects have to decide about an air fleet leasing problem for the next period, in which the only given information is a forecast about the economic conditions. The conditions can either be good or bad and will be the opposite of what they have been in the previous period. i.e., good conditions will be followed by bad conditions and bad conditions will be followed by good conditions, respectively. The authors provide several versions of this experiment. The experimental tests strongly suggest the existence of a status quo bias. Samuelson and Zeckhauser state and systemize different kinds of explanations for this phenomenon. They present three main explanation categories.

Explanation 1: Rational Decision-Making

As first aspect, they describe the status quo bias as a consequence of rational decision-making in the presence of transition costs and/or uncertainty. A preference for the status quo can be fully consistent with rational decision making, if particular conditions are fulfilled. For example, in case an individual is facing independent and identical decision settings, the only rationally consistent choice in a follow-up decision is to choose the identical option as in the first choice. In this case, we think it is questionable if one can connect this kind of behavior with the term bias, because it seems to be optimal to behave that way. For a more general explanation, one has to take into account that most consecutive decision processes are not independent. In majority of situations, the initial decision will have an influence on the preferences and the possibilities in the following choice. Transition costs can be an important reason for preferring the status quo. If the costs of changing exceed the advantages of an alternative opportunity, a rational decision maker will remain in the status quo. On societal and private level, numerous kinds of transition costs are existent. For instance, in America, nonmetric measurement is still used, even though there are substantial drawbacks compared to metric measurement, just because of the high costs of changing the measurement system. On an individual level, one often finds long-term buyer-seller relationships, e.g. in case of 1-year insurance contracts. The insured person stays with the insurance company he or she once decided for, because elsewise transition costs would occur: One has to invest time and researching effort for better offers. Again, a preference for the status quo does not necessarily have to be seen as a biased attitude. When facing high transition costs, it can be more efficient to stick to the status quo.

Another point leading to status quo bias in this context is the presence of uncertainty in decision-making. At first, identifying alternatives needs resources. Again, such transition costs decrease the attractiveness of changing the current situation. But even without any kind of transition costs, it is possible that status quo inertia occurs in a situation of uncertainty. To illustrate this, Schmalensee (1982) uses a model in which a decision between two brands is to be made. A consumer has to choose between two brands which are identical from his/her current perspective but will generate an uncertain level of utility. If the first choice brings the consumer a sufficiently high level of utility, he will stay with the decision made, because there is no guarantee that the second brand would also lead to that sufficiently high utility level. Here, the status quo bias can lead to imperfect decisions in the way that brands which are not chosen in the first step, but are leading to a superior utility level, will most likely be neglected in future decisions, if the first choice is worse, but still satisfying.

Finally, the idea that there also is a need to commit to deciding about different alternatives is a further aspect that can explain the status quo bias. People have to spend effort in analyzing whether possible alternatives could be worth to assess. Staying with the status quo, justifying this by a first, rational decision, saves the costs of a pre-decision analysis.

Explanation 2: Psychological Commitment

Due to the fact that in the experiments presented above, neither transition costs nor uncertainty play a major role, status quo bias is only insufficiently explained by rational decision-making. According to Samuelson and Zeckhauser, there must be other intrinsic reasons for the occurrence of status quo bias in their experiments. The second explanatory category deals with psychological commitment.

There is high evidence from research that people's decision processes are not fully rational. Aspects like sunk costs influence choices of the decider, even though this is not rationally explainable. Sunk costs are costs which already occurred, or will definitively occur in the future, and have to be considered as losses without the possibility of regaining them. In theory, economic decisions should depend on incremental benefits and losses. Sunk costs lead to a violation of this intuition, because they induce a status quo bias: the larger the past resource investment in a decision, the greater the inclination to continue the commitment in subsequent decisions. In a subsequent decision environment, it is difficult for the decider to change his choice if he invested a high amount of resources in this choice, and loses the resources when switching to another alternative. Even if it is rationally the right behavior, psychologically it is hard to admit that one decided the wrong way in the previous stage. To avoid a confession concerning such a bad decision, the status quo is kept. In this context, Thaler states that if one pays for a good, the degree of usage of the good increases, and calls this the sunk cost effect. He illustrates his statement with the example of a family that bought tickets for a basketball game. Even though there is a large snowstorm, they decide to go watching the game, because they already paid for the tickets. If they would have gotten them for free, they would not have taken the risk to drive through the storm (Thaler, 1980).

Samuelson and Zeckhauser add some examples from real world decisions to further emphasize the contribution of sunk cost effect on status quo effect. Amongst other political decisions, they describe the example that aircraft producer Lookhead invested high amounts of money in a new aircraft type. This new type turned out to be unprofitable. Despite realizing losses with it, the company did not stop to build the type of aircraft, just because managers still hoped they could regain some part of the investment. Sunk cost led them to not change the status quo for an inefficiently long period of time.

As a short conclusion, it is reasonable to assume that status quo bias increases with the amount that was invested in the status quo alternative, due to sunk cost problematic. How strongly one is affected by such a sunk cost effect will amongst others depend on the individual character and attitudes. In their explanation category psychological commitment, Samuelson and Zeckhauser identify regret avoidance as another important factor to strengthen the status quo bias. Bell describes that irrational decision making can be caused by a desire by decision makers to avoid consequences in which the individuals will appear, after the fact, to have made the wrong decision (Bell, 1982). This is even the case if in advance, the choice seemed to be optimal on basis of the information available at that time. Biased decision-making is the result. This is consistent with the idea that individuals are stronger regretting bad outcomes that occur due to new actions than they regret similar bad outcomes occurring due to not changing the current situation. A tendency to prefer status quo norms and regular, habitual behavior compared to innovative acting is arising. Especially, behavior in the way of conventional social norms is supported by this. People often follow the conventional norms, just because it is the way of least resistance, not because it is the optimal decision in the specific situation. These aspects again lead to the result that the status quo alternative is chosen more often than it would be rationally correct.

According to Samuelson and Zeckhauser, another element creating psychological commitment is the preference to avoid cognitive dissonance. The main idea is that people find it complicated to accept two conflicting opinions simultaneously. They state that the decision maker's tendency to avoid such dissonance contributes to status quo bias in the way that they prefer to determine one certain belief as true and want to achieve consistency in their decisions. Frequently, people see themselves as reliable, competent decision makers and because of this, rationalize past decisions. As a result, it will rarer be the case that contradictions to an earlier stated position will be accepted. Status quo then is in a stronger position (Samuelson & Zeckhauser, 1988). We suggest that the strength of a status quo bias seems to be in dependency of individual characteristics. An insecure and under-confident person will more often question own decisions and positions than a very self-confident person.

Self-perception theory provides a closely connected justification for status quo bias. The idea is that individuals evaluate their own behavior similar to the way other people would rate it, to draw conclusions about their own preferences and values. If one does that, one automatically uses the past decisions reference for future decisions and will less likely come to a new choice. The decider is of the opinion that if the past decision was consistent for him, his preferences and attitudes will still be in accordance with that choice. There is experimental evidence that even in the case of imposed decisions, one will have the tendency to legitimate the status quo resulting from the imposed choice and use it as a reference. When drawing inferences in the way described, it gets difficult for the individual to differentiate between past decisions that were randomly made, were imposed or were determined by an own appropriate decision process.

The last type of psychological commitment that is described by Samuelson and Zeckhauser is the willingness to feel in control. When deciding, the individual wants to be in control of the situation. It is stated that staying with the status quo increases the feeling of the decider to actually be in control. The hypothesis that the feeling of having control has a substantial influence on decisions and evaluations is supported by the results of an experiment: Two groups of people get football cards for participating in a lottery. Group one chooses the card on their own, people in group two get a randomly assigned card. Afterwards, from each group one card will be randomly drawn and the owner gets $50. Before drawing, every participant had to state the price which he or she would accept to sell the card. The actuary fair price was $1.85. Group one stated an average price of $8.67, more than four times higher than the average $1.96 of group two. Because group one had control over the choice of their card, they are irrationally overestimating the choice of winning the money.

DILBERT © 2005 Scott Adams, Inc. Used By permission of ANDREWS MCMEEL SYNDICATION. All rights reserved

Explanation 3: Cognitive Misperceptions

All these psychologically based deviations from rational decision making can be seen as explanations for the occurrence of status quo bias. As a third category, Samuelson and Zeckhauser present status quo bias as consequence of cognitive misperceptions. Most important in this context are the phenomenon of loss aversion, the endowment effect and the anchoring effect. Those three effects strongly support the hypothesis of a significant status quo bias. The anchoring effect in decision making describes the idea, that in subsequent decisions, an initial choice is used as a reference, one could also say as a starting point. This initial decision most likely will not be discarded in follow-up decisions but adjusted in smaller range. A relationship to status quo bias is obvious.

Applications of the Endowment Effect to the Status Quo Bias

As we have seen, whenever decisions involve a status quo alternative, individuals suffer from the bias of choosing that alternative irrationally often. This could be seen in the above described experiments and is, at least partially, explained by factors like the endowment effect or loss aversion effects in general. The severity of the status quo bias becomes obvious when considering the large amounts of decisions with a status quo alternative people are facing every day.

When facing periodical decisions, people choose their status quo in the first period, making it more likely to stick to that initial decision even if it is suboptimal. Samuelson and Zeckhauser not only proved the existence of that behavior in their laboratory experiments but also in some field studies. For that, the authors examined a panel of health maintenance plan enrollments. From the panel, it can be confirmed that new enrollments significantly differ from the plans that are chosen from old enrollees. This result is most likely going to apply to other insurance markets, e.g. house and car insurance or life insurance. Other periodic contracts like for gas, water and electricity, or cell phone contracts, tend to reinforce this status quo bias. The effect is mostly an outcome resulting from the effort it would take search for alternatives to existing contracts—thus, individuals stick with the status quo and even accept possibly higher costs.

In modern economies, however, finding relevant information and alternatives has become easier and less costly in recent years. Today, search engines like Google and apps gather and filter information instantly. With the help of search engines, we are able to efficiently acquire new information about alternatives to the status quo. Depending on the market, contract comparisons can be undertaken in milliseconds. Usually, these websites also help when it comes to switching contracts and thereby reduce transactions costs quite significantly.

Due to the status quo bias, it is highly efficient to take a deposit from customers when picking up the customers' orders. This will dramatically increase the chance of realizing the actual purchases. Buying the product becomes the status quo, thus the above described finding will apply on the chance of an actual purchase. Samuelson and Zeckhauser furthermore state the status quo bias will be enhanced if service contracts are designed such that upgrades require a one-time fee and leave the option to downgrade again for free. Subscription-based products, which can be seen within the streaming industry, do exploit the status quo bias. These services usually offer a free trial for one to three periods and require a payment method, which will be automatically triggered once the trial is over. In this way, the chance of acquiring a new customer increases since the subscription has become the status quo. Similar results are achieved on platform-based networks. Most social media and other online platforms require an account and some personal information to be usable. Once one creates an account and uses the service, it becomes the status quo such that switching to another account seems to be much harder than simply creating a new account on another platform.

In another experimental study, Kahneman, Knetsch and Thaler show that there is a strong tendency that changes are perceived as fair if the status quo is not harmed. For that, the authors asked the subjects to state whether a decrease in wages and salaries of 7% is fair, once induced due to inflation jointly with a smaller wage and salary increase, resulting in an overall decrease. This option is marked as being fair. On the other hand, if wages and salaries are simply decreased by 7% while there is no inflation, the subjects generally perceived the situation as unfair. Other questions showed similar results. The irrationality could well be explained by the status quo bias, i.e., that a certain level of wages and salaries is perceived as the status quo and loss of that status quo is generally harmful.

Samuelson and Zeckhauser additionally state that management generally suffers under the status quo bias. This leads to a continuation of non-profitable projects, divisions or products. In the extreme case, it can lead to making wrong decisions when it comes to deciding in which industry to operate in. This could also be one of the main reasons why the consulting business experiences great success. Having completely unaffected and neutral minds work on a problem, such that the status quo bias cannot occur, can lead to a higher creation of value at the end of the day. Furthermore, getting feedback while making irrational decisions increases the chance of avoiding the bias in the future.

Brand value may be driven by the status quo bias as well. Building up a strong brand loyalty among customers creates economic advantages against competition and usually leads to increased profits. Since people do make periodic decisions that are influenced by the status quo bias, building up a strong brand also depends on being among the first to offer the service or product in a market. When a brand is well established in a market, it experiences a good chance to enhance its product portfolio using the status quo bias. For that, one may consider Adidas, offering sport shoes at first in order to build up a strong brand. Afterwards, Adidas could easily release other products like shirts or trousers that will be bought partially because people already own other sportwear coming from Adidas. Other sportwear manufacturers following the same trial, e.g. Nike originally starting with selling running shoes. Being the default option is valuable in technologically related products and services. Android is being used as a smartphone operating system by almost any smartphone manufacturer except Apple. Google is offering the operating system at no charge in order to have its services preinstalled and be the default option in many different applications. Thus, triggering the status quo bias and lowering the likelihood that other search engines (or alternatives to further Google services) will be used.

Accepting changes in the status quo has further applications in fields which bring change at high pace. These changes are usually slowly accepted since it is difficult to overcome the status quo bias, even when knowing the better alternatives. Samuelson and Zeckhauser state that even the development in science might lack of pace due to the status quo bias (remember the slow rate at which Einstein's General Theory of Relativity has been accepted). Thus, if status quo bias is present, scientific advancements will need to overcome the status quo first before a result can have a real influence in its scientific area. This behavior can also be seen when technological advancements occur. It is, in general, not easy for us to get used to changes in functionality or design. However, when the new product or services become the status quo, it is difficult to think of ever going back to the previous status quo!

Investments in the stock market are another application area of the status quo bias. Usually investors are staying with their portfolio allocation for longer periods of time rather than changing the investment decisions frequently. A rational reason for this can be transaction costs and fees which incur when trading on stock markets. Besides, other transition costs, for example research effort to find other, more profitable investment alternatives, can lead to an aversion against changing the status quo. In the context of real-life investments, people tend to hold a portfolio, which shows a paper loss, for irrationally long periods of time. Two possible explanations are the sunk cost effect and regret avoidance. Selling an unprofitable portfolio and realizing the losses hereby is psychologically difficult to do (Shefrin & Meir, 1984). Even if one knows the chances are bad that losses will be regained in the future, one behaves risk-seeking in losses and hopes for an improvement of the situation, to avoid a confession to peers concerning the wrong investment decision and the loss of the money. In contrast, in case that a portfolio shows a paper gain, an investor is typically behaving risk-averse and is selling irrationally early, because he wants to secure the current status quo gains he made. Furthermore, there is empirical evidence for an increasing relative status quo bias in investment decisions if the number of alternative investment opportunities increases. In an interesting study, Kempf and Ruenzi (2006) conclude that a rising number of funds available for investors strengthens their submission to the status quo bias.

Escalation of Commitment

While inertia is a common problem, we can even do worse by increasing resources committed to a losing course of action. *Escalation of commitment* refers to an individual's or group's decision to continue a course of action that has previously been associated with negative outcomes or results. This is done despite the fact that the future might not bring the desired benefits; instead, irrationally continuing with the established course of action seems worthwhile in order to align with and justify previous decisions and actions. The economic term associated with escalation of commitment in leadership is the so called *sunk-cost fallacy*: Sunk cost is any cost that has already incurred and cannot be recovered, and thus it should not matter for future decisions—but psychologically it does! Individuals tend to take past investments and efforts into account when making decisions.

The higher the losses already incurred, the more you need to convince yourself that what has been spend already has not been in vain, which justifies future escalation of commitment. This is, unfortunately, also true when it comes to political decision of high importance such as whether to end a war or not—following the idea that "the troops who died at the beginning of the war must not have died in vain" (Sibony, 2019).

Key Takeaways for Risk Leadership

All experiments described above emphasize the importance of status quo bias in decision making. It seems that the more emotional a decision is or the higher the number of different choices there are, the more we prefer the status quo. Status quo bias influences decisions of private individuals, as presented in the health maintenance plan field study, as well as numerous strategical decisions in companies made by managers. Sometimes even the whole business model of a corporation will only be successful if a free trial period creates a status quo the costumer is willing to pay for in future periods. Spotify or Amazon Prime are examples for this kind of business model.

It is important to be aware of psychological biases, in particular the status quo bias and the endowment effect, when deciding. Doing nothing is also making a decision! The more extensive the consequences of a decision, the more thoroughly we should examine whether we are influenced by this cognitive bias. An optimal choice is more likely to be done when explicitly considering a possible status quo bias in the decision process. Especially for major management decisions with huge implications for the future development of a company, but also for important decisions of private households like selling real estate or reallocating one's investment portfolio, it is highly recommended to question whether an alternative is rationally reasonable from a neutral standpoint.

Involving an independent expert may be helpful. In corporations, consulting companies can give an independent opinion on important questions. This is one of the reasons why advisory services are highly demanded in the economy. Management has the opportunity to learn from an advisory board and avoid suffering from the status quo bias. In case of investment decisions, we should try to focus on the intrinsic value of stocks and on their expected future value development to hopefully overcome the status quo bias and the endowment effect. As a consequence, the trick is to periodically revisit our processes and ask whether we are serving their purpose in the best way. If somebody points out they have always done it like this, that does not mean they should keep doing it.

References

Bell, D. E. (1982). Regret in decision making under uncertainty. *Operations Research, 5*, 961–981.

Kahneman, D., & Tversky, A. (1979). Prospect theory: An analysis of decision under risk. *Econometrica, 47*(2), 263–292.

Kahneman, D., Knetsch, J. L., & Thaler, R. (1991). Anomalies: The endowment effect, loss aversion, and status quo bias. *Journal of Economic Perspectives, 5*, 193–206.

Kempf, A., & Ruenzi, S. (2006). Status Quo Bias and the number of alternatives: An empirical illustration from the mutual fund industry. *Journal of Behavioral Finance, 7*, 204–213.

Knetsch, J. L. (1992). Preferences and non-reversibility of indifference curves. *Journal of Economic Behavior and Organization, 17*, 131–139.

Knetsch, J. L., & Sinden, J. A. (1987). The persistence of evaluation disparities. *Quarterly Journal of Economics, 102*, 691–696.

Samuelson, W., & Zeckhauser, R. (1988). Status Quo bias in decision making. *Journal of Risk and Uncertainty, 1988*, 7–59.

Schmalensee, R. (1982). Product differentiation advantages of pioneering brands. *American Economic Review, 72*, 349–365.

Shefrin, H., & Meir, S. (1984). The disposition to sell winners too early and ride losers too long: Theory and evidence. *Journal of Finance, 40*, 777–790.

Sibony, O. (2019). *You're about to make a terrible mistake! How biases distort decision-making – and what you can do to fight them*. Little Brown Spark.

Thaler, R. (1980). Toward a positive theory of consumer choice. *Journal of Economic Behavior and Organization, 1*, 39–60.

8 Overconfidence and Self-Blindness: Why We Think We Are Better Than We Actually Are

The most important single key takeaway from this chapter is

> **The 7th Commandment of Risk Leadership:** Data analysis provides much better forecasts than human intuition—but if you have no data and need to rely on your intuition, your motto should be: Less confidence will generally lead to better results—it pays to be a pessimist!

While overconfident people are seen as being more skilled, these traits do not always result in positive outcomes for the firm. In addition, being overconfident and eager to compete may not be compatible with environments requiring cooperation and team working. The last years have seen an increasing number of studies experimenting with gender differences regarding overconfidence and the imposter syndrome.

Managerial Overconfidence

Decision-makers and especially those in higher positions are exposed to various situations in which they have to rely on their knowledge, their capabilities and the task of correctly evaluating their performances and their judgments. This can become particularly crucial, when risk-related decisions with potential high impacts or negative effects are involved. In these situations, even highly experienced managers or other decision-makers are not safe from cognitive biases and errors in their beliefs. Indeed, we know that sometimes the opposite is the case, i.e. experts and people with self-claimed expertise are prone to show even higher degrees of some psychological biases. One of the most consistent, prevalent and potentially catastrophic of these biases is the tendency to be overconfident about one's own abilities and judgments.

A. Hofmann, *The Ten Commandments of Risk Leadership*, Future of Business and Finance, https://doi.org/10.1007/978-3-030-88797-1_8

When you hear about company failures and management decisions that were made at an earlier time and turned out to be completely wrong, do you sometimes think that this mistake would have not occurred with your team or you as a leader? This chapter reflects on our tendency to significantly overestimate our abilities relative to others when it comes to a wide range of characteristics.

Chief executive officers of large corporations are often depicted on magazine covers featuring their stories and successes. This demonstrates how CEOs often cultivate their public personas as successful and self-confident leaders. While the field of social and experimental psychology has been devoted to behavioral biases such as overconfidence for a long time, corporate finance research has only recently started to catch up on these insights—somewhat sticking to the assumption of rationality in economics. It seems striking that well educated and highly trained professionals such as top managers could make systematically biased corporate investment decisions with a high impact on the firm's success and survival.

The *Overconfidence Effect* refers to the well-established psychological phenomenon of us being way too confident about our knowledge and ability relative to others—a phenomenon particularly pronounced for managers. Most of us systematically overestimate our knowledge and ability to predict future outcomes to a significant degree! Overconfidence can be defined as "greater confidence than reality justifies" (Moore & Schatz, 2017). The bias is well researched and described in the literature. In fact, "perhaps the most robust finding in the psychology of judgment is that people are overconfident." (De Bondt & Thaler, 1995) and in a recent article Moore is describing Overconfidence as "the mother of all psychological biases" (Moore, 2018). Although especially important for risk leaders, the effect is prevalent and pervasive through almost all parts of our society and population.[1]

The overconfidence effect refers not to the case whether single individual estimates are correct or not, but rather measures the (big) difference between what individuals think they know and what they really do know. The most fascinating finding in this research is that the overconfidence effect is especially pronounced for expert knowledge: Experts tend to suffer even more from overconfidence than laymen! So, if you ask me for a prediction of inflation and interest rates for the next 5 years, I will most likely be as wide off the mark as a barkeeper—however, my forecast as a professor will be communicated with just more certitude and credibility… so don't believe an expert if you can get cheaper advice somewhere else. It depends on what you are looking for. An interesting feature many of us experience is that when we read about a "failure" of a company or person, we tend to think that we would never have made that mistake and that in their shoes we would have behaved differently and ended up in a better position.

[1]Overconfidence is related to quite many negative effects in a wide field of subjects, including fraud (Rijsenbilt & Commandeur, 2013), excessive trading (Odean, 1999), investment errors (Malmendier & Tate, 2005), failed mergers and acquisitions (Malmendier & Tate, 2008), and excess entry (Camerer & Lovallo, 1999, and others).

Here are some funny general examples of the effect: In a representative survey, well more than half of the questioned drivers rated themselves as being 'above average' drivers in terms of their driving skills, which is of course incompatible with the concept of the average or expected value—and even more incompatible with the concept of median (meaning that 50% should think they are above while the other half should think they are below the middle driver (Svenson, 1981)). Most students think they are better than the lower half of their class. Wallstreet brokers think their investment decisions are better than those of others—so don't follow them except if you think they have superior information about a company. We know that about 90% of startups fail—maybe one of the reasons is that most founders of startup companies suffer from the overconfidence effect more strongly, thinking they can do better than their competitors when in fact they cannot.

Overconfidence can also show some potential advantages for the individual. Take for example increased ambition, creation of self-fulfilling prophecies, etc. This could lead to the assumption that overconfidence in itself is induced by motivational factors. In their study about desirability in self-evaluation, Alicke (1985) concludes that the term 'motivational' does not mean that reasons for this biased self-evaluation are due to affective but rather cognitive factors that induce this psychological bias, and motivation is rather the cause for maintaining this sometimes advantageous self-concept. Such a connection between a cognitive bias and motivational factors can be seen in a recent work about overconfidence and its effect on financial markets from Daniel and Hirshleifer (2015) where they describe the self-attribution bias, i.e. taking credit for the performances and abilities of positive outcomes and blaming others or bad luck at negative outcomes (Daniel et al., 1998).

Especially in earlier studies, overconfidence was mainly justified by biases in information collection and the interpretation of them (e.g. Koriat et al., 1980). In other studies, overconfidence has been explained more by unsystematic errors in the judgmental reasoning, biased information processing and also unbiased judgmental errors (Klayman et al., 1999; Soll & Klayman, 2004). Two of the factors in creating judgments are the weight and strength of underlying evidence. Researchers have found that overconfidence is stronger when the weight of evidence is low and the strength of it is high (Griffin & Tversky, 1992).

For a better understanding of this cognitive bias and in order to measure it correctly, it is crucial to distinguish overconfidence from confidence and also from optimism. While confidence is merely the trust or faith into something (e.g. the own capabilities or knowledge) or someone, overconfidence rather describes the excessive belief in someone or something. While the human decision-making processes are distorted by both inherent biases, optimism and overconfidence, optimism is described as the extent to which people hold generalized favorable expectancies for their future. Overconfidence has been studied in three distinct ways, which can be defined as *overestimation, overplacement* and *overprecision* (Moore & Healy, 2008). In the following, these three subcategories of the overconfidence bias will be defined, discussed and substantiated with examples from the literature.

Overestimation

This subcategory of overconfidence is referred to as a person's overestimation regarding their actual abilities to succeed as well as their level of control or chance of success. It has been widely studied by numerous researchers and for quite a while by now. Amongst others, the studies are structured in the way that participants have to answer questions regarding their general knowledge or have to take academic exams and subsequently give an estimation on their own performance. These studies find that in both cases, general questions and academic tests, people tend to overestimate their performance (Clayson, 2005; Harvey, 1997). While results clearly show a confidence bias towards overestimating own abilities and performance, we may be more underconfident when judgments are easy and overconfident when they are difficult.

Forecasts and the Planning Fallacy

One of the repeatedly studied cases of overestimation is the *Planning Fallacy*. This bias refers to the phenomenon that individuals often tend to overestimate the rate of work that they are able to achieve (Buehler et al., 1994). The phenomenon was originally introduced and termed by Tversky and Kahneman (1974), and extended in 2003 by the factors costs and benefits, in which benefits are overestimated whereas costs are underestimated (Lovallo & Kahneman, 2003). Indeed, planning fallacy is a very consistent specification of overestimation—in particular when large, ambitious and complicated projects are involved (Flyvbjerg & Sunstein, 2016). Planning fallacy varies in results, when adjusting for the factor of length/difficulty (or so-called hard-easy effect), i.e., for longer tasks that are perceived as harder, people tend to overestimate their future performance level or respectively underestimate the needed time, while they underestimate their performance or respectively overestimate the needed time for shorter and therefore easier perceived projects (Boltz et al., 1998).

While cognitive factors such as memory biases are mainly suspected to affect overconfident behavior (Buehler et al., 2002), even personality disorders such as narcissism have been linked to overconfidence (Ames & Kammrath, 2004; Rijsenbilt & Commandeur, 2013). In this respect, overconfidence can reflect itself as a positive feeling regarding the future—related to forecasts and planning tasks. Indeed, looking at practice, around 90% (!) of megaprojects have delays and/or multiple cost overruns before being completed. Here are some prominent examples of the *Planning Fallacy*:

- *Hamburg Concert Hall* Building a new concert hall for the northern German city of Hamburg, my home town by the way, was conceived in 2005 with an estimated cost of around EUR 186 million. This ambitious project was to turn a former warehouse into an arts venue with high expectations regarding acoustics and design. In 2016, the forecast was adjusted to have a turn-out cost around EUR 800 million—more than four times the original estimate and the difference to be paid for by German taxpayers! The contractor for the project, Hochtief, was criticized for having put in an unrealistically low bid and the architect for not sticking to schedule (Global Construction Review, 2016).

- *Berlin Airport:* Planned to open in June 2012, Berlin airport BER has missed seven opening dates since then. It is now scheduled to open in October 2021 (hopefully). After 30 years from conception to operation, it is one of the most glaring public scandals in Germany today. A few weeks before the first scheduled opening in 2012, BER was denied operating approval due to multiple technical failures and fire safety issues found by inspectors. Critics argue that an airport designed in the early 2000's may not be compatible with the technology demands and habits of today's and future travelers.[2]
- *Sydney Opera House:* Building a new opera house for Sydney was another planning fallacy. Construction begun in 1958 with a planned budget of 7 million Australian dollars. Sixteen years later, the budget had accumulated up to 102 million Australian dollars.[3]
- *Getty Center LA:* The Getty Center in Los Angeles was planned to open in 1988, and it did finally open in 1998 after consuming 1.3 billion US dollars—which was four times the initial budget.[4]

The mechanism behind why publicly financed projects often fail meeting their budgets and deadlines is simple: Companies who compete for a project by submitting their bids tend to overpromise by offering low cost and tight deadlines—which makes sense since once they have started their work they could still renegotiate at a later point in time. However, the planning fallacy is a common problem that is not limited to the business world. Students often underestimate the time they will need for a term paper or the time needed to prepare for an exam.

Illusion of Control

Another example of overestimation is a phenomenon called Illusion of Control. This is defined as the exaggerated expectancy of one's personal success probability, as compared to the objectively warranted probability (Langer, 1975). In further research, this phenomenon is often described as a consistent pattern of overconfident behavior. In fact, research on this topic finds that people tend to overestimate the level of control they have over future outcomes. A limitation of early studies of this phenomenon is the focus on cases where people had, in fact, no control at all, and newer studies indicate a less consistent pattern for the illusion of control (Charness & Gneezy, 2010).

---

[2] See https://www.dw.com/en/berlins-new-airport-finally-opens-a-story-of-failure-and-embarrassment/a-55446329

[3] See Sibony (2019), p. 65.

[4] See Sibony (2019), p. 65.

Further inconsistencies in overestimation are present in the field of individual differences. An example of individual differences is the level of expertise (and in some studies also the level of self-claimed expertise).

In an early study, Bradley (1981) found that self-proclaimed experts in certain domains show even higher overconfidence in their answers—they were unwilling to admit their ignorance especially in domains where they felt to be experts in. However, it can be stated that experts, in general, tend to be less overconfident than novices.

When expertise is set into relation with overconfidence under the premise of the hard-easy effect, it is found that experts are in general better calibrated than lay-people when predictability is reasonably high, and vice versa, they are even more overconfident than novices when predictability is low (Griffin & Tversky, 1992).

Overplacement

Another variation of overconfidence is overplacement. This is the phenomenon that people overestimate their own performance level compared to other people's performance. This cognitive bias is also known in wide fields of the literature (e.g. Larrick et al., 2007) as the *above-average-effect* or the "exaggerated belief that you are better than others".

In an early and often cited study, 93% of a sample of American drivers and 69% of a sample of Swedish drivers believed to be more skillful in driving than the median of the respective comparison group (Svenson, 1981). This statistical impossibility indicates that people tend to be overconfident regarding their general level of performance and capability as compared to other people—they are therefore subject to an individual judgment bias. In the following decades, many researchers from various domains have since replicated this type of experiment with similar results. One study on the self-assessment of a firm's professional engineers revealed that 37% placed themselves at the top 5% of performers within this firm (Zenger, 1992). Further studies have produced similar results (e.g. Alicke, 1985).

Overplacement is quite consistent when easy tasks are measured. This could also be seen as one reason for the overwhelming presence of overconfidence in a bulk of research when authors focus especially on tasks or skills that are received as comparably easy by participants. Studies have shown that, when comparing their own performance with the ones of the comparison group, people tend to focus particularly on their own skills and pay too little attention to those of their peer group. This bias results in an above-average-effect for domains where the person may find the task comparably easy due to existing high skill levels and a below-average-effect in domains where people do not locate their strengths as easily (Kruger, 1999). By combining the overestimation and the overplacement bias, we can conclude that easy tasks presumably produce underestimation and overplacement, whereas hard tasks induce overestimation and underplacement. Thus, the hard-easy effect seems to be linked to opposite effects on these two variations of overconfidence (Larrick et al., 2007).

Overprecision

The third category of overconfidence is overprecision, referring to the excessive confidence in the accuracy of one's own knowledge (Soll & Klayman, 2004). In fact, this phenomenon seems closely related to overestimation, as the individual overestimates the reliability of their knowledge. Interestingly, unlike the other two forms, there is no broad evidence of a reversal of the effect, i.e., underprecision (Moore & Healy, 2008). In order to measure and quantify overprecision, generally people and participants of studies are either asked to specify a certain confidence interval on numerical questions, which is supposed to include the correct value to a predefined level of certainty or are questioned on their certainty about having answered a binary question correctly. Overprecision occurs when subjectively estimated confidence exceeds accuracy or if intervals are narrower than one's knowledge justifies (e.g. Fischhoff et al., 1977 as well as Soll & Klayman, 2004).

One of the earlier studies where overprecision was quantified was conducted by Alpert and Raiffa (1982), in which the participants were asked to provide a 98% confidence interval, with the result that less than 50% of the answers given were correct. Similar results of overprecision were reproduced by various other researchers over the years (Klayman et al., 1999; Russo & Schoemaker, 1992 and Soll & Klayman, 2004). Overprecision is not influenced by the hard-easy effect. Further differentiation in the model structure, as for example giving a preliminary best guess or estimating the lower and upper bound separately, mostly provides for a reduction of overconfidence.

Many investigators on this topic came to ambiguous findings on the relation between expertise and overprecision. In one of the earlier studies covering this relation, Heath and Tversky (1991) find that people are particularly confident in domains of self-declared expertise, while holding their predictive ability constant, indicating a higher overprecision for experts in these domains. Only a year later, Russo and Schoemaker (1992) found that although they are better calibrated and therefore seem to be less overconfident, even experts are often unable to give precise estimations on their knowledge and show a lack of metaknowledge.

In addition to being exposed to cognitive biases that may induce overconfident behavior, we are often prone to a lack of recognizing our own judgmental errors which prevents us from overcoming them. Dunning et al. (2003) found that lesser skilled people are also lacking the metacognitive skills to recognize their mistakes.

In his prominent book "Thinking, Fast and Slow", Daniel Kahneman (2011) states that he has "made much more progress in recognizing the errors of others than my own". Ironically, this phenomenon is also discovered in research, where people rated themselves as less unlikely to be a victim of such cognitive biases resulting in the above-average-effect. Indeed, the excessive confidence in ourselves and our beliefs is resulting in ignorance of our own vulnerability to such cognitive biases. Furthermore, people seem to have problems with detecting overconfidence in specific situations even though they are aware of general overconfidence (Russo & Schoemaker, 1992).

Overconfidence and Gender

Research suggests that overconfidence levels are related to gender, with men being in general more confident than women. In particular, a large number of studies conclude that while both women and men are overconfident, men show signs suggesting that they're generally much more so than women. Dahlbom et al. (2011) conducted a survey where high school students were asked to perform a mathematics test and then guess their grades. The students' results were then compared to their actual grade. It was concluded that girls tended to be underconfident regarding their grades and boys overconfident. Another study found that despite girls' exam achievements being up to boys', girls tend to be underconfident regarding their abilities relative to their actual achievements. Pulford and Colman (1997) have tested overconfidence by asking questions divided into three categories: difficult, medium-difficult, and easy questions. He finds that men are more overconfident than women in all three levels of questions.

These differences in confidence are likely to translate into differences in outcomes, educational choices, and even labor market segregation. Studies suggest that gender differences regarding confidence may perpetuate segregated labor markets. Another outcome of such differences may also be seen at work via competition decisions and performance. Overconfidence observed in male populations is a key factor in explaining gender differences in willingness to compete, and this can be an explanation of the underrepresentation of women in top-level executive positions. Indeed, women make up more than half of the labor force in the United States and earn almost 60% of advanced degrees, yet they bring home less pay and fill fewer seats in the C-suite than men, particularly in male-dominated professions like finance and technology. Interestingly, researches find men to be more believing in their own capabilities in the financial markets, contrary to women. This bias represents a major disadvantage for women: individuals with high levels of overconfidence are perceived as more competent by their peers. Negative for the hiring companies, overconfidence of employees can be financially quite counterproductive.

Given that studies also suggest men to be more competitive than women, competition preferences of both genders may be an influential factor behind this gender gap and the lack of women in most of the highly competitive positions. If women shy away from competition, they will be less likely to succeed in competitions for better-paying jobs. But is this true? Numerous authors document that women respond less favorably to competition than men (e.g., Niederle & Vesterlund, 2007). The methodology employed by the authors is relatively similar. Experiments are based on groups of men and women. They are asked to complete various tasks under a competitive tournament compensation scheme and under a non-competitive compensation rate. These studies also point out that men are more eager to compete, and their performance tends to respond more positively to an increase in competition level. This means few women choose to enter and win competitions. It seems women are more willing to choose stable environments instead of competitive environments even if their capabilities are equal to their male counterparts. The authors also point out that, even if they don't have the needed capabilities, men choose tournaments more frequently, contrary to high-performing women.

While a general willingness to compete may well contribute to the differences observed in managerial positions taken by for men and women, a phenomenon referred to as *the confidence gap* may also play a major role.

The Confidence Gap

Linda Babcock, an economics professor at Carnegie Mellon University, evaluated the behavior of men and women when it comes to how eager they fought for career advancement and found in her studies that men tend to initiate salary negotiations four times as often as women. Furthermore, in the cases where women did negotiate, they demanded salaries up to 30% lower than men did. A possible reason for these striking differences in male and female responses to career advancement possibilities may be the so-called *Confidence Gap*. It can be consistently shown in many studies that men have a tendency for overconfidence while women have a tendency for underconfidence. These tendencies are, however, not consciously taken on but rather unconsciously manifesting themselves in different areas, e.g. salary negotiations or job applications.

Psychologists Dunning and Ehrlinger studied the relationship between female confidence and competence. They came up with what is known as the Dunning-Kruger Effect: The tendency for some people to substantially overestimate their abilities. What is really striking is that the less competent people are, the more they overestimate their abilities—a phenomenon that makes a strange kind of sense. Using a quiz where male and female students needed to rate their scientific skills, female students rated themselves less positively then male students (6.5 versus 7.6 on a scale from 1 to 10) but the science quiz revealed their competence levels were almost identical. This suggests underconfidence of female students. Going to he workplace and leaving a university context, a study by Hewlett-Packard—which was initiated to find out more about why women were missing in top management—found that within HP, women applied for a promotion only when they met 100% of the qualifications listed in the job posting while men already applied when they met 50–60%. HP concluded that underqualified and underprepared men don't think twice about leaning in, while overqualified and overprepared women tend to hold back. This effect is important and should be taken into account when making hiring decisions for upper management. The striking result of this and many similar studies is that men tend to overestimate their abilities and performance, and women tend to underestimate both—even when their performance levels do not differ in quality! This confidence gap is striking and holds women back to step up the career ladder into top management (Kay & Shipman, 2014).

Imposter Syndrome: Underconfidence in Women

It is well-known that women face a significant "gender pay gap" and do not get promoted nearly as fast as men do. So overconfidence may indeed be a contributing factor here, but is it really the only one? Clance and Imes (1978) first defined the *imposter syndrome* as a condition where high-achieving individuals either ascribe their accomplishments to luck and contingency rather than individual skill and merit, more generally defined as a lack of confidence in own ability—a phenomenon mainly found in women. It often stems from internal or external pressure to achieve. The human brain is conditioned to compare one thing against another. This is easily seen in people's personal and professional lives. Despite someone's competence, individuals might be inclined to believe that their skills, talents, or accomplishments do not accurately reflect their worth, thus, compromising their self-worth.

There are several types of imposter syndrome including perfectionist, natural genius, rugged individualist, expert, and superhero (Young, 2012). Perfectionists often set extremely high standards for themselves that they cannot fully reach. Natural geniuses are people who believe their self-worth is directly linked to how naturally they are able to pick up on skills. Those that are natural geniuses often feel like failures if they have to exert more effort to learn something. Rugged individualists believe that they should be able to complete a task independently. Individuals exhibiting this form of imposter syndrome believe that they are a failure if they ask for or receive help. Experts carry the notion that they must know everything before starting a task. For these individuals, their self-worth is tied to how much they know and how well they can comprehend a topic. Finally, there are superheroes. These individuals will work much harder than those around them in order to prove their superiority.

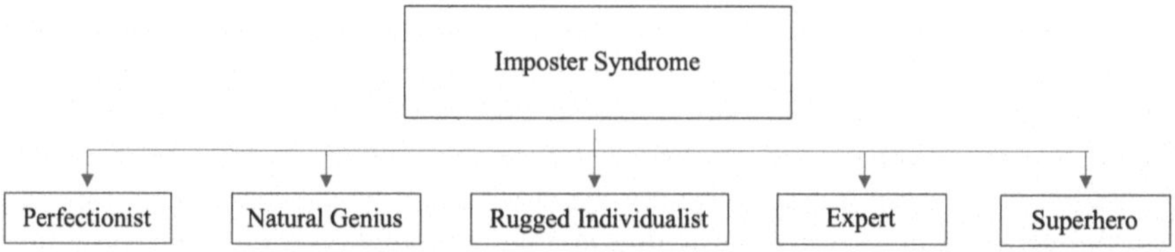

The twenty-first century, has made us believe that self-worth is contingent on achievements. The rise of social media allows us to be able to connect with people from around the world. In this day and age, everyone is trying to publish the most polished version of themselves online to "keep up with the Joneses". This leads to a rise in imposter syndrome because everyone is striving to exemplify the perfect life. Indeed, the percentage of people exhibiting forms of imposter syndrome nearly doubled during the rise of the Internet (Bravata et al., 2019). People feel validated by having the most "likes" or followers. It not only leads to our downfall due to a lapse in judgement, but also confirms fears about ourselves that we didn't know existed. This lapse in judgement can be attributed to our obsession to social media and not achieving things for ourselves, but rather to show the world that we can. The confirmation of unknown fears causes us to spiral downwards as we begin to further pick our flaws apart.

Feelings of imposter syndrome can be seen throughout all walks and phases of life. People often believe that they know everything but soon realize that they may not be the most knowledgeable about a specific subject matter. This phenomenon is known as the *Dunning-Kruger effect*. The Dunning-Kruger effect is a cognitive bias in which people believe they are smarter and more capable than they actually are (Cherry, 2019). This overconfidence yet lack of knowledge leads one to the Peak of "Mount Stupid", and from there confidence decreases as one gains more knowledge. This is because someone may realize that they actually don't know much about the topic at hand, leading to the "Valley of Despair". Symptoms of imposter syndrome start immediately after this low point with the feelings continue throughout the learning process. During this period, someone's confidence will always be below the peak because there will always be lingering thoughts of not being good enough. These ongoing highs and lows tend to frighten people as they experience a whirlwind of emotions. What starts off as excitement quickly turns to fear and desperation before one settles on satisfaction with the wealth of knowledge acquired. Thus, individuals with imposter syndrome may feel like they are never fully well versed in a subject, despite understanding more than the average person.

Men Promote Men: Narcissism or Old Boys'Club?

Harvard and UCLA economists Cullen and Perez-Truglia (2019), using data from 2015 to 2018 on 10,101 manager transitions, report in a recent study that "male bonding" may be a major contributor to this inequality. For a large multinational financial institution, they find the cumulative effect of the male-to-male employee relationship advantage in promotions to account for as much as 39% of the gender pay gap within this institution; however, female employees tend to have the same career progression regardless of the gender of their managers. Interestingly, the higher promotion rate of male employees assigned to male managers occurred despite absolutely no observable improvement in company revenues and despite any more time worked during the week; the only thing that mattered for the promotions was the fact that the two males worked closely together. The authors argue that male solidarity and schmoozing play a large part in the found career advantage, which takes time to develop and is therefore not seen in the short term.

What is even more striking is that the higher we go in a company's hierarchy, the fewer women are seen to be advanced into these positions. This is why women earn less than men on average (81 cents on the dollar). Is this really true? Maybe we are missing a part in the puzzle here. Maybe this is not all that is going on and maybe the story is more complex than simply male bonding.

Company executives tend to be disproportionately narcissistic, and narcissistic personality disorder is more pronounced in men. Narcissists are personalities with an inflated sense of self-importance, an inflated desire for power, and a propensity for manipulative behavior to others. Taking the differences in psychological traits into account, this type of personality can be found more often in men than in women, which may also contribute to the gender pay gap.

In a recent study, Rovelli and Curnis (2020) evaluate 172 Italian CEOs. They obtained each CEO's professional history and educational background, and all previous positions leading up to their appointment as CEO. They then conducted several statistical analyses to determine the likelihood of a person being appointed CEO at a given point during their career. Findings revealed that narcissism was very strongly and positively linked to the likelihood of being made CEO at a given point—regardless of the type of company. In fact, an increase in narcissism of one standard deviation was linked to a 29% higher likelihood of becoming CEO. This is a striking result given the well-known facts that higher levels of narcissism tend to be associated with negative outcomes for companies—such as financial crimes as well as less collaborative firm cultures—making narcissistic CEO appointments a risky business itself.

Managerial Overconfidence, Corporate Risk Management, and Selective Self-Attribution

Managerial overconfidence has been found to have an important impact on various corporate financial decisions. Isn't it fascinating that a driver of overconfidence seems to be past achievements, and this holds even if those achievements can be attributed to pure luck? Taking into account this so-called *Self-Attribution* bias, where people interpret their past successes as confirmation of their abilities and skills while ascribing failures to just bad luck, a person's positive performance track record may well be a major component of his or her current big ego and high level of overconfidence (Shefrin, 1999).

A recent study by Adam et al. (2015) looks at how managerial overconfidence affects corporate risk management. The authors evaluate financial risk management decisions, in particular the use of derivatives. Interestingly, managers increase their speculative activities following a speculative gain, but they do not reduce these same speculative activities following a speculative loss. This is fascinating since it represents an irrational and asymmetric response to past experience—a phenomenon referred to as *selective self-attribution*: The risk management success is attributed to one's own competence and skills, but the risk management failure is attributed to "bad luck". In this way, managers overvalue their skills by imposing a positive self-image on themselves in the cases of positive outcomes, while not imposing a negative self-image on themselves in the cases of negative outcomes. As a result, overconfidence is enhanced by selective self-attribution.

Key Takeaways for Risk Leadership

For the past 30 years, various studies have tried to explain the existing gender differences in the labor market and why men still dominate managerial positions. A potential explanation aims at female attitudes being different regarding competition and risk-taking behavior. Indeed, despite detaining the same ability, men tend to be more confident regarding their abilities. Plus, men and women differ in their willingness to compete. We have seen men are more likely to choose to be compensated for tournament schemes whereas women will mostly choose non-competitive schemes. Evidence also shows confidence plays an important role in the choice to enter into a competition. The consequences of high-ability women deciding to not enter competitions or not applying for more advanced positions are substantial. Although the willingness to enter into a competition is not innate but highly influenced by an individual's nurture (i.e. education and manner in which we are raised), an ongoing discussion among experts is on how it is possible to nurture individuals to become more competitive and more confident leaders.

However, is (over-)confidence always a desirable trait? It may help to hold a high-paying position due to the fact that overconfident people are seen as being more skilled, but these traits do not always result in positive outcomes for the firm. In addition, being overconfident and eager to compete may not be compatible with environments requiring cooperation and team working. The last years have seen an increasing number of studies experimenting with gender differences regarding overconfidence and the imposter syndrome.

But these insights may not be enough to explain the broad spectrum of what gender differences toward confidence, competitiveness and risk-related behavior generate in the economical fields (like career choices, etc.). More research is needed to understand an individual's own personality regarding these attributes in a better way. And then, we need to understand when these attributes can represent an advantage for a firm, increasing profitability or decreasing risk-taking, and when they do not.

References

Adam, T. R., Chitru, F., & Evgenia, G. (2015). Managerial overconfidence and corporate risk management. *Journal of Banking and Finance, 60*, 195–208.

Alicke, M. D. (1985). Global self-evaluation as determined by the desirability and controllability of trait adjectives. *Journal of Personality and Social Psychology, 49*(6), 1621.

Alpert, M., & Raiffa, H. (1982). A progress report on the training of probability assessors. In D. Kahneman, P. Slovic, & A. Tversky (Eds.), *Judgment under uncertainty: Heuristics and biases* (pp. 294–305). Cambridge University Press. ISBN 978-0-521-28414-1.

Ames, D. R., & Kammrath, L. K. (2004). Mind-reading and metacognition: Narcissism, not actual competence, predicts self-estimated ability. *Journal of Nonverbal Behavior, 28*(3), 187–209.

Boltz, M. G., Kupperman, C., & Dunne, J. (1998). The role of learning in remembered duration. *Memory and Cognition, 26*, 903–921.

Bradley, J. V. (1981). Overconfidence in ignorant experts. *Bulletin of the Psychonomic Society, 17*, 82–84.

Bravata, D. M., et al. (2019). Prevalence, predictors, and treatment of impostor syndrome: A systematic review. *Journal of General Internal Medicine., 35*(4), 1252–1275.

Buehler, R., Griffin, D., & Ross, M. (1994). Exploring the "planning fallacy": Why people underestimate their task completion times. *Journal of Personality and Social Psychology, 67*(3), 366–381.

Camerer, C., & Lovallo, D. (1999). Overconfidence and excess entry: An experimental approach. *American Economic Review, 89*(1), 306–318.

Charness, G., & Gneezy, U. (2010). Portfolio choice and risk attitudes: An experiment. *Economic Inquiry, 48*, 133–146.

Cherry, K. (2019). Dunning-Kruger effect: Why incompetent people think they are superior. Verywell Mind, 14 June 2019, www.verywellmind.com/an-overview-of-the-dunning-kruger-effect-4160740.

Clance, P. R., & Imes, S. A. (1978). The impostor phenomenon in high achieving women: Dynamics and therapeutic intervention. *Psychotherapy: Theory, Research and Practice, 15*, 241–247.

Clayson, D. E. (2005). Performance overconfidence: Metacognitive effects or misplaced student expectations? *Journal of Marketing Education, 27*(2), 122–129.

Cullen, Z. & Perez-Truglia, R. (2019). The Old Boys' Club: Schmoozing and the Gender Pay Gap, *NBER Working Paper*, No. w26530.

Dahlbom, L., Jakobsson, A., Jakobsson, N., & Kotsadam, A. (2011). Gender and overconfidence: Are girls really overconfident? *Applied Economics Letters, 18*(4), 325–327.

Daniel, K., & Hirshleifer, D. (2015). Overconfident investors, predictable returns, and excessive trading. *Journal of Economic Perspectives, 29*(4), 61–88. https://doi.org/10.1257/jep.29.4.61

Daniel, K., Hirshleifer, D., & Subrahmanyam, A. (1998). Investor psychology and security market under-and overreactions. *The Journal of Finance, 53*(6), 1839–1885.

De Bondt, W. F. M., & Thaler, R. H. (1995). Financial decision-making in markets and firms: A behavioral perspective, chapter 13. In *Handbooks in operations research and management science* (Vol. 9, pp. 385–410). Elsevier.

Dunning, D., Johnson, K., Ehrlinger, J., & Kruger, J. (2003). Why people fail to recognize their own incompetence. *Current Directions in Psychological Science, 12*(3), 83–87.

Fischhoff, B., Slovic, P., & Lichtenstein, S. (1977). Knowing with certainty: The appropriateness of extreme confidence. *Journal of Experimental Psychology: Human Perception and Performance, 3*(4), 552–564.

Flyvbjerg, B., & Sunstein, C. R. (2016). The principle of the malevolent hiding hand; or, the planning fallacy writ large. *Social Research: An International Quarterly, 83*(4), 979–1004.

Global Construction Review. (2016). The Elbe Concert Hall, Hamburg's beautiful disaster, is finally finished, available online: https://www.globalconstructionreview.com/news/elbe-concert-hall-hamb7urgs-beau7tiful-disa7ster/, Accessed Apr 22, 2021.

Griffin, D., & Tversky, A. (1992). The weighing of evidence and the determinants of confidence. *Cognitive Psychology, 24*(3), 411–435.

Harvey, N. (1997). Confidence in judgment. *Trends in Cognitive Sciences, 1*(2), 78–82.

Heath, C., & Tversky, A. (1991). Preference and belief: Ambiguity and competence in choice under uncertainty. *Journal of Risk and Uncertainty, 4*(1), 5–28.

Kahneman, D. (2011). *Thinking, fast and slow*. Macmillan.

Kay, K. & Shipman, C. (2014). *The Confidence Gap*, The Atlantic, May 2014 Issue. Available online: https://www.theatlantic.com/magazine/archive/2014/05/the-confidence-gap/359815/

Klayman, J., Soll, J. B., Gonzalez-Vallejo, C., & Barlas, S. (1999). Overconfidence: It depends on how, what, and whom you ask. *Organizational Behavior and Human Decision Processes, 79*(3), 216–247.

Koriat, A., Lichtenstein, S., & Fischhoff, B. (1980). Reasons for confidence. *Journal of Experimental Psychology: Human Learning and Memory, 6*(2), 107–118.

Kruger, J. (1999). Lake Wobegon be gone! The "below-average effect" and the egocentric nature of comparative ability judgments. *Journal of Personality and Social Psychology, 77*(2), 221–232.

Langer, E. J. (1975). The illusion of control. *Journal of Personality and Social Psychology, 32*(2), 311–328.

Larrick, R. P., Burson, K. A., & Soll, J. B. (2007). Social comparison and confidence: When thinking you're better than average predicts overconfidence (and when it does not). *Organizational Behavior and Human Decision Processes, 102*(1), 76–94.

Lovallo, D., & Kahneman, D. (2003). Delusions of success: How optimism undermines executives' decisions. *Harvard Business Review, 81*(7), 1–10.
Malmendier, U., & Tate, G. (2005). CEO overconfidence and corporate investment. *Journal of Finance, 60*(6), 2661–2700.
Malmendier, U., & Tate, G. (2008). Who makes acquisitions? CEO overconfidence and the market's reaction. *Journal of Financial Economics, 89*, 20–43.
Moore, D. A. (2018). Overconfidence. *Psychology Today*. Retrieved January 22, 2018. https://www.psychologytoday.com/us/blog/perfectly-confident/201801/overconfidence
Moore, D. A., & Healy, P. J. (2008). The trouble with overconfidence. *Psychological Review, 115*(2), 502–517.
Moore, D. A., & Schatz, D. (2017). The three faces of overconfidence. *Social Personal Psychology Compass, 11*, e12331.
Niederle, M., & Vesterlund, L. (2007). Do women shy away from competition? Do men compete too much. *Quarterly Journal of Economics., 122*(3), 1067–1101.
Odean, T. (1999). Do investors trade too much? *American Economic Review, 89*(5), 1279–1298.
Pulford, B. D., & Colman, A. M. (1997). Overconfidence: Feedback and item difficulty effects. *Personality and Individual Differences, 23*(1), 125–133.
Rijsenbilt, A., & Commandeur, H. (2013). Narcissus enters the courtroom: CEO narcissism and fraud. *Journal of Business Ethics, 117*, 413–429.
Rovelli, P., & Curnis, C. (2020). The perks of narcissism: Behaving like a star speeds up career advancement to the CEO position. *Leadership Quarterly*, 101489. https://doi.org/10.1016/J.leaqua.2020.101489
Russo, J. E., & Schoemaker, P. J. H. (1992). Managing overconfidence. *Sloan Management Review, 33*(2), 7–17.
Shefrin, H. (1999). *Beyond greed and fear: Understanding Behavioral Finance and the psychology of investing*. Harvard Business School Press.
Sibony, O. (2019). *You're about to make a terrible mistake! How biases distort decision-making – and what you can do to fight them, Little*. Brown Spark – Hachette Book Group.
Soll, J. B., & Klayman, J. (2004). Overconfidence in interval estimates. *Journal of Experimental Psychology: Learning, Memory, and Cognition, 30*(2), 299.
Svenson, O. (1981). Are we all less risky and more skillful than our fellow drivers? *Acta Psychologica, 47*(2), 143–148.
Young, V. (2012). *The secret thoughts of successful women why capable people suffer from the impostor syndrome and how to thrive in spite of it*. Three Rivers Press.
Zenger, T. R. (1992). Why do employers only reward extreme performance? Examining the relationships among performance, pay, and turnover. *Administrative Science Quarterly, 37*, 198–219.

The Low-Probability Puzzle: Why We Insure Our Cellphone But Not Our Home

9

The most important single key takeaway from this chapter is

> **The 9th Commandment of Risk Leadership:** Emotional events often override our rationality. Since low-probability-high-consequence events evoke strong emotional reactions, the actual risk of an event happening has little weight in the choices we make.

Our emotions often override our rationality and probabilities are not something humans are good with. When it comes to insurance decisions, our choices are not optimal: strikingly, comparing a low-probability-high-consequence risk (such a flood peril) with a high-probability-low-consequence risk (such as a bicycle theft), implies that we irrationally prefer insuring a high-probability-low-consequence risk over a low-probability-high-consequence risk. We also tend to purchase add-on coverage to our homeowner's insurance policy to cover the risk of bicycle theft rather than considering to cover the risk of loss due to flooding.

Emotions Override Probability For LRHC Events

When low-probability-but-high-consequence events evoke sharp and strong emotional reactions, the actual risk of an event happening tends to carry little weight in the choices we make. This emotional effect is especially pronounced when unlikely but very consequential events (often referred to as LRHC or Low-Risk-High-Consequence events) are involved, such as the small possibility of winning a lottery with a huge jackpot, or the possibility of cracking open a very lucrative new market. Faced with a rare event that involves strong feelings, managers are likely to either over- or under-invest their firm's resources. In particular, when it comes to extremely

A. Hofmann, *The Ten Commandments of Risk Leadership*, Future of Business and Finance, https://doi.org/10.1007/978-3-030-88797-1_9

small probabilities, managers tend to overestimate these probabilities and react irrationally.

People who are satisfied with their existing environment are also unlikely to disturb it in search of gains. This stance flows from the observation that losses tend to cause more emotional misery to people than gains of the same magnitude would cause emotional happiness. For managers, while such an attitude towards risk may infuse stability in their firm, it may also limit entrepreneurship with its associated potential for high economic profits.

The Catastrophe Insurance Market Puzzle

Given the fact that low and extremely low probabilities are often overestimated, why is it that people insure high-probability events more often than low-probability events? This interesting question is not easy to answer, although the phenomenon is rather striking. This chapter tries to summarize the most important drivers of this phenomenon and gives suggestions on how we can deal with it.

As we know from Chap. 3, the EU model predicts a rational individual to purchase insurance for a high-consequence risk, but empirical evidence shows that only a small proportion of the insured population demands insurance to protect them from natural disasters—and this is even the case when catastrophe insurance is highly subsidized. Similar effects can be observed in the long-term care insurance and agricultural insurance markets (Brown & Finkelstein, 2009; Gollier, 2005; Volkman-Wise, 2015). Another issue when thinking about rationality is that people sometimes overinsure certain risks, a phenomenon observed in the markets for homeowners and auto insurance. This behavior can only be explained when using the EU model by assuming unrealistically high degrees of individuals' risk aversion (Barseghyan et al., 2013; Sydnor, 2010).

The insurance industry creates significant value for our society. Insurers take the role of the risk transmitter from risk-averse individuals to more risk-tolerant investors and support the diversification of risks throughout our society. The industry thus "directly increases the welfare of risk-averse people, but it also induces risk-averse entrepreneurs to invest more in risky activities, thereby increasing growth and employment". The number of catastrophic events worldwide has been on a rise during the past decades. Climate change plays a big role as an accelerator when it comes to natural catastrophes, quadrupling the amount of natural disasters in comparison to the 1970's. Also, the number of man-made disasters per year soared on average and the current Covid-19 pandemic shows how catastrophic events can paralyze almost all global economies. What seems surprising in this context is the lack of insurance coverage against those low probability, extreme loss events. An example from the early 2000's is Hurricane Katrina which hit New Orleans in 2005, causing extensive damage and leaving thousands of people homeless. Despite the fact that the area is known for being exposed to frequent floods, only 40% of the people who lived in the New Orleans parish were insured against flood events.

Recent data by Swiss Re Institute demonstrate that big parts of losses caused by catastrophic events still remain uninsured.

The lack of demand for catastrophe insurance leads to high inefficiencies when it comes to risk-bearing aspects. Entrepreneurs, for instance, bear larger risks within their investments than under optimal conditions. Consequences are possible reductions in investment, employment and growth. Individuals as well as companies have to bear large economic risks and therefore provide the necessary equity. Thus, the suboptimal allocation of catastrophe risks can lead to serious negative welfare effects for the whole economy (Gollier, 2005).

The consistent missing demand for catastrophe insurance and other low-probability-high-consequence risks is often referred to as the *catastrophe insurance puzzle*. People show reluctance to insure low-probability events, and this behavior is particularly pronounced for some disasters. Individuals rather prefer to insure against high-probability losses. According to Kunreuther and Slovic (1978), one driver for that behavior could be that people think of insurance as an investment. Indeed, it may seem that insuring against hazards which do not occur in most cases might be a bad investment most of the time. Kunreuther and Slovic (1978, p.66), state that

> there is evidence that people do not voluntarily insure themselves against natural disasters even when the rates are highly subsidized. The reasons for failure of insurance markets need to be understood, as they have important implications for policy.

Indeed, after each major disaster, the question of why homeowners do not adequately insure against catastrophic losses comes up in the media again.

Economic theory suggests that it is optimal to insure catastrophe risks to a higher degree than it can be found in practice, even under liquidity constraints. In fact, according to the standard economic model of risk exchange, all non-systematic risks are diversified away throughout the economy. But there is evidence.

that the demand for insurance against events like earthquakes, floods and other natural damages is low.

Transaction Costs

One important factor to consider when it comes to practical limits of insurability are the transition costs. While the transaction costs at financial markets do generally not exceed 2 or 3%, they are far larger for insurance products. The average expense ratio of the German P&C Insurance sector mounted up to roughly 21% in 2018. For the household and residential building insurance lines (including elementary insurance), the costs are even higher with 26.4% and 33.8% on average.15 In the US, costs for home- owners insurance (which covers in general both damages on household items as well as on buildings, depending on the contract) amount to 27% in 2018.

Transaction costs often are, from a theoretical point of view, considered in insurance market models, e.g. by Mossin (1968) when he proved that full insurance coverage is never optimal when a proportional premium loading is charged. Raviv (1979) also considered transaction costs when he found that the Pareto optimal insurance contract includes a deductible and a co-insurance of losses. Hence, transaction costs may be at least a cause of partial uninsurability. The breakdown of a large risk into parts can make the sum of all parts insurable if the risk is taken by risk carriers, while the risk as a whole would be uninsurable. Yet he added that administrative and brokerage costs set a practical limit to that. Thus, there is a certain limit at which the negative cost effect compensates the positive effect of further risk-atomization.

These insights suggest that especially a portfolio of many small risks is relatively cost-intensive. That is, yet again, contradictive to real life observations. High transaction costs are specifically true for catastrophe insurance. As a high number of policy owners are affected by catastrophic risks like natural disasters at the same time, insurance companies have to deal with big waves of claims. By the nature of disaster events, claim treatments are not distributed equally over time for catastrophe insurance, such that auditing cost per customer is larger than in other insurance lines.

If the number of claims exceeds the insurance companies auditing capacity, if may be forced to randomize audits. This gives incentive to policyholders to report inflated losses in order to enrich themselves by a higher indemnity payment. This behavior does then either force the insurers to raise their auditing costs in order to check more claims or it raises the indemnity payments. In any case, the collective has to pay more, and the insurance premiums have to be raised for the following years.

The high transaction costs might be a considerable reason for the consumers to not purchase insurance coverage. Indeed, catastrophe insurance policies tend to have a low net premium due to the low loss probability, such that the premium loading (containing transaction costs and risk loading) makes out a big part of the gross premium. This makes individuals more reluctant to purchase insurance as the premium seems inappropriately high. Browne and Hoyt (2000) examined empirically the main drivers for flood insurance demand in the United States and found that the insurance price variable, measured in USD per 1.000 USD of coverage, is highly significant and, as supposed, negatively correlated to insurance demand. Ganderton et al. (2000) came to similar findings. Their experiment on the subjects confronted with low probability, high loss situations showed that high costs for insurance products are a considerable factor which lowers the demand significantly. Considering that transaction costs are a main component of the insurance premium, we can deduct that high transaction costs play in fact a big role for insurance demand.

The earlier mentioned research from Kunreuther and Pauly (2006) showed that premiums for insurance coverage on disaster events are often perceived by consumers to be priced inappropriately high, such that it is not worth their time and attention. They also claim that the high search costs for information on those insurance products are limiting insurance demand.

Possible solutions to the high transaction costs are high deductibles, which would reduce the claim waves significantly and also contribute to make premiums more affordable. Another way is to make the indemnity payment contingent to an index (like cat bonds). In this case, a basis risk remains at the policyholder. Digitalization may also be a huge driver to reduce transaction costs. Examples are the (partial) automatized processing of indemnity payment claims or digital customer service solutions like chatbots or insurance administration apps. InsurTechs and Big Tech Players like Google and Amazon entering the insurance market could be an accelerator for these changes.

Inefficient Financial Markets

As it is in the nature of financial markets to distribute risks among investors who expect an according return as compensation, also catastrophe risks can be shared and traded there. There are two common ways to participate on risk-sharing activities through the financial markets. The first one is to simply buy the stock of a reinsurance company. This way, investors own a part of the company and, hence, also a part of the risks it bears. Another way of sharing insurance risks through financial markets is the emission or purchase of a CAT bond (catastrophe bond). A CAT bond is an insurance-linked security and was issued for the first time in 1992, gaining importance since. In 2019, CAT bonds with a volume of 11.1 bn USD have been emitted.Reinsurance companies or governments can transfer parts of the risk they signed for a specific event, like a natural catastrophe in a certain region, to other market participants using a CAT bond. Thus, the risk is securitized and shared with potential investors.

Like other bonds, CAT bonds pay coupon payments to the buyers and return the notional value upon maturity. However, if the disaster the bond is based on occurs, the investors lose their investment completely or partly. The investors of a CAT bond can achieve a certain diversification in their portfolio, as they show low correlations with other securities traded on capital markets.

Asymmetric Information

Rothschild and Stiglitz (1976) first argued that heterogeneity of the population and the missing information about it heavily influence the efficiency of insurance markets. In case of natural catastrophe insurance, there are clearly differences in the risk of agents. For instance, homeowners with houses in California are significantly more likely to suffer from losses caused by earthquakes than those living in New York City. However, the amount of the loss might be higher in New York, if the house itself is worth more than the same house in the countryside of California. Insurers could charge average prices for all agents with the same observable risk attributes which however causes an adverse selection problem. If the individual risks of a group of agents are not observable (or would be very costly to observe) and the insurer asks for the same price for the entire group, those agents with lower risks than average most likely will not buy the product. If they assess their risks correctly, they notice that the price is not appropriate and thus do not transfer the risk to the insurer (or buy a policy at another insurer which applies risk-based pricing). Thus, the average risk, and therefore the average price, of the group of agents rises, when the individuals with the lowest risks leave. This results in the same discussion for the agents with the lowest risks in this smaller group. Thus, the price rises until the remaining group demanding an insurance policy only includes those agents with highest risks and the maximum individual price of the original group is reached. This is typically called *adverse selection*. The insurers would therefor need all risk-relevant in- formation in order to provide individual prices and maintain a demand for its products.

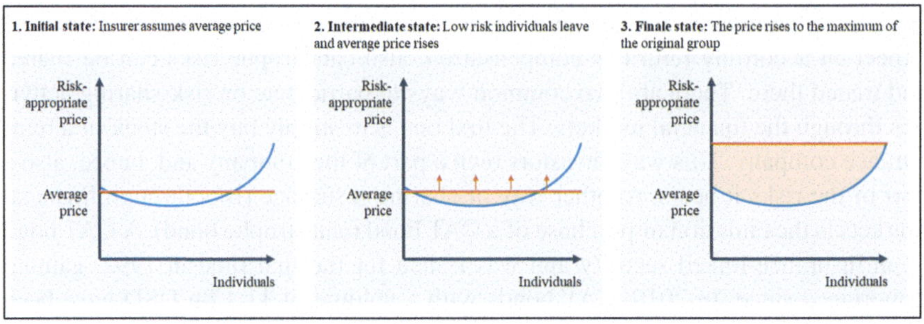

Is it fair from an ethical perspective that every citizen pays his or her individual risk-based price for an insurance product? What happens when the riskier group is on average poorer than the less riskier group? How could, for instance, individuals with cancer have health insurance when prices are based on the individual's risk? These questions raised severe ethical discussions when considering price discrimination for insurance products.

Gollier (2005) proposes two potential solutions when solving the adverse selection problem along with the arising ethical issues. The first approach is to make insurance for catastrophe compulsory (such as car liability insurance) and integrate non-discrimination regulations following the French system. In 1982, the French government integrated this system for natural catastrophe as well as insurance against damages caused by war, nuclear catastrophes as well as terror attacks. In effect, they charge an additional premium on every P&C insurance policy which insures natural catastrophes. The amount is determined by the government and reinsured by the public, state-owned reinsurer CCR (Caisse Centrale de Réassurance). The second approach proposes to use the tax system to reallocate wealth between low- and high-risk citizens. For instance, car or homeowners in Germany pay taxes which depend on the value of their car or property.

Limited Liability

Firms and individuals can generate environmental risks, which are not borne by themselves but by third parties. For instance, a manufacturer which produces its products close to a river and uses the river's water to cool machines could accidently pollute the river and thus harm others. In case of an accident in a nuclear power plant, the population of the region where the plant operates can suffer from significant damages for their possessions and bodies. When risk borne by others is realized, the originator of the risk has a limited liability. In the case of an incident, the originator of the risk usually needs to indemnify these third parties who are damaged. However, the originator can only afford as much as he owns, which means that his available financial resources limit his liability.

Firms and individuals with limited liability tend to take additional risks. When considering a lottery with a potential win of \$40 with a probability of 50% and a potential loss of \$50, risk-averse individuals would not agree to participate if having sufficient financial resources to bear the loss of 50, as the expected value of the lottery is negative. However, if they cannot afford the additional 50, individuals would participate as they can only profit from taking the risk. As illustrated in this example, firms and individuals take additional risk if they do not bear the losses. They profit from taking more risk, so they take a risk-prone attitude, even though they are intrinsically risk averse. Therefore, risk- aversion is only effective if firms are properly capitalized.

Limited liability affects the effectiveness of corporate environmental liability insurance markets. When having limited resources, firms would only limitedly suffer from losses. Thus, they do not profit from investing their limited resources in insurance policies, which are priced based on the full loss potential. Gollier (2005) presents in his paper two approaches to tackle this inefficiency 40. First, states could establish compulsory insurance for environmental risks to ensure that victims are properly indemnified in case of an incident. However, in practice, when establishing this construct, policies were mostly priced non-discriminative and non-incentive based, which resulted in low investment in risk prevention. Secondly, banks which are closely involved in managing the firm's activities could be liable for damages caused by the firm ("deep pocket"). In this case, the banks would invest heavily in monitoring the firms and raise loan interests for risky firms. The risk would thus be internalized, however the monitoring of the focal firm is very costly. For instance, CERCLA regulates the disposal of toxic waste in the US45.

Diversification in Time

Risks diversified through time via credit markets represent a second alternative for classical insurance. Individuals save money over time and take credits (or reduce their own reserves) in case of a catastrophe.

Several scholars discussed whether this strategy would be effective. Time diversification seems suitable if assuming infinite life and independent risks through time. However, when assuming finite life and borrowing and liquidity constraints (e.g., in case of 'early hit' of a catastrophe, see figure below), time diversification is not a proper alternative to classic insurance. Individuals would need to transfer risk to insurers in the short term. When having built financial reserves in the long run, agents are likely to keep their risks. To support the strategy of capital accumulation, governments could subsidize loans in order to prevent borrowing constraints.

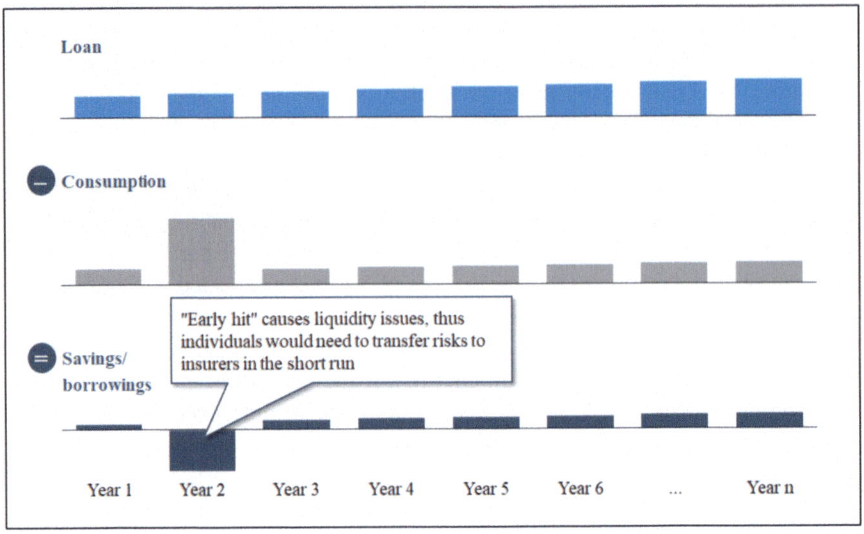

This idea can be transferred to insurers and their strategy for capital accumulation and reinsurance. A starting insurance company needs to reinsure a big part of its business, however can lower this amount when having accumulated capital. However, as managers in firms with high capital efficient than managers in those with low reserves, insurers might not accumulate capital and time diversify as theoretically assumed. The state can step in to time diversify and take the role of a reinsurer as it has sufficient credit worthiness and long time horizon.

Regret Aversion

Studies of insurance demand suggest that individuals seem to either ignore or at least undervalue low probability events. For rare but high-impact events, insurance is often not attractive. A possible explanation for this observation is that individuals may pay more attention to risks when the probability of occurrence of the event rises above some threshold.

Some studies argue that the missing demand for low-probability event insurance may indeed be due to some people ignoring risks with low probabilities. So, if this is how people evaluate risk in real world settings, maybe they do not 'ignore' small risks but consciously decide against insuring them due to other reasons - like regret aversion. As shown in several experiments and field surveys, individuals consistently buy insurance *only* when the probability of loss is above a certain threshold (e.g. Kunreuther and Slovic (1978)), even in cases where insurance is heavily subsidized.

It may be that one reason for the low demand is that consumers may not fully understand the probability of the disaster. People tend to buy catastrophe insurance more often right after a major disaster occurs, since they can then perceive the probability of the event more ('it does happen!'). This reason is based on the salience bias, which describes our tendency to focus on items or information that are more noteworthy while ignoring those that do not grab our attention. The second reason may involve the high deductible problem, according to which people feel the insurance may not cover much after a disaster occurs. A third reason may be a preference for policies with a rebate, so the person does not feel cheated in the event of a catastrophe not happening, or even probability neglect, which has been discussed before.

There are other potential reasons for why people do not participate in catastrophe insurance. A first reason is market failure including adverse selection, moral hazard, correlated risks and time consistency as potential factors. A second reason is government failure including the involvement of government relief in the case of a major catastrophe (*Samaritan's Dilemma*). However, when studying the literature, while potential contributing factors to the low demand for extreme-event insurance may be found in the high underwriting costs and limited supply as well as anticipation of government relief programs, the low take-up rates of federally subsidized flood insurance suggest that this is not a sufficient explanation. In addition, while some of these explanations might be true for the catastrophe insurance market, they do not explain the general behavior of individuals who do not want to purchase insurance for low-probability events but seem to prefer insurance for high-probability-low-impact events. A study by Browne et al. (2015) uses data from an insurer that provides coverage for both a low-probability-high-consequence risk (a flood peril) and a high-probability-low-consequence risk (a bicycle theft). They find evidence consistent with a preference for insurance for high-probability-low-consequence risks over low-probability-high-consequence risks: a significantly higher number of policyholders purchase add-on coverage to their homeowner's insurance to cover the risk of bicycle theft than to cover the risk of loss due to flooding.

While some explanations may be true for certain catastrophes, they do not explain the general behavior of many individuals not purchasing insurance for low-probability-high-consequence risks but rather for high-probability-low-consequence risks. In contrast to standard expected utility theory findings, using regret aversion can not only explain the missing demand for low- probability-high-consequence risk insurance but also the relatively high demand for insuring high- probability-low-consequence risks. The rationale of this paper is that in catastrophe insurance markets as well as other low-probability event insurance markets, due to the low probability of suffering a loss, the individual experiences high regret aversion; in other words, there is a high impact of regret aversion in the many times she does not get anything out of her insurance policy. By anticipating this relatively high ex post regret when making her insurance purchase decision, her demand for insurance is reduced for rare events. The contrary effect for insuring high-probability-low-consequence risks explains the growing market for low-value policies such as cell phone policies.

While the loss of a cellphone is usually an event of no or low consequence, the loss of a home to a family or a large property loss to a business owner can potentially be fatal. The global mobile phone insurance market has been growing substantially and its size was valued at approx. USD 18 billion in 2018. Mobile phone insurance helps individuals avoid high replacement costs in case of loss of their mobile phone or in case of a complete breakdown. A mobile phone insurance policy generally covers all physical damage, internal component failure, offers theft and loss protection, and also sometimes supports data protection.

Key Takeaways for Risk Leadership

Our emotions often override our rationality and probabilities are not something humans are good with. When it comes to insurance decisions, our choices are not optimal: strikingly, comparing a low-probability-high-consequence risk (such a flood peril) with a high-probability-low-consequence risk (such as a bicycle theft), implies that we irrationally prefer insuring a high-probability-low-consequence risk over a low-probability-high-consequence risk. We also tend to purchase add-on coverage to our homeowner's insurance policy to cover the risk of bicycle theft rather than considering to cover the risk of loss due to flooding.

References

Barseghyan, L. M., O'Donoghue, F., & Teitelbaum, T. J. (2013). The nature of risk preferences: Evidence from insurance choices. *American Economic Review, 103*(6), 2499–2529.

Brown, J. R., & Finkelstein, A. (2009). The private market for long-term care insurance in the United States: A review of the evidence. *Journal of Risk and Insurance, 76*, 5–29.

Browne, M. J., & Hoyt, R. E. (2000). The demand for flood insurance: Experimental evidence. *Journal of Risk and Uncertainty, 20*, 291–306.

Browne, M. J., Knoller, C., & Richter, A. (2015). Behavioral bias and the demand for bicycle and flood insurance. *Journal of Risk and Uncertainty, 50*(2), 141–160.

Ganderton, P. T., Brookshire, D., McKee, M., Stewart, S., & Thurston, H. (2000). Buying insurance for disaster-type risks: Experimental evidence. *Journal of Risk and Uncertainty, 20*, 271–289.

Gollier, C. (2005). Some Aspects of the Economics of Catastrophe Risk Insurance, CES Ifo Working Paper No. 1409.

Kunreuther, H., & Pauly, M. (2006). Rules rather than discretion: Lessons from hurricane katrina. *Journal of Risk and Uncertainty, 33*(1–2), 101–116.

Kunreuther, H., & Slovic, P. (1978). Economics, psychology, and protective behavior. *American Economic Review, 68*(2), 64–69.

Mossin, J. (1968). Aspects of rational insurance purchasing. *Journal of Political Economy, 76*(4 Part 1), 553–568.

Raviv, A. (1979). The design of an optimal insurance policy. *American Economic Review, 69*, 223–239.

Rothschild, M., & Stiglitz, J. (1976). Equilibrium in competitive insurance markets: An essay on the economics of imperfect information. *Quarterly Journal of Economics, 90*(4), 629–649.

Sydnor, J. (2010). (Over)insuring modest risks. *American Economic Journal: Applied Economics, 2*(4), 177–199.

Volkman-Wise, J. (2015). Representativeness and managing catastrophe risk. *Journal of Risk and Uncertainty, 51*(3), 267–290.

Fairness, Diversity, Groupthink, and Peer Effects: Why Other People Matter for Our Risky Decisions

10

The most important single key takeaway from this chapter is

> **The 8th Commandment of Risk Leadership:** Diverse teams with established rules of communication and cooperation make better decisions!

Understanding how our instinct for cooperation and our need for fairness as well as our potential weaknesses related to group dynamics influence our decisions is important. Indeed, other people matter when it comes to our risk-related and other daily decisions in business and life. Research suggests that teams need cooperative tasks, known rewards and defined goals in order to establish psychological safety and improve productivity. Conflict can be good! When we are interested in good decision-making processes, we should put together a diverse team with established rules of communication and cooperation.

Fairness and Cooperation: Lessons from Game Theory[1]

While leaders must take responsibility at the end of the day, they often interact with groups of people and need to consider decisions made by groups. Unfortunately, groups tend to make decisions that are not always best and optimal in the sense of minimizing risk and/or maximizing company profits or value. The huge mistakes are often made in a team effort. Since we are all human, we are all subject to mistakes and too often follow our inherent desires to being liked by others—which is a good thing from an evolutionary perspective but maybe not so from a business perspective. From a business perspective, it is important to be aware not only of your own biases, but also of the same defaults when it comes to risk-related behavior of

[1] See Appendix 4 for a brief introduction to game theory and its main concepts.

A. Hofmann, *The Ten Commandments of Risk Leadership*, Future of Business and Finance, https://doi.org/10.1007/978-3-030-88797-1_10

our colleagues and employees. The fear of getting fired can have an influence on the performance of your employees, concerning the upbringing of new ideas in teams, and certain conditions need to be met in order to improve team performance and persistence. This chapter is devoted to evaluating and discussing how groups make decisions, how these decisions can be flawed, and what can be done to improve group decision-making processes to minimize risk and increase firm value.

Is there anything about groups and their decision-making processes we can learn from games and game theory? How important is cooperation for humans? Are we always rational? (Well, you should know the answer to that question by now...) Economic games have become popular paradigms to evaluate social decision-making processes and optimize strategies. They provide researchers with robust behavioral patterns observed across a multitude of studies. Let me introduce you to a few famous findings from Game Theory.

Prisoner's Dilemma

Let's start with a classic among all games, the so-called *Prisoner's Dilemma*. This game can be used as a model for many real-world situations involving cooperative behavior in business practice. The characteristic feature of the game is that if the players behave in a rational way, the outcome will be unfavorable for both players. In other words, two completely rational individuals will not cooperate in such a situation, even though it appears to be in their best interests to do so! In its original version, the Prisoner's Dilemma describes the situation of two members of a criminal gang who are suspected of a crime; they are hold in solitary confinement with no means of communicating with the other. Since the police do not have sufficient evidence, they rely on a confession from one of the two guys. They can either confess to the crime or deny it. Their problem now is that their punishment depends not only on their own testimony, but also on the testimony of their colleague. While prosecutors lack sufficient evidence to convict both criminals on the principal charge, they do have enough to convict them on a lesser charge. They offer each prisoner a bargain. Possible strategies are either to betray the other by testifying that they committed the crime, or to implicitly cooperate with the other by remaining silent to the police. Referring to the criminals as A and B, respectively, they thus each have two strategies: either "stay silent" or "betray". The game can be depicted in a table as follows.

	stay silent (b_1)	betray (b_2)
stay silent (a_1)	(−5,−5)	(0,−15)
betray (a_2)	(−15,0)	(−10,−10)

We can describe the possible outcomes of the game as follows:

1. If A and B each betray the other, each of them serves 10 years in prison.

2. If A betrays B but B stays silent, A will be set free and B will serve 15 years in prison.
3. If A stays silent but B betrays A, A will serve 15 years in prison and B will be set free.
4. If both A and B stay silent, both of them will serve only 5 years in prison (the lesser charge).

The police are clever to put both criminals into this situation, since it seems that a solution to the game is as follows: Since betraying the other offers a lower sentence than cooperating, assuming purely rational self-interested criminals, the game will end in both betraying each other[2]—but this is not what their best interest would be. You see, cooperation can be tricky!

Dictator Game

The Dictator Game is a one-person decision problem but a two-player game. Player 1, called "the dictator", decides about how to "divide" a fixed amount of money—called "the pie"—between himself and one other player, player 2, called "the recipient". The task of the dictator is to decide on how to allocate $10, and the counterparty has no recourse but must accept the allocation chosen by the dictator. In game theory, we assume that both dictator and recipient are anonymous in the sense that neither knows the identity of the other.

Always assuming rationality, standard economic theory states that individuals prefer having more money to having less. Then, the dictator should offer the recipient the minimum possible amount and keep the rest for himself, right? There is no penalty for doing this in the game and leaving nothing for the recipient seems the winning strategy. Interestingly, laboratory studies of the game have not yielded this result—not even close. In fact, studies report a wide dispersion of dictator game giving amounts. While some dictators indeed do leave nothing or a very small amount to the recipient, many participants give more than zero—which is surprising given that rational dictators should give nothing. On average, is is found that dictators give around 28% of the pie (Engel, 2011). So, what is going on?

In game theory, a Nash Equilibrium is defined as a set of strategies for each player in a game such that there is *no benefit for any player to deviate from their equilibrium strategies*. In the equilibrium situation, all players are satisfied with their choices and so the game remains at equilibrium forever—therefore the name. The concept is named after the American Mathematician John Nash, winner of the 1994 Nobel Prize in Economic Sciences for his contributions to game theory.

In the game below, is [10,0] an equilibrium? Since we are talking about a dynamic setting here, where player 1 chooses first, and then player 2 does nothing except receiving the amount chose by player 1, the game is called a "dynamic

[2] The solution of this game is indeed "betray, betray" or (a_2,b_2), which constitutes both an equilibrium in dominant strategies and a Nash equilibrium. See Appendix 4.

game"—rather than a static game where both players would make a decision simultaneously. There is indeed no decision to be made by player 2 here. [10,0] is indeed an equilibrium, and this is because player 1 cannot do better than paying himself $10, and so he cannot possibly benefit by deviating from that strategy; player 2 has no power and just needs to accept player 1's give-away.

Now, what do you think will happen if we change the game and give player 2 some power?

Ultimatum Game

The Ultimatum Game, first introduced by Güth et al. (1982), involves two active players who are asked to distribute a fixed amount of money (e.g., a pie of $10) among themselves. Player 1, called now "the proposer", must decide how the pie should be divided, whilst player 2, called now "the receiver", then decides to either accept or reject player 1's offer. If the receiver accepts the proposer's offer, both players receive the amount agreed upon and the game ends; if, however, the receiver rejects the proposer's offer, both players get nothing. It is noteworthy that the Ultimatum Game—same as the Dictator Game - is a so-called one-shot game, meaning that it is only played once and so there is no repetition between the same players.

What is the (Nash) equilibrium of this game? We can find out using the concept of *backward induction*, or in other words, we can "solve the game from behind". Looking first at player 2 and his situation, it makes sense for him to accept all positive (non-zero) offers from player 1, because all such offers imply a positive amount of money for him—which is obviously better than receiving nothing at all. Now this should be anticipated by player 1, who assumes player 2 will accept all positive amounts of money $x < 10$. As a result, player 1 will offer player 2 an amount „as small as possible". In our example of a pie of $10, player 1 will thus offer player 2 exactly $1 in equilibrium—if there are 10 one-dollar bills and a one-dollar bill ist he smallest amount (otherwise, the offer should be 1cent).

The striking finding that researchers observed in the Ultimatum Game is that players do not behave according to such equilibrium predictions *at all*. In experimental ultimatum games, the average proposer offers about 40–50% of the pie to the responder with the result that these offers are most frequently accepted; in other words, most offers are to divide the pie evenly between the parties and this is generally accepted (Güth & Kocher, 2014). This is different from the dictator game where the counterparty has no choice other than accept the offer; here, the counterparty can reject and both parties end up with zero. In this way, the Ultimatum (but not the Dictator) Game includes the first party's potential for fear of retaliation in case of unfair offers. The findings of the ultimatum game are often attributed to a *fairness norm*. Studies show that individuals in the role of player 2 demonstrate a consistent willingness to forfeit gains by rejecting amounts offered by player 1 that they consider to be "unfair". It can be seen from multiple research studies that at least half of the receivers tend to reject offers below 30% of the pie. While the findings are consistent, there are some variations in gender (Eckel & Grossman, 2001), hypothetical versus real money (Fantino et al., 2007) and culture (Henrich et al., 2005).

So, we ask ourselves again, what is going on? The tendency to reject "low" offers has been attributed to individuals' preferences for *fairness* (Bolton, 1991), also named "a desire to punish socially unacceptable behavior" (Fehr & Schmidt, 1999). In the Dictator Game, individuals seem to be (at least partially) interested in a "fair" payout allocation. In the Ultimatum Game, a general "fear" of player 1 that smaller offers will possibly be rejected by player 2 may be attributed to a need for fairness in order to avoid "punishment" in the sense of player 2 rejecting the "unfair" offer. It is interesting to note that the players' age plays a role, given that children tend to play more "rationally" than adults. Possibly the behavior is learned by participating in different social environments and settings over time. This hypothesis is confirmed in a study by Benensona et al. (2007) who examine differences in developmental and socioeconomic status in young children's altruistic behavior in the Dictator Game. They find that while the majority of children displayed altruistic behavior even at the youngest age level, older children and children from higher socioeconomic status environments behaved more altruistically in general.

A question that comes to mind is: Is this tendency towards fairness and cooperation indeed an inherent human trait? How about animals? Do they strive for fairness and cooperation? If mankind has a sense for fairness, do animals have that same sense, as well? A recent contribution by Dutch-American primatologist Frans de Waal reveals interesting findings. Incorporating a few unimportant changes into the Ultimatum Game, like using bananas instead of money, he used color as the distribution key and offered two items that the monkeys could exchange for six bananas. One (blue) stood for the fair ratio 3:3, the other (red) for the ego-variation 5:1. Since the monkeys were previously trained to express their consent by exchanging objects, refusals were possible. The result of the study is that blue was almost always accepted, red was rejected in almost three quarters of all cases—similar to experiments with 2 to 7-year-old children. The fascinating conclusion is that "Chimpanzees not only behave in a similar way to humans in terms of fairness, they have exactly the same preferences as we do" (Proctor et al., 2013).

As a result, we all seem to have a preference for a "fair" and cooperative setting or simply a somewhat "homogenous" distribution in many instances, and we have inherent incentives to enable such fairness and cooperation. Unfortunately, the world is not a fair place and we often see a lot of unfairness and unevenly distributed things around us. Coming back to a corporate environment, the question comes to mind whether it would make sense to impose or foster such fairness and cooperation in business organizations, teams, committees, etc. to improve outcomes? Or should we just "let it go"? Our first step in this direction is to look at how people behave within groups in a setting where there can be different hierarchies within an organization involved but no strict official rules of team communication are established.

In the 1950s, psychologist Solomon E. Asch asked groups of people to perform an easy task: compare the length of lines on a paper, by answering out loud and in order one-by-one. There was an obvious right answer to the question and only the "last person" was the one Solomon was interested in—since this person was not let in on the experiment. While all group members one-by-one agreed on the obviously wrong answer, the last person had the choice to conform with the group or let them know they were wrong. The striking finding of this experiment was that 75% of these last persons at least once followed the group opinion. What was going on?

The Impact of Groupthink

On Saturday April 26, 1986, the worst nuclear disaster in human history occurred at a nuclear power plant in Chernobyl, Soviet Union. 120,000 people needed to be evacuated and for over a week, winds carrying toxic dust across Central and Southern Europe were reported. The estimated death toll was up to 10,000 lives lost, not counting the additional 5 million who still live on heavily contaminated lands and with radioactivity-induced illness. The team of engineers working in Chernobyl that day was extraordinary skilled, highly experienced, well respected in their field, and in every aspect an extremely competent overall team. And yet the team unintentionally brought on a disaster following their decision-making process. Indeed, despite everybody's good intentions, the accident was a result of how well they (mal-) functioned together as a team. How can the best possible team fail so dramatically?

Another disaster happened in the same year, during the morning of January 28, 1986. The Kennedy Space Center in Florida launched its space shuttle Challenger, when 73 s after launch, millions of people witnessed on TV how the rocket disintegrated in a huge explosion killing all 7 crew members, before the remains of the capsule plunged into the Atlantic Ocean. President Reagan immediately appointed a highly skilled presidential commission to evaluate the probable causes of the disaster. After several months of work, the commission identified the primary cause of the disaster to be a failure in the seal between the two stages of the rocket that allowed hot gases to escape during launch. The secondary cause identified was a flawed decision-making process including communication issues.

Just a day before the launch, the team of engineers responsible for the rocket booster performance had warned about potential risks during a teleconference. They were worried about the impact of the weather given that the forecast team announced a temperature below-freezing point the next morning. They pointed out that the seals—which had been classified as a critical component on the rocket booster before—had never been tested below 53° Fahrenheit.[3] The NASA people responded by asking them to reconsider their warning and following recommendation, since a delay was not what they wished for at this time. The directors of the Kennedy Space Center later certified that the Challenger was ready to go, and it was never mentioned at any point that the engineers had pointed out a potential problem with the seals due to cold weather conditions during launch. The person at the top of the command chain, who was responsible for reviewing

[3] The freezing point of water is 32 degrees Fahrenheit.

the flight readiness of the Challenger, had no reason to believe that there was a potential risk not considered and finally evaluated out at this point. And so, he gave it a "go"!

Yale social psychologist Irving Janis was fascinated with the question of how an acknowledged team of experts could make such terrible decisions by not taking into account important risk factors when making a final decision. He believed that the major errors were made not because of a single person being just incompetent, chief executives or corporate boardrooms being not well put together, or just a matter of some technical nature. Janis did not think of chief executives as incompetent but rather as victims of a phenomenon he called *Groupthink* (see Janis, 1991). He originally defined the phenomenon as

> a mode of thinking that people engage in when they are deeply involved in a cohesive in-group, when the members' strivings for unanimity override their motivation to realistically appraise alternative courses of action.

When Does the Phenomenon Occur?

The Groupthink phenomenon occurs when certain *antecedent conditions*, *symptoms of Groupthink*, and *symptoms of defective decision-making* are present. According to Janis, the most important antecedent condition is met when the decision makers collectively form a "cohesive group". In addition, defects in the organizational structure are considered, such as for example, the isolation of the group, which prevents outside influence. Consequently, additional opinions and advice from non-group members are not considered in the decision-making process. Fatally, this also applies to information from experts. Furthermore, the inner attitude of the group leader counts as a decisive factor of the organization. Partisan leaders, for example, tend to give preferential treatment to some group members, to give them a comparatively larger share of speech and to allow them to strictly reject alternative proposals. Another defect is when the group consists of homogeneous members who have identical social and ideological backgrounds. The third subgroup of antecedent conditions refers to provocative situational contexts. When external stressors affect the group, such as extreme time pressure, decision-makers often tend to vote for the leader's proposed solution, since there is supposedly little hope of being able to work out a more suitable alternative to the problem. In addition, individuals with low self-esteem like to seek confirmation within a group and are reluctant to contradict the supposed group consensus. Affected individuals may be permanently lacking in self-confidence on the one hand, or temporarily as a result of personal failures. Also, complex and moral conflicts can overwhelm individuals - especially when there is an obvious lack of ethically acceptable alternatives.

What Are the Symptoms of Groupthink?

Janis was interested in the symptoms of Groupthink and studied the political scenery at his time. Although competent and independent advisors advised the then U.S. President John F. Kennedy on the course of action in the conflict between the United States and Cuba, a fatal decision was made. There were some arguments that warned against the failure of the planned invasion of Cuba and the resulting consequences that would follow. Nevertheless, Kennedy and his team planned to stick with their plan to overthrow the communist government in Cuba: With U.S. support, Cuban exiles launched an attempted invasion of the Bay of Pigs in April 1961. However, the Cuban army had already been prepared and successfully repelled the attack. How did this bad decision by Kennedy's team come about?

The antecedent conditions described by Janis trigger a pronounced striving for agreement in the group members. This can be seen in the behavioral tendencies of decision-makers to achieve unanimity. These tendencies are reflected in the eight symptoms of Groupthink. A first symptom represents the illusion of invulnerability, which leads to an inflated level of optimism. This distorted perception of their own group often blinds decision-makers to warning signs of danger and impending failure. Due to the infallibility conviction, the group shows an increased willingness to take risks. In the case study of the failed Bay of Pigs invasion attempt, the illusion of invulnerability was created primarily because of Kennedy's great popularity and high approval ratings for his political goals. His election victory was celebrated as the dawn of a better future. Captivated by this euphoria, "Kennedy supporters" were convinced that nothing could stop them. Moreover, Kennedy's team felt morally vindicated in their cause, since communism was widely considered frowned upon. The conviction of the group to be morally superior, according to Janis, is likewise a symptom of his theory. In addition, stereotyping of outside groups is indicative of Groupthink, which leads to a sense of superiority over others as group members believe themselves to be more intelligent than their potential opponents. In the Cuban Missile Crisis case study, the Kennedy team believed the Cuban dictator Castro to be morally inferior because he ruled communistically. Furthermore, a negotiation with Castro as futile to them because they perceived the communist as incompetent and weak. Likewise, the Kennedy team decision-makers underestimated the strength of the Cuban army, which consisted of 200,000 soldiers. In contrast, the Cuban exiles numbered only 1400 men. Nevertheless, the Kennedy team was confident of their victory because they considered the Cuban air force to be less than functional. Based on the numerical superiority of the enemy at the Bay of Pigs, it can be seen that the Kennedy team exhibited its own collective rationalization. This behavior is generally typical of victims of Groupthink and counts as another symptom that causes groups to ignore warning signals and negative feedback. The Kennedy team even believed that the majority of Cuban soldiers were Castro opponents and would support the overthrow of the dictator. In reality, this was not the case. The illusion of unanimity was another error on the part of the Kennedy team and is among the eight symptoms of Groupthink. For example, one presidential advisor formulated criticisms of the invasion plan in a memorandum but made few critical comments during Kennedy's presence in the deliberative sessions. Moreover, others involved thought they were the only ones who viewed the plan as critical and therefore did not voice their concerns. The act of silence is referred to as self-censorship in Groupthink theory.

There are two other symptoms that can also be traced back within the decision-making process for the Bay of Pigs invasion. First, direct pressure was exerted on those who deviated from the majority thinking. For example, a foreign policy expert who expressed his concerns in a two-way meeting with his superior was admonished by the latter to fully support the President completely, since the decision had already been made. Groupthink victims often behave in such a way, feeling a need to defend the group's opinion. A contrary opinion from a member is perceived as a threat that must be eliminated immediately. Second, the admonishing superior exposes himself as a self-appointed sentiment guardian, which is the last and eighth symptom of Groupthink. These sentiment guardians feel called upon to actively protect and defend the Groupthink.

We introduced the symptoms of Groupthink using the Bay of Pigs invasion decision-making process here. In general, a decision-making process can be affected by Groupthink even if not all symptoms are detectable. For example, in all situations there is not an opposing group and consequently in these cases the symptom of stereotyping external groups will be less relevant. Furthermore, sentiment guards play a minor role when no sources of information outside the group are available.

What Are Symptoms of Defective Decision-making in Groups?

In groups influenced by Groupthink, the focus is primarily on information that supports the group opinion. As a result, the entire picture of the decision situation at hand is not considered. If this selective attitude is maintained in the further course of decision making, alternatives that have already been rejected are typically not re-evaluated. This is particularly problematic if further information is available in the meantime that speaks in favor of rejected options. However, as a rule, not only are unwanted alternatives are presented as being as unattractive as possible, but the preferred solution approach is glossed over. This comes about by ignoring costs and risks. The final symptom of defective decision-making described by Janis is mainly caused by the high level of optimism and self-confidence of a group. This is because the conviction of supposed infallibility makes the elaboration of contingency plans seem superfluous. The same applies to the introduction of monitoring and control measures.

At the end of the day, what can we conclude from this theory? Following Janis (1991), cohesiveness is one of the most important contributors to Groupthink. In other words, Groupthink requires a strong feeling of solidarity and individual desire to maintain good ongoing relationships with the other group members. Whenever this concurrence-seeking tendency is particularly high within a group, the group can make inferior decisions and not sufficiently consider risks involved. Empirical findings on Groupthink are mixed, however, which is mainly due to the difficulty of creating cohesiveness in the laboratory. It thus remains to be shown how important the phenomenon really is in practice and to what extent the contributing factors all play a major role in Groupthink.

In line with Groupthink theory, a study by Turner et al. (1992) shows that cohesive groups tend to be more confident in their decisions. Therefore, the researchers classified them as more risk averse than non-cohesive groups.[4] This phenomenon was observed in the Challenger case study, where board members had lower risk perceptions because they had completed so many successful missions in the past. In summary, there is indeed weak support for the correlation between cohesion and Groupthink.[5]

Debiasing Strategies to Limit Groupthink

What can be done to improve decision-making in teams? Every group with a strong leader can be seen as vulnerable to Groupthink. Groupthink typically arises in a work environment where employees fear having an opinion that differs from the prevailing majority. This can be the result of their own uncertainty or be caused by the methodological structure of the discussion. Therefore, the use of diverse decision-optimizing methods is crucial. Group leaders should take note of this and use such methods.

One important method to prevent Groupthink is to involve a "Devil's Advocate". This is a person who brings out the weak points of the explained proposals throughout the discussion, thus avoiding a one-sided view of the solutions. The main purpose of this is to stimulate discussion and thus promote the further development of the solutions presented. A variation of this method is the so-called "multiple advocacy" method, which, in addition to a neutral person, also consists of various group members, each of whom represents different alternatives. The neutral person acts as the decision-maker who ultimately chooses the alternative that best fits the problem at hand.

Furthermore, ensuring participation and opinion-sharing of all members within the group is important. To do this, dominant and less dominant members can be separated from each other in order to let insecure participants participate more actively in the discussion, since the inhibition threshold for participation is lower in a smaller group. Before a discussion group begins, it is primarily necessary to clarify which people will participate in the discussion. Employees who have a high need for autonomy should be represented first and foremost. This promotes independence of judgment, since people with this disposition are less likely to follow the majority. This significantly reduces the likelihood of Groupthink occurring.

Taking long-term measures is also important. These include the "Self-Leadership" method, in which participants are trained to deal better with stressful situations and to gain greater self-confidence. Thus, a smooth decision-making process is to be

[4] See Turner et al. (1992), p. 781ff.

[5] See Esser (1998), p. 130.

achieved. The use of various decision-making techniques can also reduce the extent of Groupthink. For example, the subjective perception of group members can be objectified by mathematical and economic modeling, such as utility and scenario analysis, leading to a better outcome. Finally, decision-making can be impaired if an independent, external observation is missing. In homogeneous groups, the problem can occur more often that members are limited in their mental perspective. As a result, important aspects of the decision-making process are not taken into account. It can thus be crucial to add an outside view to the inside view in order to avoid additional inside bias. An external consultant can draw attention to problems that have been neglected and thus possibly present new alternatives.

Finally, the group leader should be consulted about his/her own opinion about the best possible alternative at the end or after all group members have brought up their insights and views. Why? Laboratory studies have demonstrated a relatively strong correlation between leadership practices and Groupthink. Consistent with groupthink theory, Flowers (1977) found that groups led by a highly involved leader use less available information, propose fewer solutions, and rate their leader as more influential during the decision-making process. In addition, groups with leaders who express their preferred solutions early in the discussion tended to keep dissenting opinions to themselves and adopt the leader's opinion. Therefore, it is important to have an objective-minded discussion leader. Impartial leaders can encourage members to participate more actively in the discussion, thus creating more alternatives. With this type of leadership, the extent of groupthink can be mitigated significantly.

A recent study by Google, evaluating hundreds of teams and their decision-making processes, concluded that there is no algorithm for combining the "best mix" of types of individuals to make up excellent teams. The study was, however, able to identify one condition that mattered most to team success: psychological safety. Psychological safety needs to be high in successful teams. In other words, there needs to be a shared belief of team members that they are in a safe environment for interpersonal risk-taking and will not embarrass, reject, or punish a team member for sharing their opinion. Critical factors to establishing psychological safety are cooperation tasks, rewards, and goals. Cooperation rules need to be established and learned within a team in order to be successful. For cooperation to be learned, teams need *conflict*—differences in team members' opinions, ideas, values, or modes of thinking. Of course, nobody likes conflict since it makes us anxious and stressed out but this is exactly why it may create motivations to finally support more well-thought-through decisions.

To conclude, leadership can limit the snares of Groupthink by being mindful of the antecedent conditions, symptoms of Groupthink, and symptoms of defective decision-making. Simultaneously, it makes sense to take reasonable precautions by following the recommended debiasing strategies and, most importantly, recognize the role leadership plays in both enhancing and alleviating Groupthink symptoms.

Diversity and Independent Directors

An often-heard assumption is that boards with a majority of *independent* directors can increase company performance because of superior judgements by those directors. However, the results of empirical studies on this issue are contradictory and far from unequivocal. Looking at the impact of the financial crisis and how boards of large corporations performed during this time, it is interesting to see that then-established rules did not do anything to improve failures. The collapses of large corporations like Enron, WorldCom and others during and after the 2008 financial crisis re-opened the debate about how to improve board effectiveness. Many companies that collapsed around the financial crisis had complied with important stock exchange rules requiring the boards to have a majority of independent directors. Despite these rules, boards still failed to effectively perform their monitoring role. Apparently, being an independent director *alone* does not matter to help alleviate decision-making failures.

A study by Kamalnath (2017) analyses whether board gender diversity can possibly help corporate boards overcome Groupthink, where Groupthink is referred to as the failure of corporate board members to consider alternatives to the dominant view of the group when making important and risky decisions. It is shown that gender diversity on corporate boards can indeed help overcome Groupthink, but for board gender diversity to be successful, the *female directors need to be independent* and not bear some kind of insider status. In addition to gender diversity, other forms of diversity like race, educational and professional backgrounds etc., might offer same of the same benefits, as well.

You may ask yourself how many women are needed to effectively eliminate Groupthink. Research has evaluated the 'critical mass', that is, the minimum number required to ensure that the female director—and the corporate board as a whole in their decision-making effectiveness—does not experience the effects of tokenism.[6] A study by Erkut et al. (2008) finds that a critical mass of three female directors is necessary to avoid an effect of tokenism. These critical mass findings were further tested by Torchia et al. (2011) who studied the effect of boards with one, two, or at least three female directors on organizational innovation. Interestingly, they find that once the number of female directors increased from a few (one or two women) to a minority (consisting of at least three women), the minority board members are able to effectively influence the level of organizational innovation.

Time seems also a contributor to diminish team success. It seems another important aspect to limit the effect of Groupthink is that independent directors who serve *long terms* on the board tend to suffer from reduced independence. The reason being this is that they tend to foster fictive friendships with other directors, which in some cases leads them to not challenge their 'friends' on the board when it comes to major decisions.

---

[6] Tokenism refers to the practice of contributing only a symbolic effort to do a particular thing, which can be achieved by recruiting a small number of employees from underrepresented groups in order to give the appearance of sexual or racial or other equality within the workforce.

Peer Effects, Stereotypes, and Company Culture

How are we generally influenced by others' views and behavior? Economic theory is not helpful here since it mostly assumes that an individual follows the idea of being a homo oeconomicus by maximizing own utility without thinking about others. Social psychology tells us this is not true. It is fascinating that even something as commonly discussed in economics as individual risk aversion (which is often assumed to be constant) adjusts due to peer effects and an individual's social environment.

Peer Effects

Individual outcomes are often highly correlated with group average outcomes, a finding often interpreted as a causal peer effect or social spillover effect. In research, there are different approaches to investigate group influences on the risk attitudes of an individual. One possible approach is to test the risk aversion of an individual by means of investment decisions, where all individuals have full transparency over the decisions made by the group. It is found that an individual in the presence of the group often adopts the response of the group rather than his or her own response.

To test the influence of peers on a person's risk aversion and confidence, Ahern et al. (2011) conducted an experiment in which MBA students at the University of Michigan were first randomly assigned to six different groups. It was important that these were exogenously formed groups and not groups that had come together through self-selection. This was to avoid the possibility that individual group members already possessed similar attitudes before the start of the experiment. The individual risk attitudes of the students were determined by the use of online surveys. For this purpose, a total of two surveys were conducted. The first survey took place before the MBA program had begun. This was to ensure that the students had not yet established contact with fellow students. Consequently, it was possible to assess the individual risk attitude of a student before the start of the program. The second online survey was carried out after the first academic year and was used as a comparative value to test the influence of fellow students on individual attitudes. In the online surveys, a total of ten choices had to be made between two types of lotteries. The choice was between a less risky lottery (option A), where the values of the two payout options were closer together, and a more risky lottery (option B), where the variability of the possible payout was higher. It should be noted that the probability to receive the high payout increased as the game progressed. This resulted in a higher expected payoff for option A in the first four runs and a higher expected payoff for option B in runs five to ten. Therefore, a risk-neutral person would choose option A in the first four runs and switch to the riskier alternative from run five on. The later a person switches from option A to option B, the more risk-averse he or she is. Using this experiment, it was found that students' risk aversion was indeed influenced. Both students with a high-risk attitude and students with a high level of risk aversion approached the average risk attitude of their peers in the group after 1 year. More precisely, after completion of the first year of the MBA program, the difference between a student's and her peers' average risk aversion shrunk by 41%—which is indeed a significant peer effect in this group. Accordingly, risk attitudes became more homogeneous. Because students' risk aversion changed after only 1 year due to peer influence, it was concluded that a person's risk attitudes can change frequently during life, especially when individuals frequently change personal or work environments.

Going beyond students as a peer group, a recent study by Browne et al. (2021) uses data from the German Socio-Economic Panel to analyze peer effects in risk taking by tracking the impact of the East-West migration after the German reunification. Strong empirical evidence on peer effects in risk taking is established: Peer effects are found to be particularly relevant for women, young individuals, less educated individuals, as well as for those being married and with children. Higher social interaction tends to increase peer effects.

Interestingly, when looking at the workplace, there is growing empirical evidence on strong network effects in worker productivity. Research by Lindquist et al. (2015) contributes to the discussion on peer effects in the workplace by applying methods from the social network literature. Similar to other studies, they find that a 10% increase in the current productivity of a worker's co-worker network leads to a 1.7% increase in own productivity. This productivity spillover effect can be attributed to conformist behavior at the workplace. However, while this effect is not very large, it is interesting to know that such a positive peer effect exists and should be exploited to improve profitability of the firm.

Company Culture

Group and peer dynamics are influenced by homogeneity of a group or a given company culture. If a company establishes a strong culture with heavily communicated values, these shared values will be reflected in group dynamics and Groupthink. For instance, if it is not customary at the company to speak up in a meeting, this self-enforces Groupthink and with it inferior decision-making processes and a higher tendency to make mistakes. In a similar way, a toxic company culture can backfire when the leadership imposes goals and targets that are difficult to meet.

A prominent example for a toxic sales culture within a company was the crisis at Wells Fargo, a large US bank, 2016–2018. The bank incentivized its employees to boost their sales volume significantly by cross-selling as many products as possible to their clients, including adding insurance products, additional saving accounts or credit cards to accounts without letting clients know. The result was that the employees reacted by creating 3.5 million fraudulent bank accounts with fake addresses and even fake client signatures in order to fulfill these goals. At the end of the day, the bank had to pay billions in penalties and settlement costs.[7]

[7] See Sibony (2019), p.133–134.

The insight here is that for a company culture to work as toxic in the sense described above, deviant or non-complying behavior needs to be observed by others in order to have a peer effect. Groupthink will be established. Social pressure follows company pressure. And then more people follow a certain majority thinking or way to achieve targets set by the company. If everybody follows a non-ethical path, it becomes more and more difficult to be the only unco guid on the floor.

Stereotypes

Stereotypes refer to a set of characteristics we tend to associate with certain subgroups of the population. Evolution has told the animal world (including us) to make quick judgments about potential predators. In a similar way today, we judge others by their appearance - including hair color, skin color, weight, and gender. When it comes to gender, for instance, there seems to be a general understanding that baby boys like blue, but baby girls rather prefer pink; we think of women as soft, nice, and gentle, while considering men as strong, independent, and competitive. Then, it makes sense to assume that men will rather pursue their career goals while women are expected to stay at home and take care of the offspring.

In the workplace, this gender bias has significant impact on hiring decisions, employee performance reviews, and ultimately promotion decisions—limiting female leadership opportunities and hindering female talent to prove their abilities. Using 248 employee performance reviews across 28 companies in the technology sector, a 2014 study found that 59% critical feedback was given to men whereas 88% critical feedback was given to women. The women were mainly criticized as having a "loud" or "abrasive" personality and as being too "judgmental" (Snyder, 2014).

Looking at research on how individuals work together in groups, it is interesting to see that each individual does usually not contribute an even share of the overall work. In Germany, we have a saying relating to teamwork. A TEAM is referred to as "*T*oll! *E*in *A*nderer *M*acht's!", which translates into something like "Great! Somebody Else Does the Work!". This is supposed to be funny, of course, but there is a grain of truth to it. Teams always exhibit some elements of inertia, as team members tend to rely on others when it comes to decision-making and working on results. In addition to the inertia comes the resistance to object to the opinion of a person installing themselves as team leader. Similarly, there is some resistance to object to suggestions that are already on the table and agreed upon by the majority of the team. If everyone on the team earns the same score or level of recognition for the final result, one or two team members are often seen to have done the majority of the work while others just took the role of "free-riders". Interestingly, major workers are more often female while free-riders are more often male such that, on average, men get more credit. As a result, women often receive less credit for group work when employers cannot perfectly observe their individual contribution.

It seems that that this phenomenon should be mostly true in rather intransparent marketplaces where the exact level of an employee's competence and contribution to overall company success cannot easily be measured, and thus common biases and stereotypes will play a more important role. Then, marketplaces where performance can be easily measured and where such performance is transparent should be mostly free from such bias. For instance, academia should be a rather "fair" marketplace in the sense that academic performance can relatively easily be measured - simply by looking at the publication record of an individual researcher as well as his or her other academic achievements. Well, this is not even true in academia! Teamwork is common in academia, give that research projects often involve multiple co-authors working together on a single publication. A recent outstanding study by Sarsons et al. (2021) demonstrates the "group-work effect in academia" in an excellent way. The authors use academic observational data to test whether co-authorship matters differently for getting tenure at their employer universities for male and female economics professors. As it turns out, men and women receive the same amount of credit for solo-authored papers - which provide a clear signal of the author's ability. However, conditional on quality and other observables, while men are tenured similarly regardless of whether they coauthor or solo author, women, in contrast, are significantly *less likely* to receive tenure the more they coauthor, which represents an important disadvantage for this subgroup of economists in getting promoted to Associate Professor with tenure at their institutions.

Key Takeaways for Risk Leadership

Understanding how our instinct for cooperation and our need for fairness as well as our potential weaknesses related to group dynamics influence our decisions is important. Indeed, other people matter when it comes to our risk-related and other daily decisions in business and life.

As pointed out by Coleman (2018), research suggests that teams need cooperative tasks, known rewards and defined goals in order to establish psychological safety and improve productivity. Conflict can be good! When we are interested in good decision-making processes, we should put together a diverse team with established rules of communication and cooperation.

References

Ahern, K. R., Duchin, R., & Shumway, T. (2011). Peer effects in risk aversion and trust. *Review of Financial Studies, 27*(11), 3213–3240.

Benensona, J. F., Pascoe, J., & Radmore, N. (2007). Children's altruistic behavior in the dictator game. *Evolution and Human Behavior, 28*(3), 168–175.

Bolton, G. E. (1991). A comparative model of bargaining: theory and evidence. *American Economic Review, 81*, 1096–1136.

Browne, M., Hofmann, A., Richter, A., Roth, S., & Steinorth, P. (2021). Peer effects in risk taking: Evidence from Germany, special issue on recent developments in financial modeling and risk management. *Annals of Operations Research, 299*, 1129–1163.

Coleman, P. (2018). The science of teamwork – five actionable lessons from the lab. *Psychology Today*. June 14, 2018. https://www.psychologytoday.com/us/blog/the-five-percent/201806/the-science-teamwork

Eckel, C. C., & Grossman, P. J. (2001). Chivalry and solidarity in ultimatum games. *Economic Inquiry, 39*(2), 171–188.

Engel, C. (2011). Dictator games: A meta study. *Experimental Economics, 14*, 583–610.

Erkut, S., Kramer, V. W., & Konrad, A. M. (2008). Critical mass: does the number of women on a corporate board make a difference? Women on corporate boards of directors. In S. Vinnicombe et al. (Eds.), *International Research and Practice* (pp. 350–366). Elgar.

Esser, J. (1998). Alive and well after 25 years: A review of groupthink research. *Organizational Behavior and Human Decision Processes, 73*(2–3), 116–141.

Fantino, E., Gaitan, S., Kennelly, A., & Stolarz-Fantino, S. (2007). How reinforcer type affects choice in economic games. *Behavioural Processes, 75*(2), 107–114.

Fehr, E., & Schmidt, K. M. (1999). A theory of fairness, competition, and cooperation. *Quarterly Journal of Economics, 114*, 817–868.

Flowers, M. L. (1977). A laboratory test of some implications of Janis's groupthink hypothesis. *Journal of Personality and Social Psychology, 35*, 888–896.

Güth, W., & Kocher, M. G. (2014). More than thirty years of ultimatum bargaining experiments: Motives, variations, and a survey of the recent literature. *Journal of Economic Behavior and Organization, 108*, 396–409.

Güth, W., Schmittberger, R., & Schwarze, B. (1982). An experimental analysis of ultimatum bargaining. *Journal of Economics and Behavioral Organization, 3*, 367–388.

Henrich, J., Boyd, R., Bowles, S., Camerer, C., Fehr, E., Gintis, H., et al. (2005). In cross-cultural perspective: Behavioral experiments in 15 small-scale societies. *Behavioral Brain Science, 28*, 795–815.

Janis, I. (1991). Chapter 18: Groupthink. In E. Griffin (Ed.), *A first look at communication theory*. McGrawHill.

Kamalnath, A. (2017). Gender diversity as the antidote to groupthink on corporate boards. *Deakin Law Review, 22*(85), 86–106.

Lindquist, M., Sauermann, J., & Zenou, Y. (2015). Network Effects on Worker Productivity, Discussion Paper Series on Labour Economics, No. 10928, https://repec.cepr.org/repec/cpr/ceprdp/DP10928.pdf

Proctor, D., Williamson, R.A., de Waal, F.B, and Brosnan, S.F. (2013): Chimpanzees play the ultimatum game, Proceedings of the National Academy of Sciences of the United States of America, 110 (6): 2070–2075.

Sarsons, H., Gerxhani, K., Reuben, E., & Schram, A. (2021). Gender differences in recognition for group work. *Journal of Political Economy, 129*(1), 101–147.

Sibony, O. (2019). *You're about to make a terrible mistake! How biases distort decision-making – and what you can do to fight them, Little*. Brown Spark – Hachette Book Group.

Snyder, K. (2014). The abrasiveness trap: High-achieving men and women are described differently in reviews, Fortune, https://fortune.com/2014/08/26/performance-review-gender-bias/

Torchia, M., Calabro, A., & Huse, M. (2011). Women directors on corporate boards: From tokenism to critical mass. *Journal of Business Ethics, 102*, 299–308.

Turner, M. E., Pratkanis, A. R., Probasco, P., & Leve, C. (1992). Threat, cohesion, and group effectiveness: Testing a social identity maintenance perspective on groupthink. *Journal of Personality and Social Psychology, 63*, 781–796.

Hindsight Bias: Why We Think We Are Good Predictors Even Though We Are Not

11

The most important single key takeaway from this chapter is

> **The 10th Commandment of Risk Leadership:** Don't believe you are a good predictor. Instead, when a prediction is needed, considering the opposite may be useful!

Understanding hindsight bias is important. The cost and consequences of hindsight bias always depend on the specific context in which it is placed. Hindsight bias is deeply rooted in us and can result from various reasons. Therefore, there is no universal solution to reduce or even eliminate hindsight bias, but there are interesting approaches. The consider-the-opposite strategy seems to be most promising if it is adequately adapted to the specific situation. While expertise, on its own, does not seem to be a protection against hindsight bias, there may be a mitigating influence under the right circumstances. The key to success seems to be a high validity environment and continuous feedback.

Hindsight Bias

"No, not at all. We have it totally under control. It's one person coming in from China, and we have it under control. It's going to be just fine", was proclaimed by Donald Trump at the dawn of the corona crisis in March 2020. Only 2 months later, he completely changed his mind by announcing: "This is a pandemic, I felt it was a pandemic long before it was called a pandemic" (Rogers, 2020). Not only presidents but also sports professionals can seem doubtfully sure of their claims after an event occurred. The German soccer star Franz Beckenbauer once said: "If I look back at the 1990 world cup, I had never one spark of fear that we will not win the title" SZ Online (2020). You can probably remember more examples from your personal life where someone says: "I knew it would happen!". But did these people

A. Hofmann, *The Ten Commandments of Risk Leadership*, Future of Business and Finance, https://doi.org/10.1007/978-3-030-88797-1_11

really know or were they suffering from cognitive distortion? Even though a variety of unknown factors might have led Donald Trump to change his mind, a possible explanation for his conflicting claims could have been hindsight bias. This cognitive bias is also known as the "knew-it-all-along" phenomenon or creeping determinism.

Fischhoff (1975) was the first to study and prove the hindsight bias in isolated form. He compared the likelihood judgements of possible outcomes between hindsight groups who received outcome knowledge, and were asked to ignore it, and foresight groups who did not. The result of this experiment was that reporting an outcome increases its perceived likelihood significantly.

Hawkins and Hastie (1990) define hindsight bias to be "the tendency for people with outcome knowledge to believe falsely that they would have predicted the reported outcome of an event".[1] This definition describes hindsight bias as a unitary phenomenon. But in fact, when Fischhoff discovered the hindsight bias in 1975, he referred to it as three different empirical regularities. Scrutinizing hindsight bias at the level of these three phenomena seems crucial for understanding how it works and in what ways it affects people's perceptions. In the following, I will therefore decompose hindsight bias into the three different manifestations as they have been refined by Kelman et al. (1998). It can be shown how each of the manifestations alters people's judgments and distinguish hindsight bias from rational decision-making, as for instance when it comes to Bayesian probability updating.

The *Primary Bias* is defined as the extent to which the reporting of an outcome increases its perceived likelihood of occurrence. Fischhoff (1975) shows this effect in his first experiment where participants are asked to read a short passage about an unfamiliar event. Only a subgroup receives information about how the event turned out. After reading the passage, the participants are presented with four possible outcomes and asked to indicate the estimated probability of occurrence of each outcome. Over all outcomes reported, the reporting of occurrence of a specific outcome almost doubled its perceived likelihood of occurrence. The behavior of updating beliefs about the probability of events based on outcome information is not irrational itself. When looking in the future, as often times necessary in the case of reoccurring events, it is indeed very rational and can be referred to as "learning from experience". Also, when looking back in the past, hindsight probability estimates can be more accurate than their foresight counterparts, as the outcome knowledge provides additional insides into how to evaluate the past. The existence of primary bias is therefore questionable. It only is to be referred to as a bias if the hindsight estimation is further away from the true probability of occurrence than the original estimate. This, however, is difficult to test, as the true probability of occurrence of real-world events is rarely known. In simple examples, when the probabilities are easily calculated, hindsight bias does not occur as people then tend to form their beliefs based on common mathematical knowledge.

The *Secondary Bias* refers to the observation of people being mostly unaware that the outcome information has influenced their judgements. Fischhoff (1975) shows this in his second experiment. Again, participants are asked to evaluate the

[1] Hawkins and Hastie (1990), p. 311.

probability of occurrence of different events based on a short text, but this time they are instructed to estimate the probabilities "as if they didn't know the outcome". In 13 out of 16 cases, subjects with outcome information estimated the probability of occurrence of the actual outcome to be higher than their counterparts without outcome knowledge. Individuals here somehow fail to ignore what they have learned from the outcome and project this new knowledge into the past and by doing so commit a look-ahead bias. Moreover, they seem to be unaware of it, which mistakenly results in the feeling that "they knew it all along".

The *Tertiary Bias* can be defined as the belief that others lacking outcome information acted unreasonable, if they assigned a lower probability estimate to the actual outcome than the subjects with outcome information did themselves. This behavior is shown best when subjects are asked to evaluate the performance of others. In a study by Kelman et al. (1998), participants assess bettors to be better than their peers if the gamble was manipulated in their favor, even though the bettors couldn't know that the game was biased. On average, the participants failed to evaluate the gamblers based only on the information that was available to them, and instead relied on their own knowledge about the gamble.

Why Do People Exhibit Hindsight Bias?

Blank et al. (2008) proposed a second decomposition of hindsight bias that is closer related to the input factors, which cause it to occur. Based on an extensive study of the available literature, the authors suggest a division of hindsight bias into three distinguishable components: *Memory distortions, necessity (also referred to as inevitability)* and *foreseeability*. Roese and Vohs (2012) synthetize this framework with the comprehensive literature on the input factors of hindsight bias into a coherent whole model explaining its different components as well as the psychological mechanisms behind it.

Memory distortions describe a cognitive bias in which the remembered-reconstructed probability estimates in hindsight were on average closer to the actual outcome than the originally assigned probabilities. People tend to misremember their earlier judgments. This effect can be measured by matching a recall attempt against a recorded earlier response, as for instance done by Fischhoff and Beyth (1975). In their study, they asked subjects to estimate the outcome of several events. Sometime after occurrence of the events, they were asked to remember or reconstruct their own predictions from before as accurately as possible. The remembered probabilities were biased towards the outcome in the sense that they were higher than before for outcomes that actually occurred and lower than before for outcomes that did not occur. They also found this effect to be asymmetrical depending on the framing of the question. The hindsight bias is greater when an event is reported to have occurred than when it is not. This empirical irregularity has been reproduced in several other studies. Memory distortions are assumed to be caused by operations of memory. The first memory process involved is the recollection of one's earlier judgement. A weak memory trace for the original response is prerequisite for memory distortions to occur. When people fail to retrieve the answer they gave to an earlier question, they have to mentally reconstruct it. This gives rise to the second cognitive input factor involved: Knowledge updating. Knowledge updating refers to the way, new information is integrated into the existing memory system and how it gets connected with what is already known. New information strengthens compatible knowledge in memory, whereas inconsistent information is weakened and might even be misremembered. The knowledge base is constantly updated and there are no backups of earlier states of it, on which one can rely, when reassessing one's earlier beliefs. This is therefore assumed to be done by anchoring on the post-outcome beliefs that are based on the current knowledge base. Meaning that in reconstructing their earlier beliefs, subjects anchor on their current, post-outcome beliefs and then adjust these beliefs in order to infer their pre-outcome state of mind and usually end up closer to the actual outcome than before.

The second component of hindsight bias is *necessity* (or inevitability). Impressions of necessity are beliefs about an objective state of the world which, given the causal chain of events, could not have turned out different. Nestler et al. (2010) quantify inevitability with a four-item questionnaire capturing the participants belief in the evitability of the event. The cognitive process leading to this bias is called sensemaking. Sensemaking describes the psychological phenomenon that people feel compelled to "make sense" out of the past. This is done by causal reasoning. When investigating the occurrence of an outcome, people connect the outcome with its causal antecedents and thereby make it seem more predictable, more inevitable. The result is an oversimplification of cause and effects. In reality, many causes can interconnect with many outcomes. For instance, many symptoms could be interconnected with many diseases. Each symptom could be caused by any of the diseases. When looking in the future, people can comprehend the complexity of this structure. In hindsight however, they tend to fixate only on the different causes that are interconnected with the realized outcome. This simplification implicitly leads to a higher probability estimate of that outcome. In general, situations that can be rationalized by straightforward explanations give rise to greater hindsight bias. In contrary, situations that are more ambiguous and harder to explain usually induce much smaller bias. Roese and Vohs summarize this in a quite striking way: "The better the story, the greater the hindsight bias!"[2]

Foreseeability, in contrast to necessity, addresses the subjective representation of events. It comprises the beliefs about one's own knowledge and ability. Of particular importance in the context of hindsight bias is the belief that one personally was able to foresee a now factual event that others were unable to predict. Foreseeability can be caused by metacognitive and by motivational input factors. The metacognitive input factor associated with foreseeability is called processing fluency. It can be interpreted as an instance of the availability heuristic introduced by Tversky and Kahneman, in which a person evaluates the probability of an event by the ease with which relevant material can be brought to mind (availability). Processing fluency can influence hindsight bias in both directions. When it feels easy to come up with

[2] Roese and Vohs (2012), p. 414 f.

a plausible explanation for an outcome, this easiness is misattributed to certainty and people will show greater hindsight bias. When the situation is somehow ambiguous and it is hard to form a conclusion about a particular outcome, this difficulty is misattributed to uncertainty, resulting in lower hindsight bias. The same logic applies to possible alternative outcomes.

Sanna and Schwarz (2003) asked participants to list either 4 or 12 reasons about how a college football game might have turned out differently. Listing 12 reasons is assumed to be more difficult and should therefore increase hindsight bias. The difficulty of finding 12 reasons for alternative outcomes is thought to be misattributed in the way that there were only low chances that an alternative outcome occurs. Listing only 4 reasons should, on the contrary, evoke the feeling that an alternative outcome was very likely and therefore reduce hindsight bias. The study results confirm the assumed effects. Participants that were asked to name 12 reasons reported hindsight pre-game expectations that were closer to the actual outcome than those of their counterparts. Besides process fluency, foreseeability can also be caused by motivational input factors. They can be divided into need for closure and self-esteem. Need for closure causes hindsight bias because people have a need for order and predictability in their lives. The idea, that many outcomes are determined by pure chance feels threatening to many people. The feeling that an event was foreseeable, however, satisfies their need for order and control. As empirical results show that people with greater need for predictability show greater hindsight bias, it can be inferred that need for closure consciously or unconsciously biases people to believe that they were able to foresee an observed outcome.

Self-esteem is the second motivational input factor of hindsight bias. It is closely related to the so-called self-serving bias. In taking responsibility for desirable outcomes and externalizing responsibility for undesirable outcomes, people try to enhance positive views of themselves. For instance, workers might on average attribute promotions to their exceptional work but blame others for a denial of promotions (Shepperd et al., 2008). When applying this theory to hindsight bias, one has to distinguish between positive and negative outcomes. In the case of positive outcomes, the intuition is quite clear. People will want to take credit for that outcome, may it be for their contribution towards reaching it, or only for their knowledgeability. In both cases, they will claim to have seen it coming, thus show an increased hindsight bias. In the case of negative outcomes, it is distinguished between involved people and mere bystanders. Involved people don't want to be made responsible for the negative outcome, and therefore show reduced foreseeability. Mere bystanders, on the contrary, don't have to fear being blamed for the outcome. However, they have an opportunity to take credit for their knowledgeability and will therefore show increased foreseeability.

Blank et al. (2008) show that the three hindsight components differ in magnitude and sometimes also in direction. They also show that the three levels are largely uncorrelated and thereby deliver strong evidence to contemplate memory distortions, necessity and foreseeability as independent and fundamentally different components. Nestler et al. (2010) deliver further support for that hypotheses by showing in three experiments that each component can be addressed individually. Roese and

Vohs (2012), however, conceptualize the relationships between the components in hierarchically organized levels. Foreseeability as the highest component subsumes the two levels below it. Necessity, the middle component, is assumed to subsume memory distortions. Memory distortions are classified as the lowest component. All authors agree however, that the empirical basis regarding the dissociation and interaction of the three components remains sparse and that future research is necessary, in order to further explore the links between the components.

Consequences of Hindsight Bias in Practice

Hindsight bias can be a powerful distortion when it comes to consequences resulting from the cognitive processes within the human brain as described in the previous chapters. In order to understand more about the practical relevance of the bias, it can be useful to first gather a broad overview of possible ramifications for its manifestations.

Myopia

Myopia in a hindsight bias context can be seen as the exaggeration of one single reason in the causal chain and the neglection of other influencing factors. Because in an ex-ante view everything seems to be properly ordered and clear compared to foresight it can be easy to come to false conclusions in hindsight. In the legal punitive context, it is assumed that a myopic focus on a single outcome can harm involved stakeholders, especially the defendant. "Nulla poena sine lege", no penalty without law, is a common legal principle in all continental European legislations. Nobody can be judged by something not prohibited by law at the time of commitment. Therefore, laws in general do not apply retrospectively but are foresight-oriented. In a court review of a case, this principle must be applied backwards if it comes to the informational horizon of the defendant. Judges and jurors are asked to judge a person's behavior in a situation in the light of foresight information known to that person.

Overconfidence

The effect of overconfidence that can be induced and increased by hindsight bias when knowledge about the factual outcome of an event increases one's confidence in a priori likelihood assessment. Because the hindsight bias leads to a poor reassessment of past predictions or hypotheses, it can strengthen a person's beliefs in his or her own personal abilities. Like myopia, overconfidence is a result of hindsight bias that can account for consequences in a legal context as well, for example in the forensic assessment of eyewitness confidence, as shown by a study of Granhag et al. (2000). The authors measured overconfidence resulting from *reassessment* and *remembrance* of confidence in past eyewitness judgements given specific experiment conditions on provided feedback. In their first experiment with a solely reassessment of the situation, they not directly refer to hindsight bias, as this variation can be seen as "primary hindsight bias" according to Kelman et al. (1998) (Just the reassessment of past confidence with new information might be an effect of Bayesian updating in the light of new information). The second experiment is conducted with a variation that stressed the memory distortion of the participants with the result of stronger overconfidence for hindsight biased subjects.

A study of Biais and Weber (2009) has shown the relevance of hindsight bias and overconfidence in risk-based decision-making. In their first experiment they conducted a questionnaire with two groups of students and asked them to deliver point estimators and 90% confidence intervals (as a proxy for variances) about future spot prices of commodities, stocks and exchange rates. One week later the experiment was repeated but with different informational conditions for the two groups. One group was asked to remember their old estimates from last week (hindsight bias), the other group got their previous estimates (hindsight bias muted). But both groups got the actual spot value of the securities they needed to estimate. Biais and Weber calculate a few self-developed summary statistics that showed a less surprised hindsight group. It is seen that the upward revision of volatility forecast is stronger when one is presented with the initial forecast that is then comparable to the realized values. Although they not directly measure the effect of overconfidence, the hindsight bias group with no feedback to correct from had a lower estimation volatility. It is concluded that wrong variance estimates will lead to an incorrect hedging strategy or asset pricing when someone is not accounting for the unexpected part of the risk.

To assess the effect of hindsight bias on performance, Biais and Weber delivered a second experiment with investment bankers in London and Frankfurt branches that additionally accounts for measurements in overconfidence. The bankers were divided into two groups and asked to give estimations about economical and banking related questions (e.g. number of bankers at Lazard in 8/2001). In a second task each group needed to provide vice versa their assessment on what the other group will estimate on their questions while presented with the correct answer (hindsight bias enforced). Moreover, the participants are asked about the percentage of bankers that perform better than themselves to include a direct measurement for overconfidence.

Even though the Bankers stated on average that only 24.61% of their colleagues had better skills than themself the study resulted in no evidence of a correlation of overconfidence with the strength of hindsight bias. Meaning that there was no significant difference in overconfidence between the low and high-performance bankers although all bankers were highly overconfident. Finally, it was revealed that more hindsight leads to less performance in general as high earning bankers are the least biased in both samples. It can be summarized that overconfidence is a side effect of hindsight bias but might only manifest in a holistic sense and is not directly influenced by the strength of exhibited hindsight bias.

Effect Size

A measurement to get a deeper insight into the general effect size of the hindsight bias can be the usage of meta-analyses of the existing literature and data. There are two meta studies currently available that synthesized the results of predominant studies. The first one is Christensen-Szalanski and Willham (1991) with a selection of 122 effect sizes of 40 studies dated from 1975 to 1989 and therefore covering almost every published paper since the foundations of Fischhoff (1975). They concluded that there exists a significant effect size in the underlying literature. The strongest effect of hindsight bias was obtained from almanac questions leading to an effect that is 2.5 times stronger than the effect of case history questionnaires. The second meta study is by Guilbault et al. (2004) with a broader sample size including 95 studies with 252 independent effect sizes; it can be highlighted that all two significant moderators from Christensen and Szalanski are found to be insignificant for Guilbault et al. They speculated about the influence of the unpublished studies included by their predecessors but were not available for a novel analysis.

An interesting influence on the effect size is age. Pohl et al. (2018) conducted the second life-span study on hindsight bias with the same questions for participants from 8 to 82. The effect was measured using a multinomial processing tree fed with almanac questions that were relatively easy and generic in order to be understood by small children. Overall, this resulted in a U-Shape pattern for all ages, meaning that young children and older adults exhibiting significant higher degree of hindsight bias compared to young adults. As they account directly for input factors of the hindsight bias (e.g. recollection) they assumed the effect to be partly (but not exclusively) driven by the inhibitory control of the participants. Pohl et al. argue that because of this lack of inhibitory control, young children and older adults find it more difficult to ignore the hindsight bias information when they retrieve their original judgement.

What Can We Do About Hindsight Bias?

Now that a comprehensive insight into hindsight bias has been provided, the question arises as to what possibilities there are to mitigate it. Guilbault concludes in his meta-study that there are factors that significantly increase hindsight bias but none that generally reduce it. Nevertheless, it is worth taking a detailed look at different approaches, their strengths and weaknesses, and whether they could be the successful tool.

Consider-the-opposite

A possible input factor of hindsight bias is the recollection mechanism reporting the outcome of an event heightens the availability in memory of cues and reasons that support this outcome. This process seems to happen automatically and is therefore hard to prevent. Consequently, Fischhoffs' first debiasing attempts, where he instructed people to try harder or to ignore the hindsight bias were unsuccessful. The 'consider-the-opposite' strategy tries to use this automatic process which leads to the hindsight bias in the first place, in order to reduce it, by encouraging people to actively think about reasons why an outcome that did not occur could well have occurred. This should activate the sensemaking process of new causal chains and activate different associations which otherwise would not have been considered. The situation that is created by this strategy is more similar to the foresight situation where subjects have to consider many possible outcomes instead of trying to make sense of only one outcome (Slovic & Fischhoff, 1977). The strategy has been proven to be capable of reducing hindsight bias in multiple studies but also of being able to reduce other association-based judgement errors - like overconfidence or confirmation bias.

As already stated above, hindsight bias becomes especially relevant in courtroom settings when people are judged on decisions made in the past by an ex-post point of view. The 'consider-the-opposite' strategy and its capability of maintaining the objectiveness in courtroom settings was tested by Lowe and Reckers (1997). They divided 92 prospective jurors into three groups and asked all subjects to rate the performance of an auditor on a scale from 0 to 10. The first group was introduced to the general case scenario but was not introduced to outcome knowledge. The second group received additional outcome knowledge which revealed that the client firm had to declare bankruptcy and shareholders are suing the auditor for not reporting important disclosures. Finally, the last group was introduced to the very same outcome knowledge but also to the 'consider-the-opposite' strategy. First, they were given two alternative outcomes that could have occurred and were then asked to assign likelihoods to these alternative outcomes. Additionally, participants of the third group were asked to state other possible outcomes. As a result, the foresight group assigned a mean auditor performance of 4.91 and the hindsight group of only 2.97. The debiased hindsight group rated the auditor performance with a mean of 4.21. The ratings of both hindsight groups are significantly different on a 5% level and the strategy was capable of debiasing the hindsight ratings. Lowe and Reckers also included relevance judgements of the available information in their experiment. These revealed that the debiasing strategy significantly reduced the jurors' relevance rating of negative information cues. These findings support the hypothesis that the consider-the-opposite strategy can influence the underlying cognitive process of hindsight bias in a meaningful way.

The instructions of the 'consider-the-opposite' strategy are a narrow ridge and there are more potential pitfalls. When instructing people in such a way, it is important that they are actively encouraged to consider the opposite. In addition, care must be taken to ensure that participants do not consider too many other possible outcomes. Generating too many possibilities can be perceived as a subjectively difficult task which affects the metacognitive level of hindsight bias and can lead to the actual outcome being considered even more inevitable.

Expertise

Does expertise shield from hindsight bias? Intuitively, it would make sense that training and experience would lead to more precise predictions and therefore leave less room for hindsight bias. However, the evidence so far is mixed. In Christensen-Szalanski and Willhams' meta-analysis, they conclude that expertise can have a mitigating influence on hindsight bias. Guilbault et al., however, concluded in their meta-analysis that expertise has no significant influence. While Christensen-Szalanski and Willham defined expertise in general as familiarity with the question, Guiltbault separates a general familiarity from persons who are considered experts. Guilbault et al.s' definition seems to be more accurate in answering the question of whether expertise protects against hindsight bias, since mere familiarity with the question does not make an expert.

Several studies have already demonstrated an effect of expertise on overconfidence. Experts can tend to overestimate their own knowledge and therefore be socially-motivated to guess in case of doubt to distract from their ignorance. However, the question arises as to what influence expertise can have on the cognitive input factors of hindsight bias. An insightful answer to this question can be obtained from an experiment by Knoll and Arkes (2017). Three different participant groups had to answer a true/false quiz about a race of the MLB season in 2006. Prior to this two groups received a text with information about that race and one group received an irrelevant text. The two groups with the relevant text differed in the instructions they received. One group should try to answer the questions as best they can, the other should answer as if they had not read the text. Then all participants had to take a test on baseball knowledge which served as a proxy for the level of expertise. Even if the participants cannot be considered as classical experts, this experiment shows that as the level of expertise increases, participants become statistically significantly worse at separating their newly acquired knowledge from their previous knowledge. This supports the hypothesis that for experts, due to their greater prior knowledge, the memory distortion level is more affected via the knowledge updating mechanism compared to novices.

Overall, it is difficult to clearly assess the effect of expertise on hindsight bias. Expertise can have an impact on hindsight bias via the detour of overconfidence but can also have a direct influence on the underlying input factors of hindsight bias. Further studies will be necessary to clearly distinguish the different influences and the impact of their effects.

Visualisation Techniques

With the advancement of technology, there are better and better possibilities to reconstruct and visualize past events. Especially in courtrooms this technique is used to simulate traffic accidents. One could assume that this simulation leads to less cognitive distortions, because there is no need to imagine the situation which leaves a lot of room for interpretation but you see it accurately on video. In fact, the opposite is true. In an experiment, Roese and Vohs (2010) compare the strength of the hindsight bias in participants who are shown a traffic accident by means of text and diagrams with those who are shown the same traffic accident on video. The participants who watched the video showed double the amount of hindsight bias. One possible explanation for this could be how people perceive fluency on a meta-cognitive level. Being able to see the entire course of the accident on video makes information processing subjectively easy and the outcome is considered even more inevitable. Looking at the cognitive inputs, there is an additional potential danger that single participants or camera perspectives focus too much on specific details that distort perception. The most intuitive solution would be to show the driving error that caused the accident but not the actual collision itself. If no outcome is shown this should reduce the hindsight bias. However, this idea is strongly discouraged as it leads to the propensity effect; a reversal of hindsight bias. Foresight judgements near to a focal outcome perceive the outcome as more inevitable than hindsight judgements. A possible explanation for this could be that when the video stops an automatic process is triggered in the brain that anticipates and simulates the situation shown until the end. This can lead to the collision being considered inevitable even before it is seen.

Key Takeaways for Risk Leadership

Understanding hindsight bias is important. Kelman et al. (1998) suggest distinguishing between primary, secondary and tertiary bias. Blank et al. (2008) present a division of hindsight bias into the component's memory distortions, foreseeability and necessity, which is more closely related to the input factors of hindsight bias. The cost and consequences of hindsight bias always depend on the specific context in which it is placed. Hindsight bias is deeply rooted in us and can result from various reasons. Therefore, there is no universal solution to reduce or even eliminate hindsight bias, but there are interesting approaches. The consider-the-opposite strategy seems to be most promising if it is adequately adapted to the specific situation. It is conceivable that in some areas a systematic implementation is possible. However, expertise, on its own, does not seem to be a protection against hindsight bias, but there might be a mitigating influence under the right circumstances. The key to success seems to be a high validity environment and continuous feedback.

References

Biais, B., & Weber, M. (2009). Hindsight bias, risk perception, and investment performance. *Management Science, 55*(6), 1018–1029.

Blank, H., Nestler, S., von Collani, G., & Fischer, V. (2008). How many hindsight biases are there? *Cognition, 106*(3), 1408–1440.

Christensen-Szalanski, J. J., & Willham, C. F. (1991). The hindsight bias: A meta-analysis. *Organizational Behavior and Human Decision Processes, 48*(1), 147–168.

Fischhoff, B. (1975). Hindsight is not equal to foresight: The effect of outcome knowledge on judgment under uncertainty. *Journal of Experimental Psychology: Human Perception and Performance, 1*(3), 288–299.

Fischhoff, B., & Beyth, R. (1975). I knew it would happen: Remembered probabilities of once—future things. *Organizational Behavior and Human Performance, 13*(1), 1–16.

Granhag, P. A., Strömwall, L. A., & Allwood, C. M. (2000). Effects of reiteration, hindsight bias, and memory on realism in eyewitness confidence. *Applied Cognitive Psychology, 14*(5), 397420.

Guilbault, R. L., Bryant, F. B., Brockway, J. H., & Posavac, E. J. (2004). A meta-analysis of research on hindsight bias. *Basic and Applied Social Psychology, 26*(2–3), 103–117.

Hawkins, S. A., & Hastie, R. (1990). Hindsight: Biased judgments of past events after the outcomes are known. *Psychological Bulletin, 107*(3), 311.

Kelman, M., Fallas, D., & Folger, H. (1998). Decomposing hindsight bias. *Journal of Risk and Uncertainty, 16*(3), 251–269.

Knoll, M. A., & Arkes, H. R. (2017). The effects of expertise on the hindsight bias. *Journal of Behavioral Decision Making, 30*(2), 389–399.

Nestler, S., Blank, H., & Egloff, B. (2010). Hindsight ≠ hindsight: Experimentally induced dissociations between hindsight components. *Journal of Experimental Psychology: Learning, Memory, and Cognition, 36*(6), 1399.

Pohl, R. F., Bayen, U. J., Arnold, N., Auer, T. S., & Martin, C. (2018). Age differences in processes underlying hindsight bias: A life-span study. *Journal of Cognition and Development, 19*(3), 278–300.

Roese, N. J., & Vohs, K. D. (2010). The visualization trap. *Harvard Business Review, 88*(5), 26.

Roese, N. J., & Vohs, K. D. (2012). Hindsight bias. *Perspectives on Psychological Science, 7*(5), 411–426.

Rogers, K. (2020). Saying he long saw pandemic, trump rewrites history. *New York Times,* March 18th 2020, Section A, 1.

Sanna, L. J., & Schwarz, N. (2003). Debiasing the hindsight bias: The role of accessibility experiences and (mis) attributions. *Journal of Experimental Psychology: Learning, Memory, and Cognition, 39*(3), 287–295.

Shepperd, J., Malone, W., & Sweeny, K. (2008). Exploring causes of the self-serving bias. *Social and Personality Psychology Compass, 2*(2), 895–908.

Slovic, P., & Fischhoff, B. (1977). On the psychology of experimental surprises. *Journal of Experimental Psychology: Human Perception and Performance, 3*(4), 544.

SZ Online. (2020). Beckenbauer zweifelte 1990 nie an WM-Sieg, 8.7.2020, https://www.sueddeutsche.de/sport/fussball-beckenbauer-zweifelte-1990-nie-an-wm-siegdpa.urn-newsml-dpa-com-20090101-200708-99-712174

The 10 Commandments and How We Can Develop Strategic Risk Leadership Competencies

12

The 10 Commandments

After having read through the first eleven chapters, we can now summarize what a risk leader should pay attention to in order to avoid common decision-making biases and make better decisions:

1. Measure risk even if you think you know about it—what is measured and calculated can be optimized!
2. Reference points have significant implications for the way how you evaluate risky opportunitie!
3. Negotiating effectively means being a leader in providing information. Be the first to set an anchor by fixing an acceptable range of possible outcomes for your negotiation!
4. Losses loom psychologically twice as much as gains. Being a risk leader means embracing gains as much as losses. Embrace the risk and think twice!
5. Don't let your emotions overrun your rationality! Avoidance of a risk may be a suboptimal choice!
6. Although we prefer to keep things the way they are, change can be in our best interest. Don't let the status quo fool you!
7. Data analysis provides much better forecasts than human intuition—but if you have no data and need to rely on your intuition your motto should be: Less confidence will generally lead to better results—it pays to be a pessimist!
8. Diverse teams with established rules of communication and cooperation make better decisions!
9. Emotional events often override our rationality. Since low-probability-high-consequence events evoke strong emotional reactions, the actual risk of an event happening may have little weight in the choices you make!
10. Don't believe you are a good predictor. Instead, when a prediction is needed, considering the opposite may be useful!

A. Hofmann, *The Ten Commandments of Risk Leadership*, Future of Business and Finance, https://doi.org/10.1007/978-3-030-88797-1_12

It is noteworthy that the previous chapters mainly discussed biases in decision-making under risk that are a major focus in the business and economics literature. Taking a different perspective, like for instance a neurological one, would result in different underlying reasons for flawed decision-making. The following is an example.

Insights from Behavioral Sciences on Our Decision-Making Processes

Behavioral science offers some fascinating insights on how we can become better decision-makers. Psychologists like Daniel Kahneman, e.g. in his prominent book "*Thinking. Fast and Slow.*", describe our minds of consisting of two systems. They call these systems simply *system 1* and *system 2*. More insightfully, we can refer to the two systems as the intuitive system (system 1) and the reflective system (system 2).[1] While we can say that neither system is better than the other, we need both to be good decision-makers in practice. We use our intuitive system very often during our daily lives when it comes to following our daily routines and fulfilling regular tasks that do not require a lot of thought or calculation. The reflective system, on the other hand, is used when we need to fulfill advanced and complex tasks and calculations that we consciously focus on. This system is slow, logical, and deliberate; it requires effort by using up more energy when a person weighs all the pros and cons of a decision or problem. Note that our brain takes 30% of our energy but only takes up 3% of body weight. The intuitive system is rather automatic and fast thinking, and this is why heuristics or rules of thumb play such a big role in our daily decisions. Almost all behavioral biases stem from this intuitive system's mode of thinking; we are indeed not immune to them even though we may be considered experts in our field.

Neuroscientist Antonio Damasio is interested in the role of emotions in decision-making processes. He studies patients with lesions in their brains. Shouldn't we all follow logic and suppress our emotions in order to make more rational (risk-related) decisions? He found that the biological structure of our decision-making processes is not designed for such an approach. The main case he builds on is a patient named Elliot who had lost his intuitive system (system 1)—that part of his brain was simply gone after a necessary surgery. As a consequence, the patient analyzed everything and could not decide on simple tasks, like what to eat or drink, since there was no emotional trigger to help him decide. Before a tumor destroyed his frontal lobe tissue in the brain, Elliot was a successful businessman and a beloved husband.

After losing his system 1, Elliot's life fell apart: he lost his job (spending too much time on deciding how to organize his work instead of getting the work done), got involved in dubious financial matters resulting in bankruptcy, got divorced, and

[1] The two systems are also sometimes referred to as Intuition (system 1) and Reasoning (system 2).

finally was denied disability assistance due to the fact that no "real disease" he suffered from could be identified. He was obviously very intelligent when tested for IQ, a skilled individual with great mental capabilities, an intact short- and long-term memory, as well as great language skills. His doctors did not know what was wrong with Elliot. Damasio found that the problem was that Elliot could not plan in advance, not even very short periods of time, and that he was remembering and recounting his life with a highly significant level of detachment or complete loss of emotion. For any human, this is a tragedy. In technical terms, what happens is that the decision-making set of available options or alternatives becomes very large without any restrictions or limiting factors or weights assigned to it—the individual cannot assign values or emotional weights to the different available alternatives.[2] The consequence is that when our intuitive system and with it our emotions are impaired, so is our decision-making process. Damasio calls this the *Somatic Marker Hypothesis*. Remember that "soma" means "body" in Greek. In this way, somatic markers represent shortcuts to decision-making by filtering some alternatives out:

> without the filtering provided by emotions and their somatic markers, the data sets for any given decision—whether it's what to get for lunch or whom to marry—would be overwhelming. The working memory can only juggle so many objects at once. To make the right call, you need to feel your way—or at least part of your way—there. (Baer, 2016).

This insight is confirmed in various neuroscientific studies. For instance, as stated in Bechara et al. (2000): Emotions are often discussed in the form of a consequence of a decision (e.g. disappointment or regret experienced after a risky choice) rather than in the form of emotional reactions arising directly from the decision itself. However, following the somatic marker hypothesis, judgements are not only made by assessing severity and probability of outcomes but also in terms of "emotional quality". The researchers confirm this insight by referring to findings where brain lesions of the prefrontal cortex interfere with the normal processing of somatic signals while leaving other cognitive functions mostly unaffected.

Self-Leadership and Habits

Given the insights above, we can conclude that we need our emotional system in order to be good decision makers and leaders in practice. After being educated on decision-making and all the biases, how can we become aware of our biases and develop strategic risk leadership competencies that make us a better leader and decision maker?

As pointed out in Sibony (2019, p.163), paying attention and just trying to become aware of our biases after being educated about them is not likely to produce real results. The reason is a new bias, pointing to the fact that we will indeed

[2] See Appendix 2 on decision theory.

underestimate the general effect of biases on us in particular—called *bias blind spot*. However, if we cannot really improve in dealing with our biases, what can be done? The way to improve our decision-making is to improve the decision-making processes and practices within an organization or human being. The key here is to change the environment instead of changing the decision-makers themselves. This can be done by implementing rules for collaboration—so others can correct biases made by individuals – as wel as by implrementing processes—so groupthink will not be an issue.

Besides understanding all the common biases discussed in this book and working on actively avoiding most of them, our intuitive systems cannot easily be tricked. However, they can be changed and adjusted over time with some effort. In their interesting article, "Habits—A Repeat Performance", Neal et al. (2006) state that "approximately 45% of everyday behaviors tended to be repeated in the same location almost every day"; in other words, 45% of our daily actions are guided by our formed habits. This implies that if leaders are concerned with being the best leader possible, they need to have good practices that account for 45% of their actions.

Charles Duhigg, author of *The Power of Habit*, a book about the science of habit formation in our lives, companies, and societies, describes the process of habit formation citing several laboratory studies using rats and mazes. He states that habits can be formed in such a way that "the rat had internalized how to sprint through the maze to such a degree that it hardly needed to think at all" (Duhigg, 2014, p. 16). The study is a compelling neurological finding and implies that once we internalize activities, meaning forming established individual habits, we hardly think about them and act more unconsciously. The basal ganglia, a small group of structures within our brain, seems responsible for learning and recalling habits, and such habits are stored even while the rest of the brain is asleep. These findings confirm the impression that once we perform a particular habit, we do it unconsciously without thinking about it too much. When applying this concept to leading, we can conclude that the majority of our actions are internalized once habits have been formed. Leaders have good habits in place, which makes it seem they intuitively do the right thing. But maybe the advantage lies exactly here: when we form habits, we need less brainpower to perform a given task. This concept is critical, especially for leaders who have the responsibility to lead a group of people—having access to certain advantageous habits is less demanding for the brain, and the preserved energy can be used for other important issues.

So how long does it take to establish such a habit? A study by Lally et al. (2010) finds that forming a habit and reaching automaticity "ranged from 18 to 254 days; indicating considerable variation in how long it takes people to reach their limit of automaticity and highlighting that it can take a very long time"; this implies that the time it takes to form a habit varies among individuals and requires consistency to internalize a specific action fully. However, the good news is that even after 20 days, you will probably see a difference already.

James Clear, an accomplished researcher of habits and New York Times bestselling author of Atomic Habits, offers the positive news that small habits make a big difference over time. Using a simple compound interest equation, he advocates being 1% better every day will have astonishing long-term effects on your habits. "If you can get 1% better each day for 1 year, you'll end up thirty-seven times better by the time you are done. Conversely, if you get 1% worse each day for 1 year, you will decline nearly down to zero." He describes that small habits are part of a larger system that eventually decides the outcome. We should focus more on the progress than on the result because "ultimately, it is your commitment to the process that will determine your progress" (Clear, 2018, p. 28).

Confidence

Confidence is a powerful trait that goes hand in hand with good leadership. Fortunately, confidence is not a hereditary trait but a skill that can be improved. Even the most successful business leaders can experience feelings of doubt. The response to this feeling is what shapes a leader. Harvard Business Review published an article on the prospects of confidence building in business (Gallo, 2011). There are two key takeaways from this article. First, it's possible to build your confidence. Confidence is just like a muscle, working out and spending time on it will lead to growth. The second takeaway is that people should not be afraid to ask for help. Leaders do not have to operate on an island; there is always room for improvement.

Finally, we can learn from insights derived from studies of organizational scientists like Sunnie Giles, who is also a certified executive coach. She surveyed 195 leaders in 15 countries and over 30 global organizations on their most important leadership competencies. Interestingly, the number one most important competency identified within this survey was the following: a leader "demonstrates strong ethics and provides a sense of safety". This is interesting because it combines the need for leaders to have high ethical and moral standards as well as being able to communicate clear expectations to their environment, which makes employees feel safe so that they can relax and thereby be more socially engaged and ambitious. She points out that it is an important part of leadership to be able to make people feel safe on a deep level."

General Douglas MacArthur (1880–1964), who commanded Allied forces in the southwest Pacific during World War II, is considered one of the most successful military leaders in U.S. history. In a famous quote, he states that

> *"A true leader has the confidence to stand alone, the courage to make tough decisions, and the compassion to listen to the needs of others."— General Douglas MacArthur (Rennie, 2017)*

References

Baer, D. (2016). How only being able to use logic to make decisions destroyed a man's life, *The Cut*, June 14, 2016. https://www.thecut.com/2016/06/how-only-using-logic-destroyed-a-man.html

Clear, J. (2018). *Atomic habits: An easy & proven way to build good habits & break bad ones*. Penguin Publishing Group.

Duhigg, C. (2014). *The power of habit: why we do what we do in life and business*. Random House Trade Paperbacks.

Gallo, A. How to build confidence. *Harvard Business Review*, November 06, 2011. https://hbr.org/2011/04/how-to-build-confidence

Hackston, J. (2017). The Danger of the Overconfident Leader. *The Myers-Briggs Company*, January 06, 2017. https://www.themyersbriggs.com/en-US/Company/News/The-Danger-of-the-Overconfident-Leader

Lally, P., van Jaarsveld, C. H. M., Potts, H. W. W., & Wardle, J. (2010). How are Habits formed: Modelling Habit Formation in the Real World. *European Journal of Social Psychology, 40*(6), 998–1009. https://doi.org/10.1002/ejsp.674

Neal, D. T., Wood, W., & Quinn, J. M. (2006). Habits – A repeat performance. *Current Directions in Psychological Science, 15*(4), 198–202. https://doi.org/10.1111/j.1467-8721.2006.00435.x

Rennie, J. (2019). The four C's of leadership. John S Rennie.com, April 20, 2017. https://jonsrennie.com/2017/06/01/the-four-cs-of-leadership/

Sibony, O. (2019). *You're about to make a terrible mistake! How biases distort decision-making – and what you can do to fight them, Little*. Brown Spark – Hachette Book Group.

Appendix 1: Probability Fundamentals

The Axioms of Probability Theory

There are many situations that are not deterministic or in which the decision-maker does not recognize the underlying mechanism (for instance, look at the price development of a stock at NYSE). The individual possible coincidental events are called *elementary events* (e.g.: rolling a dice has the elementary events ["1", "2" ...., "6"]). The *event space* Θ is the union of all elementary events. Θ covers thus all possible events (E), whereby an event can contain several elementary events (e.g. roll a dice to find an even number). So E is always a subset of Θ. Now let's assign probabilities to these events. This happens by means of axiomatization of probability theory as introduced by Kolmogorov in the 1930s. Note that axioms by definition do not need to be proven: they are assumed to be true.

A function p, which assigns a real number to each event E, is called *probability measure*, and $p(E)$ is called *probability of event E*. Then the following axioms are assumed to hold:

Axiom 1 $0 \leq p(E) \leq 1$. In words a probability is a number between zero and 1.

Axiom 2 $p(\Theta) = 1$. In words the probability of the event space (all events) is 1.

Axiom 3 For all countable events $E_1, E_2, \ldots.$ with $E_i \cap E_j = \varnothing \; \forall \; i \neq j$ (i.e., for all mutually exclusive events), the following holds:

$$p\left(\bigcup_{j=1}^{\infty} E_j\right) = \sum_{i=1}^{\infty} p\left(E_j\right).$$

In words the probability of the union including all mutually exclusive events is equal to the sum of all probabilities.

A. Hofmann, *The Ten Commandments of Risk Leadership*, Future of Business and Finance, https://doi.org/10.1007/978-3-030-88797-1

Probability Interpretations

Mathematically, the probability is defined by the Kolmogorov axioms. A completely different question is the interpretation and measurement of probabilities. Here there is a controversy between different schools that continues to this day. In the literature there are essentially three different interpretations of probability:

1. *Logical (or objective a priori) probabilities*
2. *Frequentistic (or objective a posteriori) probabilities*
3. *Subjective probabilities*

ad (1) This is the idea that certain probabilities can be objectively determined a priori. When a fair coin is tossed, there are two possible outcomes: heads and tails, and thus we can conclude that the likelihood of each coming up is ½ or 50%. Another example is as follows. When a single die is thrown, there are six possible outcomes: 1, 2, 3, 4, 5, 6. As a result, we can conclude that the probability of any one of them is 1/6. However, this interpretation of probability is not very satisfying, since for most problems such objective a priori probabilities do not exist (an exception possibly is gambling). Therefore, this interpretation of probability is hardly used anymore in the social sciences.

ad (2) Frequentists consider probability as a limit value of relative frequencies. Such a conception is intuitively convincing but requires (arbitrary) repeatability of (identical) random experiments. Since this is usually possible in the natural sciences, the frequentistic interpretation of probability prevails there. In the social and economic sciences, however, a repeatability of random experiments is generally not possible. Therefore, an adoption of the frequentistic probability interpretation for economic sciences would imply that for economic questions enormously important random experiments (economic development, sales opportunities for a new product, etc.) cannot be treated in terms of probability theory, since no reasonably interpretable probabilities exist. Therefore, a purely frequency-based interpretation of probabilities is not very satisfying for economic questions.

ad (3) Subjective probabilities stand for credibility numbers, which the decision maker attributes to the occurrence of the individual credibility numbers. They are therefore dependent on the estimations of the decision maker and are not inter-personally comparable, but this also applies—as seen—to the other components of the basic model of decision theory. The subjective concept of probability was first axiomatized by Savage in the 1950s and is compatible with the Kolmogorov axioms above. Since economic decisions under uncertainty depend crucially on how credible individuals consider the occurrence of relevant environmental conditions to be, subjective probabilities are a natural basis of decision theory. However, decision theory takes the frequentist approach into account when individuals modify their subjective probabilities in accordance with Bayes' theorem (see below) when new information becomes available, i.e., they learn from the "objective" data. This means that, where repeated random experiments take place, individuals re-evaluate their prior assessment of the underlying probability distribution and adjust it if necessary.

Basic Rules and Definitions for Calculating Probabilities

Given that probabilities always add up to one, the probability of event A must be equal to one minus the probability of the complementary event *not* A or A', in written form.

$$p(A) = 1 - p(A')$$

Two events E_1 and E_2 are called *(stochastically) independent*, if.

$$p(E_1 \cap E_2) = p(E_1) \cdot p(E_2).$$

Here, the "∩" means "and" in the sense that events E_1 and E_2 occur together. For example, the probability of throwing a "1" and a "2" using two dice is ½ · ½ = ¼.

The *conditional probability* that E_1 occurs given E_2 has already occurred is defined as.

$$p(E_1 | E_2) := \frac{p(E_1 \cap E_2)}{p(E_2)}.$$

The conditional probability indicates the probability of the occurrence of an event E_1, under the condition that an event E_2 occurs. For example, the probability that it will rain the day after tomorrow under the condition that the sun will shine tomorrow. For stochastically *independent events* follows immediately.

$$p(E_1 | E_2) = \frac{p(E_1 \cap E_2)}{p(E_2)} = \frac{p(E_1) \cdot p(E_2)}{p(E_2)} = p(E_1).$$

In other words, for stochastically *independent* events, the probability of occurrence of an event E_1 is independent of the occurrence of the event E_2. Here is an example: the probability of throwing an even number using dice is independent of whether an even number has fallen on the previous roll. The conditional probabilities lead us to the *Law of Total Probability*:

Be E_j, $j = 1,2....$ is a countable family of pairs of disjoint events and let C be an event such that.

$$C \subseteq \bigcup_{j=1}^{\infty} E_j.$$

Then follows

$$p(C) = \sum_{j=1}^{\infty} p(E_j) \cdot p(C | E_j).$$

This means, that the sum of all conditional probabilities for the occurrence of an event C must be equal to the unconditional probability of occurrence of C.

Theorem of Bayes

By defining the conditional and the total probabilities, we can derive the *Theorem of Bayes*, which is extremely important for probability theory. It reads:

$$p\left(E_k \middle| C\right) = \frac{p\left(E_k\right) \cdot p\left(C \middle| E_k\right)}{\sum_{j=1}^{\infty} p\left(E_j\right) \cdot p\left(C \middle| E_j\right)}$$

Here $p(E_k)$ is called "a priori" probability of E_k and $P(E_k/C)$ is called "a posteriori" probability of E_k with knowledge of C. The usefulness of Bayes' Theorem becomes apparent by using it such that with its help, a *probability adjustment* can be made when new information becomes available.

Let's apply the Theorem to some real-world scenarios; I would like to introduce you to two fascinating applications of the Theorem:

The Monty Hall Problem

Let's apply Bayes' Theorem to the Monty Hall Problem in Chap. 1. Let $P(E_k)$ be the unobservable event: "where is the car?" and let C be an ex-post observation: "which door does the quizmaster leave *closed?*". Inserting into the *Theorem of Bayes*:

$$p\left(E_k \middle| C\right) = \frac{p\left(E_k\right) \cdot p\left(C \middle| E_k\right)}{\sum_{j=1}^{\infty} p\left(E_j\right) \cdot p\left(C \middle| E_j\right)}$$

- $P(E_k)$ = probability that the car is behind door k, where k is part of the set {1,2,3}; since there is one car out of three doors, this value is 1/3.
- $P(C)$ = denominator; probability with which a door remains closed after the quiz master has chosen it; since the quizmaster opens one of two closed doors, this value is ½.
- $P(C/E_j)$ = probability with which the quizmaster will keep a door closed if there is a car behind it; since the quizmaster only opens a door with no car behind it, this value is 1.
- $P(E_k/C)$ = probability that there is a car behind the closed door left unopened by the quizmaster. This is the a posteriori probability we are looking for.
  Inserting into the *Theorem of Bayes* now leads to.

$$= \frac{1 \cdot \frac{1}{3}}{\frac{1}{2}} = \frac{2}{3}$$

Inserting the probability values into the theorem reveals that the probability that the car is behind the door left closed by the quizmaster is thus 2/3, whereas it is only 1/3 behind the original door. So, it is clear that if you switch, you double your chances of getting the car. Vos Savant was right. Bayes' Theorem seems complex but it is not really that complicated when you think about it a little further.

Assume that your first choice is Door 1. The situation is as shown in the following table. The chance of gain if you stick with Door 1—and so you do not switch doors after being shown what is behind the other closed door—is only 1/3. If, however, you decide to switch, your chance of gain is 2/3. As a result, by switching, you can double your chance of winning from 1/3 to 2/3.

Example: assume your first choice is Door 1.

Door 1	Door 2	Door 3	*Result: not switch*	*Result: switch*
Car	Goat	Goat	*Car*	*Goat*
Goat	Car	Goat	*Goat*	*Car*
Goat	Goat	Car	*Goat*	*Car*

To illustrate this insight even more, assume that there are one million doors to choose from and assume you choose Door 1. Now you are asked whether you would like to stick to your original choice or whether you would like to switch doors. The moderator, who knows what's behind the doors and who always avoids the one door with the car, opens all doors except door number 666,666. Now you would immediately switch to this door, wouldn't you? This is because you have updated your guess about where the car might be after learning about the other doors with goats behind them.

The Monty Hall Problem is not a multiplayer game but a game against nature (i.e. against the probability distribution of cars and goats behind doors). The quizmaster is not a decision maker who has to decide between two doors based on his own preferences, but he acts like an executing algorithm by always opening that door where there is certainly no car. Now—it seems easy to understand why this is about probability updating, and maybe you can see why people tend to have problems with it.

The Paradox of the False Positives

This more serious application of Bayes' Theorem introduces you to the wide world of testing. Assume we know that a newly discovered rare but nasty disease (whose treatment has very serious side effects and a chance of death) infects one out of every thousand people in a given population. There is a *pretty good*—but not perfect—test available to find out whether a person has the disease. If a person has the disease, then the test comes back positive in 99% of the time; on the other hand, the test unfortunately also produces some false positives. About 2% of uninfected individuals also test positive. Now you just found out that your test was positive. Instead of freaking out and getting emotional ("why me???"), let's try to stay rational and find out what the chances really are that you do have the disease.

We define two events: A: "patient has the disease", and B: "patient tests positive". Then, we know that.

- $p(A) = 0.001$ (one person in 1000 has the disease)
- $p(B/A) = 0.99$ (probability of a positive test, given infection, is 0.99)
- $p(B/A') = 0.02$ (probability of a false positive test, given no infection, is 0.02) and we are looking for
- $p(A/B) =$ what?? (probability of having the disease)

From above, we know that the conditional probability we are looking for is given by

$$p(A/B) = \frac{p(A \cap B)}{p(B)} = \frac{0.00099}{0.02097} = \mathbf{0.0472}$$

where the numerator above is from

$$p(A \cap B) = p(B/A) \cdot p(A) = 0.99 \cdot 0.001 = 0.00099$$

and the denominator is from

$$p(B) = p(B \cap A) + p(B \cap A'),$$

where

$$p(B \cap A') = p(B/A') \cdot p(A') = 0.02 \cdot (1 - 0.001) = 0.01998$$

and so

$$p(B) = p(B \cap A) + p(B \cap A') = 0.00099 + 0.01998 = 0.02097.$$

As a result, *despite the high accuracy of the test*, we find that **less than 5%** of those who test positive actually have the disease!!

This result is often referred to as the *Paradox of the False Positives*. The test is thus not very helpful to really confirm your having the disease. The following table illustrates what happens in a group of 1000 patients undergoing testing, on average. You can see that 21 patients test positive while *only one* of them actually has the disease; 20 false positives are generated from the much larger uninfected group of patients being tested.

	Disease	*No disease*	
Tests positive	1	20	21
Tests negative	0	979	979
	1	999	1000

The test is not very helpful but does provide some information: you can update your knowledge by concluding that with a positive test result, your chance of having the disease increased from 1 in 1000 up to 1 in 21. The educated you may stop worrying too much and instead you may decide on getting more information on whether you have the disease before starting treatment. However, a patient not educated about conditional probabilities may have a few sleepless nights and the medical industry may earn a fortune by convincing him or her to undergo a costly preventative treatment for a disease he or she doesn't have.

Appendix 2: Decision Theory Fundamentals

What Is Decision Theory?

Decision theory can be broken down into two subfields: *normative* decision theory, which studies the optimal decisions for an individual decision-maker under constraints and assumptions, and *descriptive* decision theory, which studies how agents actually make decisions in practice. In this way, normative decision theory answers the question "how would the optimal decisions (theoretically) look like?—how should the world be doing?", while descriptive decision theory answers the question "how do individuals make their decisions in practice?—how is the world doing?". Decision theory is closely related to game theory, another normative science, and is more interdisciplinary than game theory. Decision-making is studied not only by economists, but also by data scientists, psychologists, political and other social scientists, as well as philosophers.

The Basic Model

The basic model of decision theory depicts the decision-making process of a *Homo Oeconomicus*. This theoretical rational human being aims to maximize economic profit and has complete knowledge about the environment; he calculates costs and benefits; he lacks passion or altruism or any emotion. The model neglects moral values (Brzezicka & Wiśniewski, 2014).

A basic model of decision theory allows for a basic structure of arbitrary decision problems under risk. The model has the following ingredients:

First, a space of alternatives (A), consisting of the set of all available alternatives (a, a ε A) that the individual considers possible. Any rational individual tries to make the best of his or her situation, taking into account the restrictions that apply. It should be clear that these restrictions differ between individuals. For example, many individuals will not seriously consider the alternative "acquisition of a brownstone in Brooklyn Heights" when deciding on suitable living space, while it may be relevant for well-heeled contemporaries. Note that different information levels can lead to different restrictions: To reduce his tax burden, a tax consultant considers

A. Hofmann, *The Ten Commandments of Risk Leadership*, Future of Business and Finance, https://doi.org/10.1007/978-3-030-88797-1

options for action that other individuals would not even think of. For these individuals, the alternative action of "consulting a tax advisor" could be relevant. We can therefore see that the definition of the action area is only subjectively possible. Further, the individual action alternatives must exclude themselves mutually.

Second, a set of states (θ, $\theta \varepsilon \Theta$), consisting of all environmental states considered possible by the decision-maker and relevant for the decision (θ). By environmental conditions we understand mutually excluding constellations of expressions of the decision-relevant data, of which the decision-maker believes that exactly one of them will occur. The set of environmental conditions can be both finite and infinite. Both the definition of the decision-relevant data themselves and their possible characteristics lie in the subjective discretion of the decision maker. It is therefore easily possible that different decision-makers make a different definition of the relevant environmental conditions with one and the same decision problem. As pointed out in Chap. 1, decision models are often subdivided according to the probability premises contained in them. If a decision-maker is able to assign probabilities to the states considered by him as relevant for his decision, then we speak of *decisions under risk*. In contrast, *decisions under uncertainty* in the narrower sense describe situations in which the decision-maker has no idea about the probabilities of the states or conditions he or she is looking at.

Third, a set of results (*X*), consisting of all possible results (x, $x \varepsilon X$). The set X of all possible consequences of action. Now there is still such an abundance of different measures to choose from for the description of consequences of action, even if they are restricted to objectively measurable circumstances, that every clear representation of expected results of action requires a restriction to certain characteristics. Which these characteristics are, cannot be determined generally with the requirement on intersubjective validity, but depends on the individual goal conceptions of the decision maker. So that a decision-maker can compare the consequences of actions on the basis of his objectives, the selection of characteristics should therefore be determined in such a way that the results take into account all relevant aspects of the objectives aimed at by the decision maker. It must be presupposed that the decision-maker has a weak order on X. Under these conditions, only the probability distribution of results is relevant for the decision.

Fourth, a function $g : A \times \Theta \rightarrow X$ that uniquely assigns a result $x \in X$ to each pair (a,θ) with $a \in A$, $\theta \in \Theta$ such that $x = g(a, \theta)$. The requirement that the meeting of a handling possibility and an environmental condition leads to a clear result can be fulfilled by a suitable choice of the condition roughness in principle always. If, for example, a result of the first formulation of a decision model is not clearly determined by an alternative action and an environmental condition, this problem can be eliminated by a further differentiation of the state space.

The basic model of decision theory is now characterized and illustrated below.

	θ_1	θ_2	...	θ_j	...	θ_n
a_1	x_{11}	x_{12}	...	x_{1j}	...	x_{1n}
a_2	x_{21}	x_{22}	...	x_{2j}	...	x_{2n}
...	...	...	...	...	...	...
a_m	x_{m1}	x_{m2}	...	x_{mj}	...	x_{mn}

Dominance Principles

There are two basic dominance principles that can help decision-makers achieve at least an idea of which alternatives should *not* be chosen. These principles are *statewise dominance* and *stochastic dominance*. They are defined as follows.

Statewise Dominance Principle

The principle of statewise dominance, also referred to as *state-by-state dominance*, is defined as follows:

An alternative a_1 dominates an alternative a_2 if a_1 does not lead to a worse result in any state but leads to a better result than a_2 in at least one state. Then, we can more formally say that a1 is preferred to a_2 if and only if.

$$x_{1_j} \geq x_{2_j} \quad \forall j \text{ and } \exists j : x_{1_j} > x_{2_j}$$

In other words, an alternative A is called statewise dominant over an alternative B if and only if A gives at least as good a result in every state (every possible set of outcomes), and a strictly better result in at least one state.

This rule is immediately understandable and can hardly be argued with from a viewpoint of a person who prefers more to less. However, according to this easy criterion of state dominance, oftentimes no optimal alternative can be determined, but usually only some possibilities of action can be excluded from further consideration and no final decision can be made. Consider the following example:

	θ_1 $p(\theta_1) = 0.4$	θ_2 $p(\theta_2) = 0.4$	θ_3 $p(\theta_3) = 0.2$
a_1	10	5	10
a_2	10	10	10
a_3	0	0	11

An individual confronted with the decision situation depicted in the table cannot find an overall optimal alternative. The principle of state dominance helps the individual a little bit since a_1 is dominated by a_2, but the criterion cannot decide between a_2 and a_3—it does not help out here.

The following principle of probability dominance can help in such situations by making weaker demands on a dominance relationship than state dominance. It is based on the idea that, at the end of the day, probability distributions of results are important, and so it is not important that one alternative is at least as good as another alternative for each individual environmental state.

(First-Order) Stochastic Dominance Principle

The principle of statewise dominance is a special case of the (first-order) stochastic dominance principle. The principle of stochastic dominance is defined as follows. *An alternative a_1 has first-order stochastic dominance over random variable a_2 if for any outcome x, a_1 gives at least as high a probability of receiving at least x as does a_2, and for some x, a_1 gives a higher probability of receiving at least x.* In notation form,

$$1 - F_1(x) \geq 1 - F_2(x) \forall x \in X \text{ and } \exists \hat{x} \in R : 1 - F_1(\hat{x}) > 1 - F_2(\hat{x})$$

	θ_1 $p(\theta_1) = 0.4$	θ_2 $p(\theta_2) = 0.4$	θ_3 $p(\theta_3) = 0.2$
a_1	10	20	10
a_2	20	10	20
a_3	0	0	25

We can see that a_2 dominates a_1, while there is no dominance relationship between a_2 and a_3. Stochastic dominance is a very plausible concept (i.e., why should a decision-maker prefer a_1 if he considers alternatives 1 and 2 equally probable?). Similar to the principle above, using the principle of stochastic dominance, often only a preselection of alternatives can often be made, even if it is more comprehensive than with state dominance; this is because each state dominance represents at the same time a stochastic dominance, while this is not the case vice versa.

The stochastic dominance principle can be illustrated graphically. An alternative a_1 dominates an alternative a_2 according to this principle, if and only if the distribution function of the results $F_1(x)$ is nowhere above and at least in one place really below the distribution function of the results of the alter-native $F_2(x)$. Graphically, the principle is equivalent to saying that for all x: $F_1(x) \leq F_2(x)$.

The importance of the dominance principles can be seen in the fact that they serve as a yardstick for other decision criteria. Every criterion that clearly selects an alternative should at least guarantee that the selected alternative is not dominated according to the principles above.

Classical Principles of Decision Theory

Classical decision rules deal with the question which alternative a decision-maker should take given all the options available to him. Thus, it is no longer a matter of a preselection, as in the case of the dominance principles, in which alternatives that are obviously unsuitable are eliminated without specifying the preferences of the decision-maker in more detail. Rather, the preferences of the decision-makers should be specified and then the optimal alternative for action should be determined. With the classical decision principles, the preference function is derived from one or more key ingredients of the probability distributions of alternatives. We will introduce two classical decision criteria here: namely the expected value rule or μ-principle and the expected value-variance rule or μ-σ-principle.

The Mean-Principle (μ-Principle)

In the world of the μ-principle, the probability distributions of results are evaluated according to their expected values. The mean is the expected value of a probability distribution and it can help an individual to choose between different risky alternatives. The alternative action with the highest expected value is selected. The expected value of a discrete probability distribution $\tilde{X}$ is defined as:

$$\mu_{\tilde{X}} = \sum_{j=1}^{n} x_j \cdot p_j$$

	θ_1 $p(\theta_1) = 0.4$	θ_2 $p(\theta_2) = 0.4$	θ_3 $p(\theta_3) = 0.2$	μ
a_1	10	20	10	14
a_2	20	10	20	16
a_3	0	0	25	5

Alternative 2 has the highest expected value and is selected according to the μ-principle. Even if the criterion in the above example leads to a very rational behavior, it only represents rational behavior to a very limited extent, since it only considers the first moment of the probability distribution of results. The scatter of the results is not considered. For example, most decision-makers, if they were asked to make a choice, would prefer rather a million dollars with a 50%-chance over 2 million dollars and 0 otherwise, although they would have to be indifferent after the μ-criterion. This weakness of the *μ-criterion* is at least somewhat solved by the following, more sophisticated rule.

The Mean-Variance-Principle (μ-σ-Principle)

Expected value already has been used as a simple decision principle. Its main drawback is that it ignores the riskiness of different alternatives, as dramatically illustrated by the St. Petersburg paradox. As a consequence, it seems reasonable to consider not only the expected value of a probability distribution, but also take into account variability of outcomes in the form of the variance .According to the μ-σ-principle (also often referred to as simply mean-variance principle), variance is also considered as a second criterion in addition to the expected value. The variance is defined for discrete distributions as:

$$\sigma^2\left(\tilde{X}\right) = \sum_{j=1}^{n}\left(x_j - \mu_{\tilde{X}}\right)^2 \cdot p_j$$

Occasionally, the standard deviation (σ), the square root of the variance, is also used instead of the variance. The μ-σ-principle becomes a decision rule once the exact functional relationship between expected value and variance is specified. This relationship will depend on the risk preferences of the decision-makers. A concrete decision rule could be, for example "choose the alternative that maximizes the following preference function.

$$\Phi\left(\mu,\sigma\right) = \mu - 0{,}05\sigma^2$$

As a result, a decision principle only defines, which arguments appear in the preference function. As long as there is a functional relation between the arguments, we can call this a decision rule or decision principle. As an example, consider the following situation:

	θ_1 $p(\theta_1) = 0.4$	θ_2 $p(\theta_2) = 0.4$	θ_3 $p(\theta_3) = 0.2$	μ	σ^2	$\mu - 0.05\sigma^2$
a_1	5	5	5	5	0	5
a_2	20	0	0	8	96	3,2
a_3	0	0	25	5	100	0

Although alternative 2 has the highest expected value, alternative 1 is chosen due to the high dispersion of results in alternative 2. The μ-σ-principle takes different risk preferences of the decision-maker into account. It is therefore much more variable than the μ-principle; however, it is important to note that the μ-σ-principle only takes into account limited information about the probability distribution. In other words, a probability distribution usually has more than two parameters. Two probability distributions can have the same expected value and variance but an investor would strictly prefer one over the other—the one with more probability mass on higher outcomes.

Despite this criticism, both principles enjoy great popularity in the economics and decision theoretical literature—maybe because they are so easy to handle. For instance, as pointed out above, the μ-σ-principle is applied throughout modern capital market theory, and now you may be able to criticize this theory.

Appendix 3: Risk Aversion and Expected Utility Fundamentals

Expected Utility Theory and Risk Aversion

Remember that while the outcomes of choosing between risky alternatives tend to be objective, their resulting utility is rather subjective and specific to each individual, depending upon individual risk preferences. The expected-utility principle, despite often referred to as the *Bernoulli principle*, was developed by John von Neumann and Oskar Morgenstern (1944) and has proved to be a powerful technique for analyzing choices under risk. The Bernoulli principle is an axiomatically based decision criterion. It is based on a set of formal axioms, and we will see that it can be used to provide some very important preliminary insights into risk-management problems. Bernoulli arrived at the following decision principle for risky outcomes called.

Bernoulli Principle. *An individual should choose the alternative that maximizes the expected value of utility over all states of the world.*

Formally, for the discrete case, the Bernoulli principle is therefore.

$$E\left[u\left(\tilde{X}\right)\right]=\sum_{j=1}^{n}u\left(x_j\right)\cdot p_j \rightarrow \max$$

where p_j = *probability of outcome* x_j and $u(x_j)$ = *utility value of outcome* x_j.

Under this principle, the possible outcomes are weighted according to their respective probabilities and according to the utility scale of the individual. The substitution of outcomes measured in utility terms for money outcomes ensures that individual risk preferences can be impressed on the decision process. Clearly, a higher level of wealth should induce a higher level of utility. Thus, the utility function is increasing in wealth W. In particular, it is generally not only increasing but also concave in W.[1] When an individual's utility function is concave in W, it reflects

[1] A twice-differentiable function is concave if and only if its second derivative is negative, i.e., marginal utility $U'(W)$ is decreasing in W.

A. Hofmann, *The Ten Commandments of Risk Leadership*, Future of Business and Finance, https://doi.org/10.1007/978-3-030-88797-1

risk aversion. This is because the individual prefers receiving the expected value of a lottery with certainty, rather than the lottery itself. Risk aversion is important in order to explain decision making under risk. It is also the most common argument for explaining insurance demand. We can define risk aversion as follows.

Risk Aversion. *A risk-averse individual at any level of wealth dislikes every lottery with an expected payoff of equal to zero. Formally, for any wealth level W and any lottery* $\tilde{X}$, *with* $E(\tilde{X})=0$, $EU\left(W+\tilde{X}\right)\leq U\left(W\right)$.[2]

The above definition states that a risk-averse individual dislikes zero-mean risks. Furthermore, since any lottery $\tilde{X}$ with a non-zero expected payoff can be decomposed into its expected payoff $E\tilde{X}$ and a zero-mean lottery $\tilde{X}-E\tilde{X}$, we may generally say that an individual is *risk-averse whenever he prefers receiving the expected value of a lottery with certainty, rather than the lottery itself.* Hence, for a risk-averse expected-utility maximizer with concave utility function $U(\cdot)$, for any initial wealth W and any lottery $\tilde{X}$, we must have

$$EU\left(W+\tilde{X}\right)\leq U\left(W+E\left(\tilde{X}\right)\right).$$

Utility Function under Risk Aversion. *An individual with utility function* $U(\cdot)$ *is risk-averse, i.e., the inequality above holds for all W and* $\tilde{X}$, *if and only if* $U(\cdot)$ *is concave.*[3]

If the utility function is linear or convex, an individual is said to be risk-neutral or risk-loving, respectively. Consequently, we find that for a very small level of risk, individual behavior towards risk approaches risk neutrality.

Certainty Equivalent and Risk Premium

Risk aversion tends to vary by age and gender. As demonstrated by Riley and Chow (1992), risk aversion first decreases with age and then increases after the age of 65, when individuals enter retirement. Similarly, Halek and Eisenhauer (2001) discuss a negative relationship between relative risk aversion and age, sharply increasing after the age of 65. Interestingly, they find that at the margin, education increases an individual's aversion to pure risk but also increases the willingness to accept a speculative risk. They also find that women tend to be more risk-averse than men, in particular when it comes to financial investments. Since individuals generally differ in their preferences towards risks, even a risk-averse individual might not want to purchase insurance if the price of insurance is "too high" . It seems therefore useful to determine the optimal trade-off between the expected utility gain of having

[2] See Eeckhoudt et al. (2005), Definition 1.1, p. 7. Observe that the concept of risk-aversion follows directly from Jensen's inequality stating that for any real-valued function $f(\cdot)$, we must have $Ef\left(\tilde{X}\right)$ is smaller than $f\left(E\tilde{X}\right)$ for any random variable $\tilde{X}$, if and only if $f(\cdot)$ is concave. In other words, any arc linking two points on curve U must lie below the curve.

[3] See Eeckhoudt et al. (2005), Proposition 1.2, p.8.

insurance and the degree of risk without it. A common way to measure the individual degree of risk aversion is to ask how much an individual with utility function $U(\cdot)$ is ready to pay to get rid of a zero-mean risk $\tilde{X}$. The outcome is referred to as the *risk premium r*, defined by Pratt (1964), via the equation

$$EU\left(W+\tilde{X}\right)=U\left(W-r\right).$$

To eliminate all riskiness, the individual is willing to pay a nonrandom cost that exceeds expected loss by an amount not higher than the *risk premium r*. In this way, *r* denotes the maximum an individual is willing to pay to securely receive the expected value of the risk $\tilde{X}$ instead of being exposed to the risk $\tilde{X}$ itself. The risk premium is positive for any concave utility function. It is negative in case of a convex utility function and it is zero in case of linear utility.

In analogy, we may define the *certainty equivalent* of the risk $\tilde{X}$ as the payoff *e* that an individual would have to receive to become indifferent between that payoff and the risk $\tilde{X}$. Hence, *e* represents the certain increase in wealth that has the same effect on individual welfare as being exposed to risk $\tilde{X}$, i.e.,

$$EU\left(W+\tilde{X}\right)=U\left(W+e\right).$$

When $\tilde{X}$ has a zero mean, the certainty equivalent *e* of $\tilde{X}$ is equal to minus its risk premium *r*. As an example, consider facing a lottery where you can win \$100 with probability 0.5 or nothing at all. Assume you are *risk-averse* with utility function $U(x) = x^{0.5}$. The situation is depicted graphically below. The expected value here is \$50. The certainty equivalent is found by calculating

$$e=u^{-1}\left\{0.5U\left(100\right)+0.5U\left(0\right)\right\}=5^2=25.$$

and the risk premium is then $r = 50–25 = 25$.

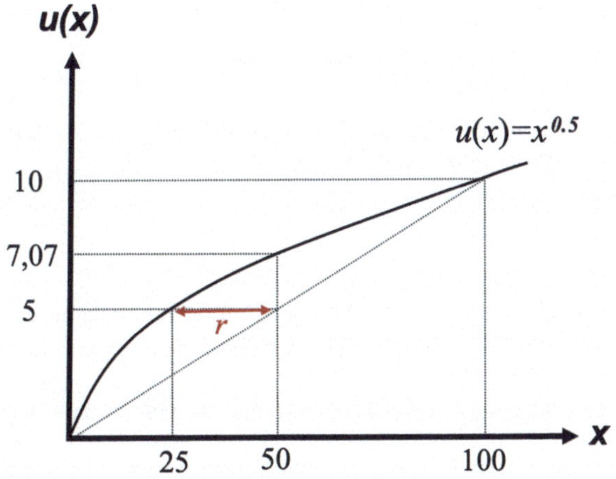

The Arrow-Pratt Coefficients of Risk Aversion

How can we measure risk aversion? Since the risk premium is generally a complex function of initial wealth, the utility function and the risk $\tilde{X}$, it seems convenient to estimate r by considering *small risks*. By using a second-order and a first-order Taylor approximation for the left-hand side and the right-hand side of Pratt's equation, we obtain[4]

$$r \simeq \frac{1}{2}\sigma^2 A(W)$$

where $A(W)$ is defined as

$$A(W) = \frac{-U''(W)}{U'(W)}$$

which is positive under risk aversion, zero and negative for a risk-neutral and a risk-loving individual, respectively. $A(W)$ is known as the *Arrow-Pratt approximation*. It has been developed independently by Arrow (1965) and Pratt (1964). It measures the degree of concavity of the utility function. It is therefore generally referred to as the degree of *absolute risk aversion* of an individual.[5] An individual with a larger absolute risk aversion $A(W)$ would be more reluctant to accept small risks. Hence, when we constrain ourselves to small risks, we can derive that if two individuals have the same initial wealth W, individual 1 with utility function U_1 is more risk-averse than individual 2 with utility function U_2 whenever

$$A_1(W) \geq A_2(W)$$

for all W. As shown by Pratt (1964), we may extend our analysis to any risk, not only to small risks, and the following conditions are equivalent:

1. *Individual 1 is more risk-averse than individual 2, i.e. the risk premium r of any risk is larger for individual 1 than for individual 2.*
2. *For all W, $A_1(W) \geq A_2(W)$.*
3. *Function U_1 is a concave transformation of function U_2: there exists $\phi(\cdot)$ with $\phi' > 0$ and $\phi'' \leq 0$ such that $U_1(W) = \phi(U_2(W))$ for all W.*[6]

[4]The left-hand side of becomes $U(W - r) \simeq U(W) - rU'(W)$ and the right-hand side $EU\left(W + \tilde{X}\right) \simeq E\left[U(W) + U'(W)X + 0.5\tilde{X}^2U''(W)\right] = U(W) + 0, 5\sigma^2 U''(W)$, respectively, where $\sigma^2 = E\tilde{X}^2$ indicates the variance of the lottery $\tilde{X}$.

[5]Given that the index of *absolute risk aversion* $A(W)$ is measured in monetary units, it is sometimes useful to measure sensitivity in a more general way. Thus, we may define the index of *relative risk aversion* $R(W)$ of an individual as $R(W) = -WU''(W)/U'(W)$. It measures the rate at which marginal utility decreases when wealth increases by one percent, i.e., the wealth-elasticity of marginal utility.

[6]See Eeckhoudt et al. (2005), Proposition 1.5, p.14.

Hence, in order to ensure that a change in the utility function makes an individual indeed more reluctant to accept risks, while it is sufficient to determine the degree of concavity of the utility function *locally* at a current wealth level W in case of small risks, the degree of concavity of the utility function must be increased at *all* wealth levels in the case of large risks.

If the Arrow-Pratt measure of local absolute risk aversion $A(W)$ is decreasing in wealth, preferences are said to exhibit decreasing absolute risk aversion (DARA). Similarly, we define constant absolute risk aversion (CARA) and increasing absolute risk aversion (IARA). While the case of CARA is often used as a base case (since these preferences eliminate any wealth effect), a more common and realistic assumption is DARA, which implies that insurance is an inferior good. That is, the demand for insurance decreases when wealth increases.

By keeping in mind the definition of risk aversion above, let us suppose a risk-averse individual may find an insurance company that offers full insurance coverage at an actuarially *fair* price of $E\tilde{X}$. He will indeed be better off by purchasing the insurance policy than by being exposed to the risk of the lottery, due to his risk aversion. Indeed, individual welfare is improved by introducing "fair insurance".

Appendix 4: Game Theory Fundamentals

What is Game Theory?

Game theory is used to analyze decision problems involving multiple actors with different objectives. For this reason, game theory can also be referred to as "interactive decision theory". The interactive decision problem consists of the fact that the result of one's own actions here depends on the actions of others. The concept of a "game" refers to economic and social conflict situations of various kinds. Game theory can be described as the formal modeling of interpersonal conflicts of interest. Within economic theory, the importance of game theory has increased rapidly over the last 30 years. Today, hardly any modern microeconomic textbook lacks a section on game theory, and entire subdisciplines, such as industrial economics, are now dominated by game-theoretic methods. We discuss non-cooperative games here. This means that we are dealing with situations in which cooperation between players is either not possible or players cannot make any binding agreements. In contrast to non-cooperative games, cooperative games deal with groups of players and subsets of individuals who are able to achieve certain outcomes through binding cooperative agreements or contracts that can be enforced.

Basic Assumptions or "Rules" of a Game

For a game, we need at least two decision-makers, whom we call "players", and some basic rules. We assume that the rules of the game are common knowledge to all players. In addition, players have perfect recall of all their moves (their own and those of their opponents) at any time during the game. A game can then be completely described by:

1. the set of players $N = \{1, \ldots, n\}$
2. the strategy space $S = \{S_1 \times S_2 \times \ldots \times S_n\}$, which is the Cartesian product of the strategy sets of the individual players. S is the set of all possible strategy combinations, $s = (s_1, s_2, \ldots, s_n)$, where in each case a permissible strategy of player i is given by $s_i \in S_i$.
3. A set of payoff or utility functions of the players $u = \{u_1(\cdot), u_2(\cdot), \ldots, u_n(\cdot)\}$.

A. Hofmann, *The Ten Commandments of Risk Leadership*, Future of Business and Finance, https://doi.org/10.1007/978-3-030-88797-1

The game is common knowledge to all players. In principle, random moves (so-called moves of "nature") can also occur. In some situations, players may randomize, i.e., they choose their actions with a given probability (we refer to these games as games in mixed strategies) and the players' payoffs will be random variables.

The Normal Form of a Game

The normal form is the usual representation for a static game. A game is called "static" if the players decide on their move only once and simultaneously. This means that the players do not receive any information during the game, for example about the decisions of the opponents. In the normal form, the results of all possible strategy combinations are displayed in a table (matrix). The strategies of player 1 are usually shown in the rows and those of player 2 in the columns. In the result vectors, the first element denotes the payoff for player 1 and the second element denotes the payoff for player 2. Here is an example:

	b_1	b_2
a_1	(10,0)	(5,2)
a_2	(10,11)	(2,0)

If both players choose their first strategy, player 1 receives a payout of 10 and player 2 receives a payout of 0. If both players choose their second strategy, player 1 receives a payout of 2 and player 2 receives a payout of 0

The Extensive Form of a Game

The extensive form is the natural representation form for dynamic games. On the one hand, a dynamic game exists when the moves are sequential and at least one player can determine his moves knowing the moves of an opponent. A dynamic game is also present, on the other hand, when a game is repeated several times and the players can observe the results of the previous games. The structure of such games is mostly captured with the help of a game tree and this is called extensive form. As an example of the extensive form, please see the game below. This is a static game, but of course static games can also be captured in the extensive form, just as dynamic games can also be represented by the normal form. However, we will see that it is more convenient to represent static games by the normal form and dynamic games by the extensive form.

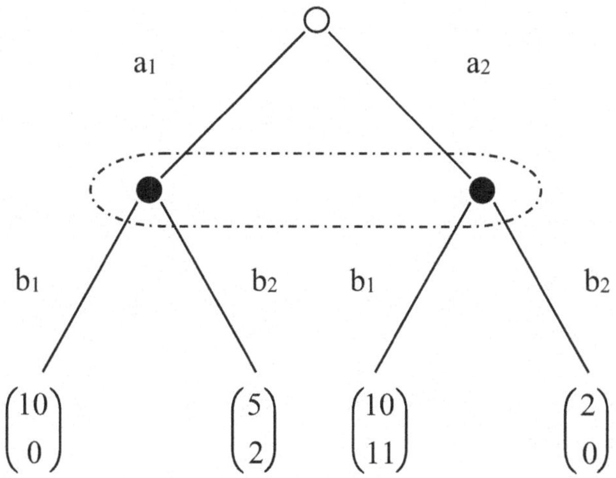

First the decision of player 1 and then that of player 2 is shown. Our example is a static game. This means that the players decide simultaneously or, more precisely, that player 2 does not know which move player 1 has chosen (before) when making his decision. This is denoted in the extensive form by an information set. The dashed line means that player 2 does not know at which of the two decision nodes he is located.

Information Set. *A player's Virgil M. Schwarm Associate Professor of Finance and Investments information set H is a set of decision nodes such that 1) the player has a move at each decision node of the information set, and 2) if one of several decision nodes of the information set is reached during the game, the player does not know which of the decision nodes has (not) been reached.*

While the normal form is clearer in static games, the extensive form is much more practical in dynamic games. To illustrate this, we modify example 1 in such a way that first player 1 executes his move. Player 2 can observe him and then decide to make his own move. The information sets of player 2 are now one-element because he knows at which decision node he is. This can be seen in the extensive form by the fact that the dashed line is omitted.

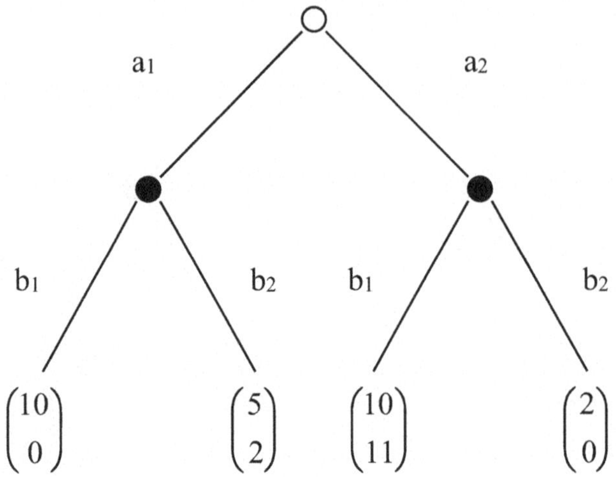

A game in which all previous moves are known to each player at the time of his decision is called a *game with perfect information*. If, on the other hand, at least one player does not know a previous move at the time of his decision, it is called a *game with imperfect information*. In principle, dynamic games can also be represented in the normal form. However, it should be noted that player 2 has much more possibilities to act, since he can make his decision dependent on the decision of player 1. Therefore, for the representation in normal form, we first have to introduce the notion of strategy.

Strategy. *A strategy is a complete conditional behavioral instruction that determines ex ante what actions a player will take during the course of a game.*

Thus, a strategy is an "if-then" instruction by which a player determines ex ante how to respond to certain information he receives during the game. If a player does not receive any information during a game, and if it is only his turn once, the move and the strategy are identical. In dynamic games, on the other hand, a strategy is more comprehensive because it involves a complete plan of behavior. Thus, in our example 1, player B has the following four strategies:

- $\mathbf{b_A}$: If a_1, then b_1; if a_2, then b_1
- $\mathbf{b_B}$: If a_1, then b_1; if a_2, then b_2
- $\mathbf{b_C}$: If a_1, then b_2; if a_2, then b_1
- $\mathbf{b_D}$: If a_1, then b_2; if a_2, then b_2

The above game can then be written in its normal form as follows:

	b_A	b_B	b_C	b_D
a_1	(10,0)	(10,0)	(5,2)	(5,2)
a_2	(10,11)	(2,0)	(10,11)	(2,0)

In this example, the normal form is still relatively simple. This changes drastically as soon as the players have more options, since the number of strategies of the second player is the square of the options available to the players A and B. For example, in a dynamic game, if both players have three moves each, the normal form of the game is a 3x27 matrix

A Famous Game: The Prisoner's Dilemma

Let's start with a classic among all games, the so-called *Prisoner's Dilemma.* This game can be used as a model for many real-world situations involving cooperative behavior in practice. The characteristic feature of the game is that if the players behave in a rational way, the result is unfavorable for both participants. In other words, two completely rational individuals will not cooperate in such a situation, even though it appears to be in their best interests to do so. In its original version, the Prisoner's Dilemma describes the situation of two members of a criminal gang who are suspected of a crime; they are hold in solitary confinement with no means of communicating with the other. Since the police do not have sufficient evidence, they rely on a confession from one of the two guys. They can either confess to the crime or deny it. Their problem now is that their punishment depends not only on their own testimony, but also on the testimony of their colleague.

	Stay silent (b_1)	Betray (b_2)
Stay silent (a_1)	(−5,−5)	(−15,0)
Betray (a_2)	(0,−15)	(−10,−10)

While prosecutors lack sufficient evidence to convict both criminals on the principal charge, they do have enough to convict them on a lesser charge. They offer each prisoner a bargain. Possible strategies are either to betray the other by testifying that the other committed the crime, or to implicitly cooperate with the other by remaining silent to the police. Calling the criminals A and B, respectively, we can describe the possible outcomes of the game as follows:

1. If A and B each betray the other, each of them serves 10 years in prison.
2. If A betrays B but B stays silent, A will be set free and B will serve 15 years in prison.
3. If A stays silent but B betrays A, A will serve 15 years in prison and B will be set free.
4. If both A and B stay silent, both of them will serve only 5 years in prison (the lesser charge).

The police are clever to put both criminals into this situation, since it seems a solution to the game is as follows: Since betraying the other offers a lower sentence than cooperating, assuming purely rational self-interested criminals, the game will end in both betraying each other.

Equilibrium in Dominant Strategies

Let's illustrate the famous *Prisoner's Dilemma* by adding more economic relevance for corporate managers. Assume a competitive situation for duopolists. To simplify, we assume that the two suppliers can only choose between two strategies, a *high price* (a1 and b1, respectively) and a *low price* (a2 and b2, respectively). If both take a high price (a1, b1), the market is divided and both make a profit of 10. If both take a low price (a2, b2), the market is also divided and both make a profit of 5. If one supplier chooses a low price while the other chooses a high price (a1, b2) or (a2, b1), he can attract higher demand and make a profit of 15, while the competitor's profit is zero.

	High price (b_1)	Low price (b_2)
High price (a_1)	(10,10)	(0,15)
Low price (a_2)	(15,0)	(5,5)

How can we solve this game? The outcome for each player depends on the action chosen by the other player. One could now be tempted to assign probabilities to these actions—analogous to the treatment of risk situations—and then make the optimal decision according to the preferences of the players. However, such an approach does not make sense, since the individual players do not act randomly but strategically, i.e., to their advantage. Therefore, a game solution must in principle take into account the decision situation of the opponents. In this special case, however, the situation is much simpler. To see this, let us consider the situation of player 1 a little more closely. With a low price (a2), he gets 15 if 2 demands a high price (b1) and 5 if B decides for the low price (b2). If, on the other hand, player 1 asks for a high price (a1), he receives 10 and 0 if 2 asks for a high price (b1) and a low price (b2), respectively. This means that for every decision made by B, it is better for A to choose the low price

Player 2's situation is completely equivalent to player 1. Therefore, he will also choose the low price. Thus, the game solution is that both players choose their low-price strategy. This result, however, has an interesting implication, to which the game owes the name *Prisoner's Dilemma*: In which both players pursue their strictly dominant strategy, they achieve a rather unsatisfactory result overall. This is because if they both opted for the high price strategy, they could improve significantly. However, the solution in which both opt for a high price is highly unstable, since each player has the possibility to increase his profit at the expense of the other players by switching to a low-price strategy. Thus, a prisoner's dilemma is characterized by players reaching a situation that is unsatisfactory for them when they choose their strictly dominant strategies

Such prisoner's dilemma situations do occur frequently in practice: For example, they are characteristic for dealing with public goods such as the environment. Everyone would be better off if they refrained from environmentally damaging behavior, even if this entails costs. But since individual behavior has no noticeable effect on environmental quality, polluting behavior becomes the strictly dominant strategy for everyone

Nash Equilibrium

Let us first consider only *pure strategies*. This means that each player selects a very specific strategy with certainty (with 100% probability). We will later describe situations where players assign positive probabilities to multiple strategies, so-called mixed strategies. Look at the following example:

	b_1	b_2	b_3
a_1	(1,1)	(0,1)	(10,0)
a_2	(0,0)	(3,2)	(0,0)
a_3	(3,3)	(1,0)	(7,7)

First of all, it is easy to verify that there are no dominant strategies in this game. Player 1's best response to 2's first strategy would be a3, to the second strategy a2, and to the third strategy a1. The best response of 2 to the first strategy of 1 would be b1 or b2, to the second strategy b2, and to the third strategy b3. Therefore, when choosing their strategies, both players have to consider how the opponent is likely to behave. In such situations, a completely convincing and unassailable solution, as we have learned in the case of dominated strategies, is no longer possible. The most common equilibrium concept in non-cooperative game theory is the Nash equilibrium. It defines a situation in which no player can improve given the strategy choices of the opponents. In the Nash equilibrium, it is not worthwhile for any player to deviate from his equilibrium strategy. Let us illustrate the idea with an example: An intuitively obvious solution is the strategy pair (a3,b3), since both players receive a high payoff. Let us therefore assume that 2 chooses b3. If player 1 anticipates this, however, his optimal answer is a1 and player 2 would receive a low payoff. The same is true for the strategy combination (a3,b1) another candidate solution. B's best response to a3 would be b3, but then again player 1 would have the incentive to choose his strategy a1. As you can see, both game solutions proposed so far are unstable, since one player at a time can improve by switching strategies unilaterally. Let us now consider the combination (a2,b2). Here, no player is able to improve by a unilateral strategy change, (a2,b2) consequently form a Nash equilibrium. This implies, and herein lies the meaning and justification for the Nash equilibrium as a solution concept, that the players receive exactly the payoff they expect if the opponent correctly anticipates their behavior. This is otherwise not the case: if 2 plays b3 expecting to realize (a3,b3) and this is anticipated by 1, the result is (a1,b3) and player 2 gets a nasty surprise. After this introductory example, we can now formally introduce the concept of Nash equilibrium.

Nash equilibrium. *A Nash equilibrium is a strategy combination s^* where each player chooses his optimal strategy s_i^*—given the optimal strategies of all other players. Formally:*

$$u_i\left(s_i^*,s_{-i}^*\right) \geq u_i\left(s_i,s_{-i}^*\right) \forall i, \forall S_i \in S_i$$

where $s_{-i}^* \equiv \left(s_1^*,\ldots,s_{i-1}^*,s_{i+1}^*,\ldots,s_n^*\right)$

In plain English: A strategy combination s forms a Nash equilibrium if and only if it is not profitable for any player to unilaterally deviate from the equilibrium strategy. This is equivalent to each player in equilibrium receiving an expected payoff that is no smaller than if any other strategy were chosen, provided the other players maintain their equilibrium strategy (Osborne & Rubinstein, 2016)

Nash equilibria can be found most reliably via the *Best Response Functions* of all individual players $BR_i(s_{-i})$. For each strategy combination of the opponents, player i determines her best answer:

$$BR_i\left(s_{-i}\right) = \left\{s_i \in S_i : u_i\left(s_i,s_{-i}\right) \geq u_i(s_i^{'},s_{-i}) \forall s_i^{'} \in S_i\right\}$$

In other words, we can say that a strategy profile $s = \{s_1,\ldots,s_n\}$ constitutes a Nash equilibrium if and only if $s_i \in BR_i \; \forall \; i$

So how can we easily identify Nash equilibria? Well, just follow two basic steps: First, find the *Best Response Functions* of all players to all possible strategy combinations of opponents; Second, identify strategy combinations which are *Best Response Functions* of all players. These are then all Nash equilibria of the game

How can we evaluate the Nash equilibrium of a game? On the one hand, it is obvious that the Nash equilibrium concept sems a necessary condition to be fulfilled in order to ensure a reasonable game solution. One can hardly accept a solution in which at least one player can improve her situation by unilaterally deviating from the equilibrium strategy. On the other hand, this does not mean that every Nash equilibrium is a reasonable solution

Multiple Nash Equilibria in Pure Strategies

Let's start with an example with multiple equilibria, where players are expected to head for exactly one equilibrium. The following game has multiple equilibria:

	b_1	b_2
a_1	(10,10)	(0,0)
a_2	(0,0)	(1,1)

The game has 2 equilibria (a1,b1) and (a2,b2). The players must form expectations as to which of the equilibria will be targeted by the other player. In the example, there is a lot to be said for both players assuming that the teammate will target (a1,b1) and play their first strategy. Therefore, they will play their first strategy and (a1,b1) will indeed turn out to be the game solution. In other cases, things become more difficult. To this end, let us consider an example that is referred to in the literature as a battle of sexes. Let us consider a pair of lovers who want to spend the evening together but have not made an exact appointment where the meeting should take place and now have no means of communication. The discussion was about attending a ballet evening (a1 and b1, respectively) and a boxing match (a2 and b2, respectively). While the woman (player 1) prefers the boxing match, the man (player 2) is more into ballet. As befits a pair of lovers, however, they would like to spend the evening together in any case. The following game is called *Battle of the Sexes*:

	b_1	b_2
a_1	(10,20)	(0,0)
a_2	(0,0)	(20,10)

This game has two Nash equilibria: both meet at ballet (a1,b1) and both meet at boxing (a2,b2). In this case, game theory cannot provide a meaningful prediction of which equilibrium will be chosen, since both are equally plausible. Worse, it is by no means guaranteed that an equilibrium will be reached at all. For this would require the players to correctly anticipate the behavior of their game partner. But this is not possible without further assumptions. If, for example, both players back down and submit to their partner's preferences, the woman ends up doing ballet and the man boxing, and this leads to a highly unsatisfactory state of affairs. As you can see, purely game-theoretical considerations will not get you anywhere here. The only way out of this situation is to create secure behavioral expectations in the form of social norms. If, for example, the norm exists that in relationships the preferences of women are weighted higher, the equilibrium (a2,b2) is reached, which impressively documents the sense of social norms

No Nash Equilibria in Pure Strategies

We have seen that predicting the outcome of a game can become problematic when a game has multiple Nash equilibria in pure strategies. On the other hand, there are also many games in which no Nash equilibrium exists in pure strategies. Again, we will first illustrate this with an example. For this purpose we go back to the roots and consider the well-known children's game *rock-paper-scissors.* This famous hand game is played between two players, in which each player simultaneously forms one of three shapes with an outstretched hand: scissors, rock, or paper. If both players display the same symbol, the game ends in a draw. Otherwise, rock wins against scissors because it blunts it, paper wins against rock because it wraps it, scissors wins over paper because it cuts it. Let the payoff be 1 for a win 0, for a draw, and −1 for a loss. The game looks as follows:

	Scissors	Rock	Paper
Scissors	(0,0)	(−1,1)	(1,−1)
Rock	(1,−1)	(0,0)	(−1,1)
Paper	(−1,1)	(1,−1)	(0,0)

It is easy to see that this game cannot have a Nash equilibrium in pure strategies: For example, if player 1 chooses scissors, stone is the best response of B. Given this, it is attractive for 1 to switch to paper, whereupon player 2, anticipating this, chooses scissors, and so on. If a player anticipates the other player's strategy (and this is the premise of the Nash equilibrium), he can adjust his behavior so that he wins.

However, the other player can anticipate this and change his behavior to his own advantage, which in turn can be anticipated, and so on. Therefore, this game obviously has no Nash equilibrium in pure strategies. On the other hand, every child knows how this game must be played. It is crucial to keep the opponent guessing about one's strategy. Therefore, playing a pure strategy cannot be useful here, but players choose their strategies randomly

Nash Equilibrium in Mixed Strategies

In mixed strategies, players *randomize*, i.e., they define a probability distribution over their possible actions. Which action is actually taken is then decided by the random mechanism defined in this way. Equilibrium in mixed strategies follows the same ideas as the equilibrium in pure strategies in the sense that no player can improve his expected utility by choosing a different probability distribution if the other players stick to their (mixed) equilibrium strategy. If one includes mixed strategies in the consideration, the following reasonable statement can be derived:

Nash equilibrium in mixed strategies. *Every game with a finite number of players has at least one Nash equilibrium in mixed strategies.*

Despite this pleasant feature, the concept of mixed strategies is not very popular among many economists. The reason for this is perhaps best understood by looking at the structure of equilibrium in mixed strategies. Let us illustrate it with a simple example.

	b_1	b_2
a_1	(3,2)	(1,3)
a_2	(2,4)	(3,1)

Consider the situation of player 2. If he chooses b1, he receives a payoff of $2p + 4(1 - p)p2$, where p and $(1-p)$ are the probabilities with which player 1 plays a1 and a2, respectively. Accordingly, if he chooses b2, he gets $3p + (1 - p)$. This means that the pure strategy b1 (b2) is advantageous for him if $2p + 4(1 - p)> (<) 3p + (1 - p)$. For player 2 to even consider a mixture, he must be indifferent between b1 and b2. Consequently, we have that $2p + 4(1 - p) = 3p + (1 - p)$. This results in $p = 3/4$ as well as $(1 - p) = 1/4$. Player 2's indifference condition gives rise to player 1's equilibrium strategy, which is central to understanding the concept of mixed strategies. For any other mixed strategy, player 2 would benefit from using one of his pure strategies. To a pure strategy of 2, however, the best response of player 1 would of course be a pure strategy. For player 1, the reasoning is completely analogous. In order for him to play a mixed strategy, it must hold that $3q + (1 - q) = 2q + 3(1 - q)$, where q and $(1 - q)$ denote the probabilities with which player 2 chooses his strategies b1 and b2. This results in $q = 2/3$ as well as $(1 - q) = 1/3$. If both players play their derived strategies, the result is a Nash equilibrium in mixed strategies

The concept of mixed strategies is ultimately based on the idea that a game is played multiple times. Then, it is easy to see that in *rock-paper-scissors* any deviation from the uniform distribution could be detected and exploited by the opponent, so that the expected payoff decreases. In a static game, which by definition takes place only once, the concept of mixed strategies seems a little more difficult to justify. The Nash equilibrium is the most important solution concept in game theory, but it is not free of problems. For one thing, a game can have multiple Nash equilibria, and it is unclear which of these equilibria is the game solution, or whether players even reach equilibrium in such a situation. Second, a game cannot have a Nash equilibrium in pure strategies. At least one equilibrium in mixed strategies then exists, but the concept of mixed strategies in at least controversial. Apart from these problems, there are games where Nash equilibria do exist, but where it seems indeed doubtful that the players will be heading for a Nash equilibrium. Look at the following example:

	b_1	b_2	b_3	b_4
a_1	(200,6)	(3,5)	(4,3)	(0,−1.000)
a_2	(0,−10.000)	(5,−1.000)	(6,3)	(3,20)

This game has two Nash equilibria in pure strategies, namely (a1,b1) and (a2,b4). In addition, there is another equilibrium in mixed strategies, where the strategies b1, b2 and b4 are mixed. Nevertheless, it is difficult to accept one of the equilibria as a game solution. On the contrary, there is a lot to be said for player 2 choosing b3, the only strategy that does not appear in any of the equilibria. But also (b3,a2) can hardly be accepted as a solution, because why should player 2 then not improve by choosing b4. A generally acceptable solution does not exist for this game

The concept of a Nash equilibrium constitutes an important criterion for a "reasonable" game solution. It is unlikely that we can generally accept a game solution that is *not* a Nash equilibrium, since then at least one player can improve by deviating unilaterally. Therefore, if we can accept a strategy combination as a solution, it is a necessary condition that this strategy combination forms a Nash equilibrium. However, as seen, a Nash equilibrium is by no means a sufficient condition for a strategy combination to form a plausible game solution. Therefore, it seems a good idea to eliminate implausible equilibria by defining some additional requirements that a Nash equilibrium needs to fulfill in order to be called "reasonable".

Subgame Perfect Equilibrium

So far, we have looked at games that are static in nature. In contrast to these *static games*, *dynamic games* are characterized by players who can—and will—make their actions dependent on information they receive during the game. We will restrict ourselves here to games in which the players make their moves one after the other and player 2 makes his move knowing about player 1's move. As an example, assume the following situation: A company (player 1) is considering whether to enter a previously monopolistic market and thus has the strategies "do not enter" (a1) and "enter" (a2). If it decides to "enter", the previous monopolist (player 2) also has two options: It can engage in a price war (b1) or it can choose not to engage in a price war (b2) . If one assigns reasonably plausible payoffs to the individual strategy combinations, the following extensive form could result, for example:

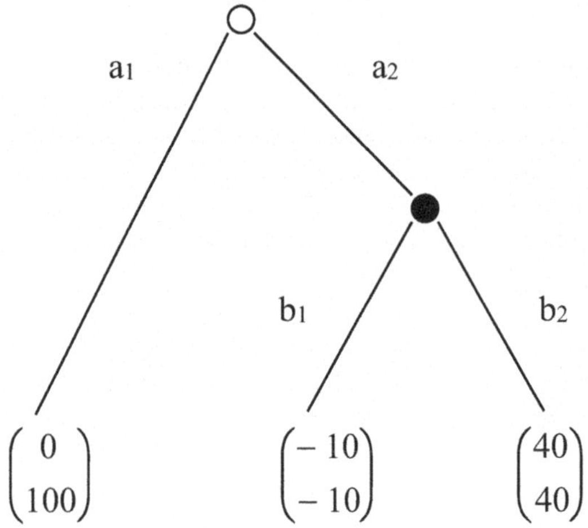

Apparently, this game has two Nash equilibria, namely (enter, do not fight) (a2,b2) and (do not enter, fight) (a1,b1). But let's take a closer look at the strategy fighting: The monopolist has to decide only if the other player enters the market. But if this is the case, he will never fight. Therefore, the Nash equilibrium (do not enter, fight) is not very plausible, since not entering is only reasonable if the monopolist would fight. But since he would never do so in an emergency, the threat implicit in the move "fight" is empty. Using this introductory example, we can define the concept of subgame perfect equilibrium:

Subgame in extensive form. *This means any subset of a game that starts at a one-element information set. If a decision node x of an information set H is part of the subgame, then all other decision nodes in H must be elements of the subgame. A Nash equilibrium is called "subgame perfect" if it also forms a Nash equilibrium for each subgame.*

The concept of subgame perfection is able to rule out certain implausible Nash equilibria as solutions based on empty threats. It is a weakness of the Nash equilibrium concept that the plausibility of equilibrium strategies is not investigated. In the partial-game perfect equilibrium concept, on the other hand, they are subjected to scrutiny. For example, in the market entry game (do not enter, fight) a Nash equilibrium forms. If we assume this equilibrium, the situation in which the firm enters the market does not occur (with zero probability) along the equilibrium path. However, if we now consider this situation outside the assumed equilibrium path, we see that the monopolist would not struggle if confronted with market entry (move outside the considered equilibrium path). Therefore, the considered equilibrium is implicitly based on an empty threat of player 2 and is therefore implausible. The concept of subgame perfect equilibria can rule out such implausible Nash equilibria based on empty threats: Since the monopolist, when he comes to move, would never fight, an equilibrium that implicitly assumes exactly this behavior is also dubious. (Please remember that this is a one-time game. If the game is repeated infinitely often, "fighting" can be a reasonable strategy.) The only partial game perfect equilibrium is (enter, do not fight).

Interestingly, very dynamic or sequential game with perfect information has a subgame perfect equilibrium:

Subgame perfect Nash equilibrium. *Every finite (sequential) game with perfect information has a subgame perfect Nash equilibrium in pure strategies. If no player reaches the same payoffs at any two endpoints, then a unique subgame perfect Nash equilibrium exists.*

But how do we find the subgame perfect equilibrium of a dynamic game? Here is a safe way (called *backwards induction* or *Bellman's principle*) to determine subgame perfect equilibria in dynamic games with perfect information:

1. Start with the last decision node of a game and determine for the considered subgame the optimal action of the player whose turn it is;
2. replace the start of the subgame by the payoffs resulting from the optimal decision of the player whose turn it is;
3. continue points 2. and 3. until you have reached the beginning of the game.

The requirement of subgame perfection is widely accepted as a necessary condition for a solution. A Nash equilibrium that is not subgame perfect is hardly an acceptable solution. Therefore, it seems a reasonable tightening of the Nash equilibrium for dynamic games. However, as with the Nash equilibrium, not every subgame perfect equilibrium is a convincing solution, as the following example (*centipede game*) shows:

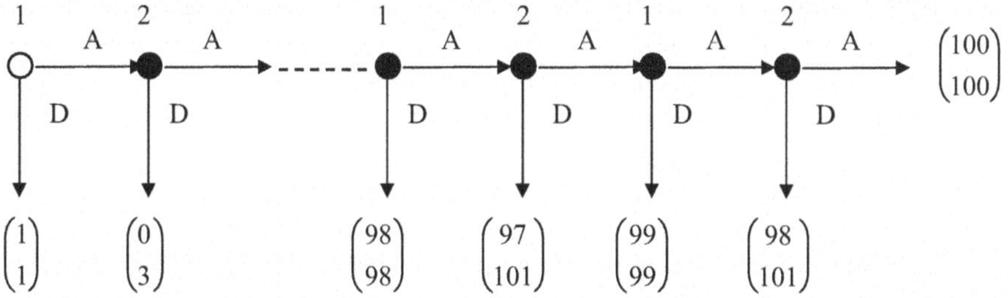

The extensive form can be interpreted as follows. Player 1 first decides between his strategy A and D. If he chooses D, the game ends and both players receive a payoff of 1. If he chooses D, the game is over and both players receive a payoff of 1. If, on the other hand, he chooses A, player 2 takes his turn and can choose between his strategies A and D. If he chooses D, the game is over and he receives a payoff of 3, while player 1 receives 0. If he chooses D, the game ends and he receives a payoff of 3, while player 1 receives 0. If player 2 chooses A, player 1 takes his turn. This continues until player 2 has to choose between A and D in the last round. If he chooses A, both players get 100, if he chooses D, he gets 101, while player 1 only gets 98. To determine the subgame perfect equilibrium, we start at the end of the game tree and then work our way forward (*backward induction*). If player 2 were to make a move in the last round, he would choose D. This would be the first move of the game. This is anticipated by player 1 and, if it got to that point, would also choose D in the round before. Since player 2 sees this coming, he would not let it get that far and would choose D in the round before. Having worked our way forward in this way, we find that in the only partial game perfect equilibrium player 1 chooses D on the first move and both receive a payoff of 1. This result is both unpleasant, since there are much nicer payoffs, and not particularly believable. We would not expect the players to actually play this way, and there is a good and game theoretically very interesting argument for this.

Let's assume that player 2 expects with certainty that player 1 is heading for the subgame perfect equilibrium and therefore expects with certainty D. But player 1 chooses A. Now player 2 is puzzled and has to think about it. For it to be reasonable for him to choose D now, he must assume that player 1 has made an inexplicable mistake and will correct it at the next opportunity. If, on the other hand, player 2 assumes a sufficiently high probability (which can be very small in this case) that player 1 wanted to send a signal to climb the tree a good bit and therefore plays A the next times it is his turn, it is better for him to play A himself. Of course, player 1 can anticipate these considerations of player 2 and will play A first if there is a sufficient probability that player 2 does not play D at the beginning. Such considerations in information sets outside the equal weight path are summarized under the term "forward induction". Generally speaking, for dynamic games interesting questions arise with respect to the equilibrium concepts used. In Nash equilibrium and, of course, in subgame perfect equilibrium, players anticipate the strategies of their opponents. In a dynamic game, however, at least player 2 can observe at least one move of player 1 before making his own decision. The question arises what conclusions player 2 draws when he observes a move of player 1 that the latter should not choose if he follows his equilibrium strategy, i.e. if he makes a move outside the equilibrium. Two possible interpretations are obvious:

1. player 1 has made a mistake. On his next move, he will choose his equilibrium strategy for the rest of the game.
2. player 1 has deliberately played the move and sent a signal that he is willing to deviate from his equilibrium strategy in future rounds (even if not forever).

Which interpretation one prefers is ultimately a matter of taste. To me, the second interpretation seems to be much more convincing, since the assumption of mistakes by the players seems very ad hoc in a context where game solutions are derived with the help of very high demands on the players' ability to anticipate. The subgame perfect equilibrium is not necessarily a convincing solution here. But this is also true for any other strategy combination. Even if we expect players to play A for quite some time, they are unlikely to do so until the end. It is to be expected that at some point a player will choose D and end the game. Experimentally, this was mostly the case when the players' payoffs were between 80 and 90. However, it is not possible to make a theoretically based statement about when the game will end. However, since the game was originally introduced by Rosenthal (1981), many researchers have put the game into a more practical perspective; for instance, it is argued by Dulleck and Oechssler (1997) that play may be continued almost to the end if one player is known to be absent-minded.

References

Arrow, K. J. (1965). Aspects of the Theory of Risk Bearing, in: The Theory of Risk Aversion. Helsinki: Yrjo Jahnssonin Saatio. Reprinted in: Essays in the Theory of Risk Bearing, Markham Publ. Co., Chicago, 1971, 90–109.

Brzezicka, J., & Wiśniewski, R. (2014). Homo oeconomicus and behavioral economics. *Contemporary Economics, 8*(4), 353–364.

Dulleck, U., & Oechssler, J. (1997). The absent-minded centipede. *Economics Letters, 55*(3), 309–315.

Eeckhoudt, L., Gollier, C., & Schlesinger, H. (2005). *Economic and financial decisions under risk*. Princeton University Press.

Osborne, M., & Rubinstein, M. (2016). *A course in game theory*. PHI Press.

Pratt, J. W. (1964). Risk aversion in the small and in the large. *Econometrica. 32*(1/2), 122–136.

Rosenthal, R. (1981). Games of perfect information, predatory pricing, and chain-store paradox. *Journal of Economic Theory, 25*, 92–100.

Von Neumann, J., & Morgenstern, O. (1944). *Theory of games and economic behavior*. Princeton University Press.

A. Hofmann, *The Ten Commandments of Risk Leadership*, Future of Business and Finance, https://doi.org/10.1007/978-3-030-88797-1

Index

A
Adverse selection, 103, 104, 107
Allais paradox, 23–37
Anchoring effects, 29, 31, 39–49, 71, 77
A-posteriori probability, 10
A-priori probability, 10
Asymmetric information, 103–104
Availability heuristic, 52, 132

B
Backward induction, 114
Bernoulli principle, 24, 25, 28

C
Catastrophe insurance market puzzle, 100–103
Cognitive misperceptions, 77
Company culture, 123–126
Completeness, 25
Confidence gap, 91
Confirmation bias, 12, 39–49, 137
Continuity, 25
Cooperation, 83, 95, 111–116, 121, 126, 141

D
Debiasing strategies, 120–121, 137
Decision theory, 143
Defective decision-making, 117, 119–121
Dictator games, 113–115
Diversity, 111–126
Dunning-Kruger effect, 91, 93

E
Ellsberg Paradox, 8
Endowment effect, 67–81
Enterprise risk management (ERM), 2, 3
Escalation of commitment, 80
Expected utility, 8, 23–37, 107

F
Fairness, 111–126
Forecasts, 8, 55, 73, 84, 86–87, 116, 135, 141
Framing effects, 29, 34, 51–53, 55, 58

G
Game theory, v, 111–116
Groupthink, 111–126, 144

H
Habits, 87, 143–145
Heuristics, 1, 6, 23, 37, 44, 52, 142
Hindsight bias, 129–139
Homo Oeconomicus, 123, 155
House Money Effect, 19, 20

I
Illusion of control, 87–88
Imposter syndrome, 83, 92–93, 95
Independence, 25, 28, 35, 120, 122
Insulation effect, 36
Insurances, 3, 7, 8, 13, 18, 26, 27, 46, 55–58, 61, 64, 71, 72, 74, 77, 99–108, 124
Isolation effect, 33–34, 36

L
Leadership, 1–4, 80, 121, 124, 125, 145
Limited liability, 105

A. Hofmann, *The Ten Commandments of Risk Leadership*, Future of Business and Finance, https://doi.org/10.1007/978-3-030-88797-1

Loss aversion, 23, 29–34, 37, 53–54, 59, 63, 64, 67–71, 77

M
Monty Hall Problem, 10, 11
Myopia, 134

N
Nash equilibrium, 113

O
Ostrich effect, 51–59
Overconfidence effects, 43, 84, 85
Overestimation, 85–89
Overplacement, 85, 88
Overprecision, 85, 89

P
Peer effects, 111–126
Planning fallacy, 86–87
Primary bias, 130
Prisoner's dilemma, 112–113, 171, 172
Processing fluency, 132
Prospect theory, 23–37, 52, 68
Psychological commitment, 72, 74–77
Pure risks, 3, 19

R
Rational decision-making, v, 51, 73–75, 77, 130
Reference points, 23–37, 44, 47, 59, 68, 141
Reflection effect, 35
Regret aversion, 106–108
Risk aversion, 2, 5, 16–21, 26, 27, 30, 35, 46, 73, 100, 123, 124
Risk leadership, 1–5, 20–21, 23, 37, 48–49, 51, 59, 64, 80–81, 94–95, 108, 126, 139, 141–146
Risk literacy, 1, 2, 4
Risk management, v, 2–6, 12, 17, 20, 21, 25, 26, 46, 94
Risk metrics, 14–16
Risks, v, vi, 1–21, 23–31, 33–37, 46, 53, 55–59, 61–64, 71, 72, 75, 84, 99–108, 111, 112, 116–120, 123, 124, 135, 141

S
Safety effect, 34–35
Secondary bias, 130
Selective self-attribution, 94
Somatic marker hypothesis, 143
Speculative risks, 3, 18, 19
Status quo bias, 67–81
Stereotypes, 123, 125–126
St. Petersburg Paradox, 17
Sunk-cost fallacy, 80
System 1, 142
System 2, 142

T
Tertiary bias, 131, 139
Theorem of Bayes, 10, 11
Transitivity, 25

U
Ultimatum games, 114–116
Uncertainty, v, 1, 2, 4–9, 12, 20, 23, 24, 26, 29, 34–37, 48, 51, 72–74, 120, 133

V
Value functions, 29, 33, 68

W
Weighting function, 29

Z
Zero-risk bias, 21, 33, 61–64

The manufacturer's authorised representative in the EU is Springer Nature Customer Service Centre GmbH, Europaplatz 3, 69115 Heidelberg, Germany. If you have any concerns regarding our products, please contact ProductSafety@springernature.com

Printed and bound by CPI Group (UK) Ltd, Croydon, CR0 4YY
30/09/2026
02225699-0001